S0-AHT-253

Hmong and American

Hmong and American

From Refugees to Citizens

EDITED BY VINCENT K. HER AND MARY LOUISE BULEY-MEISSNER

CABRINI COLLEGE LIBRARY
610 KING OF PRUSSIA ROAD
RADNOR, PA 19087

Minnesota Historical Society Press

#765881591

©2012 by the Minnesota Historical Society. All rights reserved. No part of this book may be used or reproduced in any manner whatsoever without written permission except in the case of brief quotations embodied in critical articles and reviews. For information, write to the Minnesota Historical Society Press, 345 Kellogg Blvd. W., St. Paul, MN 55102-1906.

www.mhspress.org

The Minnesota Historical Society Press is a member of the Association of American University Presses.

Manufactured in the United States of America

10 9 8 7 6 5 4 3 2 1

♾ The paper used in this publication meets the minimum requirements of the American National Standard for Information Sciences—Permanence for Printed Library Materials, ANSI Z39.48–1984.

International Standard Book Number
ISBN: 978-0-87351-848-2 (paper)
ISBN: 978-0-87351-855-0 (e-book)

Library of Congress Cataloging-in-Publication Data

Hmong and American : from refugees to citizens / edited by Vincent K. Her and Mary Louise Buley-Meissner.
    p.   cm.
  Includes bibliographical references and index.
  ISBN 978-0-87351-848-2 (paper : alk. paper) — ISBN 978-0-87351-855-0 (e-book)
  1. Hmong Americans—Ethnic identity. 2. Hmong Americans—Social conditions. 3. Hmong Americans—Social life and customs. 4. Community life— United States. 5. United States—Ethnic relations. I. Her, Vincent K. II. Buley-Meissner, Mary Louise.
  E184.H55H555   2012
  305.895'972073—dc23

2011048666

The text of this book is set in Arno Pro, a typeface designed by Robert Slimbach in 2007. Book design by Wendy Holdman.

Tsheej ib cuab vim muaj yawm qhuab.
Tsheej ib yig vim muaj puj plig.

A household is stable because of a grandfather's teachings.
A family thrives because of a grandmother's patience.

Contents

Acknowledgments

We would like to acknowledge the steadfast support of our families throughout this project. This Hmong American proverb reminds us of how important they are to our lives:

> *Ntoo ib tsob*
> *Xyoob ib txooj*
> A tree stands alone. (One person is not a family.)
> Bamboo flourishes in a grove. (Families form villages.)

Our parents, spouses, and children have truly given our lives meaning and purpose. With our families, we are glad to join in helping to make multicultural America a dynamic, vibrant reality. We stand and grow because of them:

> Wang Xiong, Chaomee, Chia, Alesha, Katie, and Kristin Her
> Ray and Louise Buley, Daniel, Michelle, and Lisa Meissner,
> LaRoy Hoard

Also, we thank our students for asking good questions and our teachers for helping us in the ongoing search for answers.

> Vincent K. Her and Mary Louise Buley-Meissner

< ix >

Hmong and American

< 1 >

Hmong American Studies

Bringing New Voices into Multicultural Studies

VINCENT K. HER AND MARY LOUISE BULEY-MEISSNER

Hmong and American: From Refugees to Citizens offers a much-needed, updated look at Hmong American life through essays that open the door to a new way of understanding who Hmong people are becoming in this country. Groundbreaking in its approach, this book goes beyond previous anthologies on the Hmong American experience by taking a contemporary look at the life journeys of Hmong American individuals, families, and communities. Dating back to the 1980s, earlier accounts tend to take an outsider's view of Hmong people, either through political assessment of their involvement in the Vietnam War or sociological evaluation of the assistance that refugee families and communities have required to survive in the United States. In fact, from the mid-1970s to the present, most studies of Hmong adjustment to American society adhere to this narrow under-standing of Hmong culture, identity formation, and community advance-ment. Consequently, many stereotypes of Hmong people persist: they are the least prepared of all refugee groups to succeed in modern society; they are resistant to change, holding on to time-honored traditions; and they are unable to assimilate fully into American culture. Long overdue is a well-informed reassessment of Hmong lives in modern society, including a concerted effort to overcome such stereotypes by dismantling the falla-cies underlying them. This collection fills the need for a new approach. As a whole, *Hmong and American* brings new voices to multicultural studies as it strives to:

- Emphasize the experiences of Hmong Americans as U.S. citizens rather than perpetual refugees. Foundational to the collection is the realization that because they have settled here for three gen-erations, this country has become their permanent home.

< 3 >

- Underscore the agency of Hmong Americans in identity formation, community building, and cultural renewal and reform.
  Across the collection, the authors highlight the voices and viewpoints of Hmong Americans themselves.
- Purposefully interrelate experiential and scholarly perspectives
  as contributors speak from their specific locations not only in
  academic disciplines but also from their experiences in family,
  community, and social settings. These diverse perspectives are
  creatively developed and thematically linked.
- Critically assess how the past and the present are continually
  being interpreted and re-interpreted in the dynamic process of
  being and becoming as Hmong Americans situate themselves
  within the ethnic and racial landscape of the United States.[1]

Hmong American studies is becoming a respected area of research
within the field of Asian American studies and the broader discipline of
ethnic studies. Aside from highly specialized anthropological studies,
foundational works on the Hmong were published in the late 1980s to the
mid-1990s. The cultural revitalization, socioeconomic advancement, and
rising political influence of Hmong Americans have produced a flurry of
books since 2000.[2]

Missing until now, however, has been a teachable collection, accessible to
college students as well as general readers, with broad coverage of compelling topics linked to the theme of multicultural America—a theme increasingly important in university courses and public discourse. In response to
that need, *Hmong and American* provides an engaging series of essays with
a range of writing styles by authors who are leading scholars, educators,
artists, and community activists. History, culture, gender, class, family,
and sexual orientation are all part of its consideration of Hmong American identities in modern society. In fact, by the very title of the collection,
we are asserting that Hmong people are here to stay. Understanding how
they have arrived in this country and what they are choosing to make of
their lives is a fascinating story emblematic of and inseparable from the
American experience.

More than three decades have passed since Hmong refugees began arriving in the United States in 1975. How have their lives changed? What are

the social, cultural, and economic signs suggesting that Hmong have in fact been assimilating into American society? In multicultural America, where change is expected of all immigrants, how is Hmong identity being re-imagined and re-constructed by Hmong Americans across generations? As people rebuild their communities and orient themselves to modern society, does knowledge of history, culture, and tradition remain central to their collective identity? As citizens, how are Hmong Americans contributing to the advancement of American society? In our view, sustained discussions of these questions can promote a more balanced representation and understanding of Hmong American lives as informed by events of the twentieth and twenty-first centuries. By bringing together authors with diverse personal perspectives and interdisciplinary expertise, we hope to lay new ground for scholarship recognizing and framing Hmong experiences as contemporary and global.

Hmong and American aims to participate in the exchange of ideas on Hmong American identity development and to contribute to the growing scholarship on Hmong history and culture. We also would like to see this collection open the door for the inclusion of Hmong and Hmong American studies as a vital aspect of Asian American studies, ethnic studies, and multicultural studies. We undertook this endeavor as a respectful reflection on the meaning of a complex, compelling, and ever-evolving idea called the Hmong American experience. Indeed, *Hmong and American* presents a groundbreaking array of contemporary viewpoints on identity formation, community reformation, and cultural renewal in modern society. Affirming that the United States is now a Hmong homeland, each essay reveals an important facet of the journey that Hmong people have embarked on to reinvent themselves as citizens of this country. Wholeheartedly, we believe that each chapter adds important details about the lives of Hmong Americans to public education. The viewpoints and possibilities presented in this book highlight a conundrum that many at the start of the twenty-first century find intriguing: what does it mean to be Hmong *and* American?

Through our research, teaching, and service, we and our contributors have positioned ourselves at the intersections where different life experiences often converge; in the process, we have gained much-needed insights into the elusiveness underlying the concept "Hmong." We hope to encourage constructive debates regarding its many meanings as a way to promote a better understanding of the multidimensional lives of Hmong Americans. Although we readily acknowledge that "Hmong" as a marker of identity and difference can be (and has been) essentialized, inspiration for this project comes from our interest in its infinite manifestations. Beyond historical and sociopolitical influences on Hmong destinies, we intend in this collection to honor the memories and wisdom that Hmong people across generations continue to cherish.

Community-Based Research:
Inquiries into Hmong American Lives

Our paths to Hmong American studies crossed more than a decade ago at a campus event to show the documentary *Split Horn: The Life of a Hmong Shaman in America*. Since then, we have collaborated on many projects to promote better understanding of Hmong history, heritage, and community concerns; across these projects, we have investigated both identity formation and cultural reformation as ongoing processes with important consequences for Hmong Americans today. Along the way, we have obtained firsthand knowledge of such important topics as the complicated relationships between our students and their parents; the changing roles of Hmong women in the United States; the complexity of Hmong American lives across generations; and the evolving nature of Hmong culture in modern society.[3]

As researchers interested in community-based issues, we are personally as well as professionally connected to our students and their families in many ways. They are people that we know in and out of our classrooms, whether through clan affiliations, church services, social events, community celebrations, or the deeply felt commitments to social justice that often bring us together. As we meet people and learn about their lives, we are compelled by their stories to take whatever small steps we can toward educational reform. In our classrooms and at professional conferences, Hmong American undergraduates continually remind us that they feel invisible on university campuses. Rarely if ever do they see their history or heritage incorporated into the curriculum. Seldom do they see a Hmong American professor in any department. "Are you Chinese? Korean? Vietnamese?" is asked not only by other students but also sometimes by their teachers.

Because Hmong American student enrollment represents a small percentage of the overall student population, a low priority is assigned to addressing their needs; "equity and access" policies, hiring practices, and curricular designs tend to exclude serious consideration of their presence. Consequently, the quality of education for all students, Hmong and non-Hmong, is negatively affected; when any minority group is treated as insubstantial, a message goes out to everyone on campus about who belongs and who does not.

This situation has left us profoundly affected. Through our teaching and scholarship, we insist that Hmong American students belong on campus just as much as their families belong in American society; none of them should be made to feel like a foreigner or an outsider. At the same time, we remain mindful of the painful history of civil rights leading to integrated campuses today. Only through steadfast effort to include community perspectives, particularly those of our students' families and clans, can we conscientiously attempt to build cross-cultural bridges of understanding.

To encourage reflection and self-discovery, we have been persistent in asking students to develop an informed understanding of their cultural heritage. In addition to reading books and carrying out class projects, we believe they should enrich their education by learning about the "Hmongness" woven into the fabric of their everyday lives. What stories can their grandparents and parents tell about growing up Hmong? What values would their elders say are quintessentially Hmong? What Hmong customs would they like to see their children and grandchildren follow? How does Hmong language convey cultural meanings that cannot be expressed in English? What changes have their parents and grandparents seen taking place in Hmong families and communities over the past thirty-five years of American life? Far beyond what is contained in any books, people themselves make "Hmongness" real, vibrant, and vital.

By incorporating family- and community-based research into our courses, we have created a structured environment for students to acquire firsthand knowledge of Hmong lives; to extend their knowledge of Hmong history and culture; and to nurture their intellectual growth and development. For example, we have paired Hmong American students from different religious backgrounds to learn more about similarities and differences in their families' guiding values and spiritual practices. A lifelong Catholic student could be matched with a student whose family continues to maintain Hmong religious traditions, or a student whose own parent is a *txiv neeb* (shaman) could be matched with a classmate whose family recently has converted to Christianity. Learning how to ask culturally sensitive, nonjudgmental questions—and to listen with an open mind to whatever answers are given—is a life skill that undergraduates can practice and improve. "*How* have you come to believe what you believe?" can be much more revealing than "*What* do you believe?" Furthermore, these are questions that students often ask their own parents and grandparents for the first time when they realize how much they do not know about their own family backgrounds. Equally important in today's multicultural classrooms, non-Hmong students who participate in such collaborative research with Hmong classmates also report that the insights they gain prompt them to continue learning. Consequently, when questions about Hmong life today come up at home, in school, and at community forums and public events, our students can be better prepared to speak constructively about community challenges made vivid by person-to-person encounters.

In our experience, research—as a quest for knowledge—is not an undertaking that unfolds neatly. From start to finish, its uncertainties, tensions, and disagreements call for continual negotiation. For us, this reality has been made most clear in our interactions with elders and community leaders, who are remarkably forthcoming in their inquiries about our underlying commitment to community advancement. Persistently, they seek answers to questions such as these: (1) What can you offer in return for access to people's lives? (2) How will the knowledge that you gain be reinvested into the community? and (3) What are you doing to achieve a view of Hmong life that goes beyond what people are telling you in interviews or what you see in family and community settings? From their point of view, a researcher possesses knowledge, skills, and expertise that can make a difference to the lives of people—a negative or positive difference, depending on how those skills are wielded.

For example, in preparation for a research conference presentation, we interviewed a number of Hmong American women in the community regarding their changing roles and responsibilities. Equally important, we collaborated with some of the same women to put together the first public forum at our university featuring Hmong American women's voices. Listening to and learning from them in both cases was crucial. Later, when they asked for assistance with an art and oral history exhibition, we were glad to participate, especially because they wanted to reach both a campus and a community audience with new cultural representations of Hmong womanhood. Another recent example of mutual assistance is the cooperation offered to coeditor Vincent Her in his research on funeral rites and rituals. In return for allowing him to learn about these rites and rituals from the inside—through personal interviews, close observation, and detailed documentation—Hmong American elders and practitioners left no doubt that they expected him to put what he was learning into use. Honoring that trust, as well as fulfilling family obligations, Her has been active in chairing funerals, playing *qeej* (a traditional Hmong instrument), and taking on duties prescribed by marriage or clan relations.[4]

Living up to the expectations of the community, which calls for critical consciousness of a kind rarely expected in academia, has pushed us to consider the purposes of research while developing a participatory, collaborative approach to understanding Hmong lives. Accepting our academic credentials, Hmong American elders nonetheless have been adamant that we must strive to achieve a well-informed awareness of how decisions influencing family and community life are made from the inside; only then, in their view, is it possible for us and our students to appreciate what it means to be Hmong in modern society. Only then, in fact, will we be fully prepared to counter the stereotypes, prejudices, and misconceptions circulating even on college campuses.

After more than a decade of working in the Hmong American community, we are convinced that when a mutually respectful relationship is the foundation of inquiry, people influence each other's ideas and perspectives in ways that are rarely predictable but always eye opening, whether we agree with each other or not. Among those who have been helpful in sharpening our insights are leaders and members of the Hmong American Women's Association, Inc. (HAWA); Hmong American Friendship Association, Inc. (HAFA); Hmong Educational Association (HEA); Hmong Consortium; Hmong National Development, Inc. (HND); Hmong Women's Circle (HWC); campus branches of Hmong Student Association (HSA); Lao Family Community, Inc. (LFC); Milwaukee Christian Center (MCC); Shee Yee Community of Milwaukee, Inc.; and Hmong Professional Network of La Crosse. Diverse as these organizations are in their goals, we have been encouraged by their shared vision that choosing to be Hmong and American is a very promising path.

Perhaps this is the most important lesson we have learned as community-based teachers and scholars: research changes not only what we know but who we are. Influencing the questions we ask, the answers we find persuasive, and the sources we come to trust, research remakes what we learn into what we do. Accordingly, a central aim of this book is to suggest productive ways to push the boundaries of intellectual engagement beyond the conventions of a researcher carefully observing informants. In this way, *Hmong and American* adds to the work of interdisciplinary scholars who are intrigued by the insights to be gained through exploring potential intersections of their personal and intellectual lives.[5]

Roots of Hmong and Hmong American Studies

The origin of Hmong studies can be traced to the impressions of missionaries Samuel Pollard and F. M. Savina in the early 1900s. Writing about Hmong in China, Father Savina observed:

> From time immemorial there has existed in China a race of men whose origin we do not know. *Living continuously on the heights,* away from all other Asiatics, these men speak *a language unknown* by all those who surround them, and wear a *special dress* which is seen nowhere else.[6]

Although this widely quoted passage offers valuable clues regarding Hmong origin, it also has reinforced enduring images of Hmong as fixed in time and place. Nearly one hundred years ago, a powerful link was made by Savina between Hmong and the natural environment that had for many generations provided them refuge. As recently as the 1970s, Hmong were still referred to as "migrants of the mountains." Viewed through a historical lens, Hmong people have long been imagined to inhabit only the margins of more dominant societies. Yet, identities are forged not in isolation but in environments of intergroup contact and interaction. Identities also gain prominence at times of conflict. In this light, Hmong identity development always must be examined with acknowledgment that its assessment reflects the presuppositions of those drawing conclusions about its characteristics. In the 1990s, Anne Fadiman, writing decades after Savina, presents these conclusions as definitive:

The history of the Hmong yields several lessons that anyone who deals with them might do well to remember. Among the most obvious of these are that the Hmong do not like to take orders; that they do not like to lose; that they would rather flee, fight or die than surrender; that they are not intimidated by being outnumbered; that they are rarely persuaded that the customs of other cultures, even those more powerful than their own, are superior; and that they are capable of getting very angry.[7]

As the world around them has undergone dramatic changes, so have the lives of Hmong people. Many traits that were once helpful to historians and anthropologists in delineating Hmong as the Other should now be reconsidered. We believe that narrow characterizations, such as those highlighted above, are no longer sufficient to convey the full spectrum of Hmong identities in existence today. Here, we return to the question of representation not as a criticism of the scholarship done to date on Hmong history and culture; rather, we are interested in extending knowledge of Hmong people by broadening the discussion to include a look at how much more fluid Hmong identities have become, especially since their resettlement in the West. Our approach to this issue can be described succinctly with this question: what are new and productive ways of imagining Hmong life?

Given recent controversies filtering across Hmong American communities throughout the United States, this question is appropriate and timely. In the Clint Eastwood movie *Gran Torino,* Hmong American youth are portrayed as gang members and thugs. The "good" Hmong boy is in need of a father figure and role models outside the Hmong community. Moreover, Hmong culture is depicted as primitive, even to the extent that Hmong people are obsessed with offering food, symbolic of their spiritual indebtedness, to a white savior. In media coverage of the Chai Soua Vang shootings in the north woods of Wisconsin in 2004, the sensationalism went beyond what happened between him and the other hunters. Ultimately, the root cause of the incident was linked to Hmong immigration, creating a backlash against Hmong culture and Hmong Americans. Central in that debate was whether or not this group could assimilate into American society. Questions such as "Do Hmong Americans understand hunting rules (written and unwritten)?" and "Do they have any regard for private property?" suggested that they could not. Prior to the entrapment case against Vang Pao and others in 2007, for allegedly plotting to overthrow the government of Laos, Hmong Americans were categorized as terrorists under the Patriot Act. Only through subsequent actions taken by Congress to change the language of that law were Hmong eventually removed from the list. In higher education, when a University of Wisconsin System law professor made inappropriate comments regarding Hmong cultural practices in the United States, much of the public debate surrounding that controversy sent the message that principles of academic freedom were incompatible with initiatives to improve campus-community relations through curriculum development and hiring Hmong American faculty.[8]

To us, these are clear examples of how Hmong identity has been subjected to definition by forces outside of the Hmong American community. All too often, stereotypes are a reality that Hmong in the United States confront in the news, in school, at work, and in other settings where their citizenship is overlooked and their image as an unwelcome refugee remnant of the Vietnam War is reinforced. As we reflect on family and community life, we are continually perplexed by the mismatch between how Hmong view themselves and how others perceive them. Like all other immigrant groups, Hmong people have changed, as has their culture. Yet, this fact proves difficult to communicate when preconceived notions of their identity remain prominent.

Representation of Hmong Reconsidered: A More Complicated View

In our assessment, Hmong life has become a blend of the traditional and the modern. Consequently, we cannot sum up Hmong ways of life quite as neatly as Father Savina did eighty-six years ago. No longer are Hmong found exclusively in remote places on the "heights"; they have settled across the globe. In addition, recognized as part of the Miao–Yao family of languages, Hmong is spoken by at least several million people. Now fluent in the language are missionaries, anthropologists, and countless others. Much has occurred since Savina's time. In Laos, Hmong endured French colonial rule, survived Japanese occupation in World War II, and fought in the Vietnam War on the U.S. side, paving the way for Hmong immigration to this country as refugees. Moreover, through the efforts of

a U.S. linguistic anthropologist, William Smalley, and a French missionary, Yves Bertrais, a Hmong writing system was established in 1954. The
first Hmong-French dictionary appeared in 1964; a Hmong-English dictionary followed in 1969. The most widely recognized symbol of Hmong
identity today is no longer the "special dress" that captured Savina's attention in the 1920s but the story cloth whose origin dates to the 1970s and
1980s in the refugee camps of Thailand. This Hmong art and the creativity
of Hmong women have earned international recognition. (See Mary Louise Buley-Meissner's chapter in this volume.) In the United States, story
cloths hang on the walls of museums, schools, libraries, and government
offices. Hmong clothing, needlework, embroidery, and jewelry have been
cataloged by anthropologists, museum curators, and art exhibitors. All of
these developments are evidence of the host of changes that people collectively have experienced as refugees and the ongoing impact of local,
national, and international influences on Hmong lives.[9]

While a majority of the world's Hmong population continues to maintain a traditional life in rural villages across Southeast Asia and China,
hundreds of thousands have settled permanently in the West. (See Kou
Yang's chapter in this volume for information on Hmong populations in
the United States.) Today, Australia, Canada, France, Germany, and the
United States have become home for Hmong people across at least three
generations. As citizens of these nations, Hmong have gained newfound
perspectives on who they are in relationship to the rest of the world. To
find their place in history, to understand the changes affecting their lives,
they are on the move to retrace their roots, tell their stories, and write
down their families' histories. Unlike the first generation, younger people
see themselves as urban, cosmopolitan, and technologically savvy. Their
identities are a complex weaving of traditional practices and contemporary
values. While stories told by their parents and grandparents remain central
to who they are, modern communication technologies have also enabled
them to build social networks that extend beyond the boundaries of the
family and clan to include others across the United States and around the
world. Consequently, for many young people today, what is Hmong has
become much more flexible, perhaps more so than at any point in the past.
At the same time, we see that some of our students, particularly those who
are close to their culture, are becoming strikingly conservative about what
is Hmong because they are worried that the language is being lost, the

customs are not being honored, the rituals are not being practiced, and so on. We talk in class, for example, about the consequences of an identity becoming so elastic that it holds everything and nothing.[10]

More and more, people in the United States are adopting an "American" frame of reference to articulate a Hmong place in the modern world. Hmong are a people with a long history, rich culture, and new possibilities. Their horizons, which once were limited to the surroundings of their highland villages, now stretch all the way from the United States to Southeast Asia and China. At community gatherings, we frequently have heard Hmong elders remind one another that in the Midwest, the land is flat and people can see far into the distance. What is implied by this metaphor is that the terrains of Hmong life have changed: the Hmong imagination now more than ever is expanding into new territory. As a people displaced around the world, Hmong have adopted new means of connecting with one another through technology. Locally, rituals and ceremonies—such as funerals, *ua neeb* (shamanic performances), and *hu plig* (soul-calling ceremony)—continue to bring people together, especially on weekends, to eat, fulfill family obligations, and affirm social relationships. Globally, they are forging new bonds based on values, ideals, and experiences that wield symbolic, political, and ideological significance. In this interpretive lens, we see Hmong as actively engaged in maintaining what Benedict Anderson refers to as an "imagined" community, with roots anchored in not one but many places around the world.[11]

Hmong Identity Development in the United States

In a nation where diverse cultures crisscross and Hmong lives are open to the influences of new opportunities, ideas, and values, each person's identity is a kaleidoscope of possibilities for development. Since their arrival in the United States beginning in 1975, one of the most significant changes for Hmong Americans has been the emergence of an educated group literate in English. People of the first and second generation are the first to include writing as artistic and creative expressions of their identities. Such an example is unmistakable in the groundbreaking book *Bamboo Among the Oaks: Contemporary Writing by Hmong Americans,* the first anthology of prose and poetry by Hmong Americans to be published for a national audience. In her introduction, Mai Neng Moua underscores reasons Hmong Americans must write:

> Why are we always waiting for others to tell our stories, to define us, to legitimate us? . . . It is essential for the Hmong . . . to express themselves—to write our stories in our own voices and to create our own images of ourselves. When we do not, others write our stories for us, and we are in danger of accepting the images others have painted of us.[12]

To write is to have a voice. In their conversations with us, Hmong American elders who cannot read and write clearly realize their disadvantage in American society. Although they may not have attended school, they are keenly aware of the politics of representation, always seeing themselves in light of how others see them and their families in American society. They recognize that to possess writing ability is to be perceived as culturally advanced and thus progressive and attuned to modern times. Looking to the future, most are optimistic that their children and grandchildren will be highly literate in English. Indeed, second and third generations are taking advantage of educational opportunities that very few of the older generation ever had. Raised and educated in this country, younger Hmong Americans are much more prepared than their parents and grandparents to engage in public discussion of what it means to be Hmong and American. In fact, reading and writing have become essential for anyone trying to keep up with debates about the meaning of both "Hmong" and "American" in educational, political, social, and cultural contexts.[13]

Undoubtedly, the meaning of "American" has been highly contested throughout American history, as scholars across disciplines have documented. Informing this debate is legislation that has been used from the eighteenth to twenty-first centuries to define and redefine the grounds of American citizenship. (See Vincent Her's chapter in this volume for a more extensive discussion of citizenship debates, including relevant U.S. legislation.) Yet, the plurality of meanings for "American" cannot be stabilized because the country's lifeblood is its multicultural citizenry. Regardless of political affiliation, more people than ever in the United States seem to be aware that "American" is a dynamic, ever-evolving term. Who could have predicted during the Civil Rights Movement of the 1950s and 1960s that we would elect an African American president in 2008? Moreover, the growth of the minority population of the United States (defined as "non-white" in the U.S. Census for 2010) is outpacing that of the majority (defined as "white," "single race," and non-Hispanic) to a highly significant extent: by 2042, the minority and majority populations are expected to be approximately equal in number; by 2050, the minority will be on the rise to becoming the majority. Even sooner, by 2023, the Bureau of the Census anticipates that more than half of the children in the country will be from minority ethnic groups.[14]

As Hmong Americans increasingly pursue professional careers, they cannot help but assess who they are and how they must adapt socially and culturally to American society. In our view, linking "Hmong" and "American" is both a right of citizenship and a bold undertaking. Particularly because they are a relatively new group in the United States, the term "Hmong" also is continually under question and subject to redefinition. Perhaps Hmong identity should be unearthed one layer at a time through careful consideration of its cultural, historical, linguistic, political, social, and other elements. In that case, to search for identity is to engage in philosophical excavation. For many Hmong Americans, this entails digging up the past and piecing together fragments to form a coherent view of the self in the present. Through the act of reassembling the self, the building blocks of a person's identity may come more clearly into focus. However, as our research suggests, Hmong identity is not premade in a predictable form awaiting discovery. Instead, it comes in many shapes and shades, often with surprising variations from person to person and family to family. A good starting point for its exploration, which we have suggested to our students, has been this question: what is the difference between Hmong, Miao, and Meo? All of these labels refer to the same ethnic group, but they differ in cultural origin, meaning, and perception of what is Hmong. The first term is indigenous; the latter two originated in China and Southeast Asia and are commonly used there—although not without controversy— to this day.

In a distinctly modern development, Hmong American identities also are visibly marked by cultural and generational tensions. Such conflicts are part of working out where people belong and who they want to be— whether as individuals or as families—in a multicultural society. Identities flourish in the present because they have vital, vibrant histories. Cultural theorist Stuart Hall speaks of identity as making the most sense when we plot points of identification along a historical continuum. Moreover, identities are living webs of relationships and events, rooted in the past, reaching out to the present, and extending into the future as sources of contemplation and inspiration for people in the twenty-first century, including scholars of Hmong and Hmong American studies. Following their own path toward becoming American, young people experience the growing pains of dealing with the demands of families and clans as well as the larger society. Bee Cha vividly describes this situation in "Being Hmong Is Not Enough," where he proposes the "Theory of Necessary Return":

> (W)hat we are (i.e., our will to succeed) cannot free us from who we are (the obligations of being Hmong). Essentially, because needs take precedence over wants, we cannot pursue the "American dream" and simultaneously neglect the Hmong culture without grave consequences. In the end, it becomes necessary to return home and attend to immediate needs rather than face the uncertain price of wanting something different.[15]

As we interpret Cha's essay, collective Hmong identity can no longer be plotted on a collective continuum because "freedom" and "sacrifice"—terms interlinked for older generations—seem opposed to each other in modern society. In his view, it makes sense to say, "Hmong means Free" before and during the Vietnam War; and "Hmong means Surviving" in the fifteen years immediately after the war. From 1990 to the present, however, he thinks that "Hmong means ????" because no common ground exists for older and younger generations to agree on a distinct, authentic Hmong identity.

Our students also find it very difficult to balance competing expectations in their lives. Listening to their stories, we recognize that identity conflicts too often are the result of cross-generational misunderstanding that neither they nor their elders are equipped to resolve. For many young people, we are sad to say, knowledge of what it means to be Hmong is limited to what they are able to discern from popular media; accounts of the Vietnam War in grade school and high school textbooks; and websites where they can chat with their peers about current events. Some of what they learn is useful, but few are prepared by the time they start college to question the veracity of stereotypes such as illiterate refugee, intractable fighter, and ignorant outsider. Concurrently, they may view their own parents and grandparents as out of place in modern society, deeming them irrelevant to the pursuit of social status and material success.

For college students, the clarity of their identity as Hmong American does not occur until they are given opportunities to investigate in depth the sacrifices, courage, and determination of their parents and grandparents to make a new life in the United States possible. Moreover, such an investigation can initiate a lifelong process of exploring not only the proud history and rich heritage of Hmong people but also their contemporary roles and responsibilities, particularly their outspoken advocacy of democracy and human rights in the United States and abroad. Hmong Americans, for example, have spoken out for Vietnam War veterans' rights; the inclusion of Hmong history and language in public school curricula; and the reform of U.S. immigration law. Hmong American elected officials (such as former Senator Mee Moua of Minnesota) have become role models for working alongside other citizens in local, state, and federal policy making. On university campuses, new alliances between Hmong American and other students have been forged through multicultural groups focused on issues such as international human rights and global environmental protection. Within this exciting new context of identity formation, convictions of who they are become most powerfully evident when students discover a meaningful place for themselves within their families and communities and join in shaping an American future that includes their hopes and dreams.

Hmong American Studies: A Convergence of Voices

In the late 1970s and early 1980s, information on Hmong Americans was scarce (as Kou Yang notes in his chapter for this collection). Following the publication of *The Hmong in the West* in 1982, the literature on Hmong history and culture has grown substantially to cover a wide range of topics, including history; resettlement, adaptation, and identity; community life and cultural renewal; health care; education and youth; and myth, legends, and folktales. Since its inception in 1996, *Hmong Studies Journal,* a peer-reviewed online academic publication, has been a chief source of information on Hmong and Hmong Americans. In his well-respected bibliographic review of the literature from 1996 to 2006, Mark Pfeifer has confirmed the expansion of research into many areas of Hmong and Hmong American life, from traditional music, storytelling, and oral history to contemporary Hmong American cultural arts, community formation, and race relations. Through bibliometric analysis of Hmong-related publications across disciplines, Nancy K. Herther has concluded that Hmong studies to date can be characterized as "a field that is still emerging, growing and developing." She finds neither defined boundaries nor discipline-distinct research materials to be common. Moreover, Herther suggests that the work of scholars in Hmong and Hmong American studies has yet to gain recognition in wider academic circles. Much more positively, she emphasizes,

> The developing "invisible college" of researchers, that includes Hmong and non-Hmong participants, is a strong sign of vitality and growth. The development of significant research activity in geographical areas that are also home to large populations of Hmong people, speaks to the strength that these relationships can engender to the mutual benefit of both communities.[16]

While the future remains uncertain, the origins of Hmong and Hmong American studies can be linked to the need to convey changes taking place in the Hmong American community. Hmong immigration to the United States in the 1970s and 1980s gave rise to a wide range of challenges that the U.S. government and sponsoring agencies (mainly Catholic and Lutheran services) did not anticipate. As Hmong refugees began the slow process of rebuilding their lives in this country, their efforts and determination caught the attention of others, from reporters to schoolteachers and scholars to social service providers and health care professionals. As the interests of these groups converged, the lives of Hmong Americans were opened up for discussion in relationship to debates over immigration, refugee resettlement, secondary migration, assimilation, and cultural renewal.[17]

From the mid-1980s to the mid-2000s, we have seen a gradual rise in undergraduate college enrollment of Hmong Americans, particularly in Wisconsin, Minnesota, and California, the three states ranked highest for Hmong population. This change has translated into concrete efforts on the ground. On campuses with a sizeable Hmong American presence, student leaders have asked for courses related to Hmong history, culture, and life experiences. Many community leaders have spoken in support of their efforts, stressing the need for more collaboration between campus and community. With this impetus, universities have begun experimenting with Hmong language courses, which have sometimes led to more substantial offerings. As part of the regular course rotations, the University of Wisconsin–Milwaukee currently offers an undergraduate course that focuses exclusively on Hmong American life stories and Hmong American history, culture, and contemporary life. In 2006, Concordia University (St. Paul, Minnesota), with the help of a private grant, established the Center for Hmong Studies and is now offering a minor in Hmong studies. To promote ongoing research and disseminate knowledge in Hmong studies, the center also has been bringing together scholars from across the country and around the world for a well-respected biannual conference. The center is certainly not alone in its efforts. In 2009, the University of Wisconsin–Milwaukee launched a certificate in Hmong diaspora studies. Finally, crucial to the development of Hmong American studies is the rising number of scholars of Hmong descent who are pursuing research in many areas of Hmong and Hmong American life.[18]

Not until the 1970s and 1980s did Hmong individuals earn academic credentials to address Hmong experiences in scholarly publications. Paving the way were two major figures: Dao Yang, who researched social and economic developments among the Hmong of Laos, and Gary Yia Lee, who carried out ethnographic fieldwork on Hmong villages in northern Thailand (as described in Lee's chapter for this volume). Since then, many others have followed their footsteps, marking an important milestone in the Hmong transition from the mountain villages of Laos to urban metropolitan areas across the United States. Today, scholars, researchers, and other writers of Hmong descent take active roles in telling the stories of their people. Their ongoing work adds to our knowledge of culture, religion, spirituality, gender relations, and community life. They enrich the perspectives and approaches in Hmong American studies by bringing in their life experiences as cultural insiders. Additionally, through their creative and literary work, young Hmong Americans question traditional practices as a way to foster gender equality within the Hmong American community. Founded in 1994 by Mai Neng Moua, the literary journal *Paj Ntaub Voice* has brought national attention to the emerging talents of young writers and their views on such subjects as war, immigration, religion, manhood, and womanhood. Moreover, autobiographical accounts supply a rich sampling of life stories to amplify our understanding of what Hmong refugees endured in their journey from Laos to the United States. Hmong history and life experiences also have been incorporated into contemporary novels.[19]

Laying New Ground for Interdisciplinary Research

Contributors to this volume include anthropologists, creative writers, artists, educators, historians, and community activists. In vividly rich detail, *Hmong and American* examines experiences of war, transnational migration, and refugee resettlement from a cross-cultural, intergenerational, and interdisciplinary perspective. Our aim is to convey—in an intellectually relevant and yet personally meaningful way—how research can take the form of constructive dialogue where all participants share the responsibility for what is learned and presented. To this end, we have asked each author to situate himself or herself not as an outsider looking in but as someone who weaves in and out of the lives of those he or she studies. Accordingly, each speaks from a specific location within the community, incorporating his or her personal perspective to render an understanding of Hmong lives that is situated, practical, and experientially informed.

As a contribution to the field of Hmong American studies, the significance of this collection is twofold. First, it points to the diversity of voices that are now emerging in the interpretation of Hmong history and culture. Second, it promotes an approach to Hmong studies that combines academic analysis with life histories, community engagement, and day-to-day experiences. As outlined below, we focus on themes related to identity and history; challenges and community transitions as Hmong Americans adapt to American society; and cultural integration through education and the arts.

Intrigued by the cross-influence of culture, place, politics, and history on identity development, Vincent Her draws on his teaching, research, and life story to explore the ongoing process of becoming Hmong American in modern society. In his view, identity development is a process that brings together an informed understanding of the forces that shape the past and present. Discovering that Hmong Americans answer the question "Where are you from?" very differently than European Americans do, sociologist Jeremy Hein considers the importance of refugee and immigrant history in understanding the meaning of home and homeland. Using what he calls "homeland narratives," he compares the experiences of Hmong Americans to those of European immigrants to see how place names can significantly influence identity development. A prominent philosopher, political scientist, and historian, Keith Quincy traces the path taken by Hmong from the Vietnam War to the present in becoming allies and then citizens of the United States, highlighting what may be lost as well as what is to be gained through cultural adaptation. One of the most influential scholars in international Hmong studies, Gary Yia Lee incorporates his unique life story into observations on the complexity of Hmong individual and collective identities, supporting his conclusions through a review of social, economic, and political developments in Hmong American communities since 1975.

An award-winning creative writer and community activist, Ka Vang finds that living up to the concept of being a "good Hmong girl" is a continuing struggle for many women, including those who conform to and those who resist its powerful hold on their self-identities. An educational researcher with a deep interest in better understanding the lives of younger Hmong Americans, Bic Ngo focuses on the experiences of gay, lesbian, bisexual, and transgendered (GLBT) youth and their families to show how alienation, conflict, and support are all part of the changing meaning of being Hmong in modern society. With a background in family therapy and counseling, Song Lee draws on her experience as a Hmong daughter and popular radio talk show host to show how elders have special needs but also irreplaceable wisdom to offer as family dynamics change with the pressures of urban life. Active in national and international education, Pao Lor traces a remarkable progression in professional identities through cultural, social, and educational markers of achievement. One of the first Hmong Americans to earn an EdD and now an internationally known scholar of Hmong studies, Kou Yang reviews community achievements since 1975 to show how Hmong Americans contribute to the social, economic, and political vitality of the country.

Tracing her history from refugee to urban educator, May Vang reflects on the conflicted development of her own bicultural, bilingual identity as she urges readers to keep Hmong language alive in families and public schools. In collaboration with young artists working in dance, drama, animation, painting, and singing, cross-cultural educator Don Hones investigates how individual identity arises from family relationships, Hmong history, and ongoing experimentation in cultural creativity. A nationally known multimedia artist, Kou Vang also is a community activist whose paintings, photography, and oral history projects demonstrate the importance of bringing women's life stories out of silencing and shaming into public recognition and respect. The award-winning author of *The Late-homecomer: A Hmong Family Memoir*, Kao Kalia Yang reflects in prose and poetry upon the people, events, and dreams that have shaped her life journey from Thailand to the United States. Incorporating lessons learned from teaching Hmong American life stories at a midwestern university, cross-cultural educator Mary Louise Buley-Meissner explores the cultural creativity connecting women's traditional sewing in Laos, the emergence of story cloths in Thailand refugee camps, and the contemporary identity development of her students.

At this moment in history, choosing to be both Hmong and American signals a breakthrough to new and exciting possibilities. The passing of former general Vang Pao on January 6, 2011, marked the end of an era of Hmong American life and the start of another. As people reflect on his life, his contribution to Hmong society, and his place in history, it is also important for us to recognize the scope of Hmong adaptation to urban American life. Hmong have come a long way since the 1970s.

While America is changing Hmong people, it is no less true that Hmong are changing America in ways that we believe are still unfolding. Across the United States, from California to Massachusetts, Minnesota to Texas, Wisconsin to Mississippi, and Michigan to North Carolina, Hmong culture is now an essential attribute of the new multiculturalism. Overall, our intention is that *Hmong and American* will become a major contribution to Hmong American studies as an emerging, interdisciplinary field. Through essays that are insightful, accessible, and eye opening, the collection demonstrates how Hmong Americans across generations are developing complex identities as they participate in helping to create the ethnic and social fabric of this nation.

NOTES

1. Previous anthologies include Bruce T. Downing and Douglass P. Olney, eds., *The Hmong in the West: Observations and Reports* (Minneapolis: University of Minnesota, Center for Urban and Regional Affairs, 1982); Glenn Hendricks, Bruce T. Downing, and Amos S. Deinard, eds., *Hmong in Transition* (New York: Center for Migration Studies of New York, 1986).

2. Anthropological studies: Jacques Lemoine, *Un Village Hmong Vert du Haut Laos* (Paris: Éditions du Centre National de le Recherche Scientifique, 1972); Dao Yang and Jeanne L. Black, *Hmong at the Turning Point* (Minneapolis, MN: Worldbridge, 1993). Foundational works include See Sucheng Chan, *Hmong Means Free: Life in Laos and America* (Philadelphia, PA: Temple University Press, 1994); Jane Hamilton-Merritt, *Tragic Mountains: The Hmong, the Americans, and the Secret Wars of Laos, 1942–1992* (Bloomington: Indiana University Press, 1993); Jo Ann Koltyk, *New Pioneers in the Heartland: Hmong Life in Wisconsin* (Boston: Allyn and Bacon, 1997); Keith Quincy, *Hmong: History of a People* (Cheney: Eastern Washington University Press, 1988); Nicholas Tapp, *Sovereignty and Rebellion: The White Hmong of Northern Thailand* (New York: Oxford University Press, 1989). More recent publications are Fungchatau T. Lo, *The Promised Land: The Socioeconomic Reality of Hmong People in Urban America* (Lima, OH: Wyndham Hall Press, 2001); Mai Neng Moua, ed., *Bamboo Among the Oaks: Contemporary Writing by Hmong Americans* (St. Paul: Minnesota Historical Society Press, 2002); Patricia V. Symonds, *Calling in the Soul: Gender and the Cycle of Life in a Hmong Village* (Seattle: University of Washington Press, 2004); Nicholas Tapp, Jean Michaud, and Christian Culas, eds., *Hmong/Miao in China* (Chiangmai, Thailand: Silkworm Books, 2004); Jeremy Hein, *Ethnic Origins: The Adaptation of Cambodian and Hmong Refugees in Four American Cities* (New York: Russell Sage, 2006); Yer J. Thao, *Mong Oral Tradition: Cultural Memory in the Absence of Written Language* (Jefferson, NC: McFarland & Company, 2006); Kao Kalia Yang, *The Latehomecomer: A Hmong Family Memoir* (Minneapolis, MN: Coffee House Press, 2008); Paul Hillmer, *A People's History of the Hmong* (St. Paul: Minnesota Historical Society Press, 2010); Chia Youyee Vang, *Hmong America: Reconstructing Community in Diaspora* (Champaign: University of Illinois Press, 2010).

3. *Split Horn: The Life of a Hmong Shaman in America*, VHS, directed by Taggart Siegel and Jim McSilver (San Francisco, CA: Independent Television Service, Corporation for Public Broadcasting, 2001). For other work by these authors, see, for example, Vincent K. Her and Mary Louise Buley-Meissner, "'Why Would We Want Those Students Here?': Bridges and Barriers to Building Campus-Community Partnerships," *Hmong Studies Journal* 7 (2006): 1–43; and Vincent K. Her and Mary Louise Buley-Meissner, "Hmong Voices and Memories: An Exploration of Identity, Culture, and History through *Bamboo Among the Oaks: Contemporary Writing by Hmong Americans*," *Journal of Asian American Studies* 13.1 (2010): 35–58.

4. Vincent K. Her, "Animal Sacrifice and Social Meanings in Hmong American Funerals," in *The Impact of Globalization and Trans-Nationalism on the Hmong*, ed. Gary Yia Lee (St. Paul, MN: Center for Hmong Studies, Concordia University, 2009), 3–11.

5. See, for example, Ruth Behar, *An Island Called Home: Returning to Jewish Cuba* (Piscataway, NJ: Rutgers University Press, 2009); Ruth Behar, *Translated Woman:*

Crossing the Border with Esperanza's Story, 2nd ed. (Boston: Beacon Press, 2003); and Ruth Behar, *The Vulnerable Observer: Anthropology That Breaks Your Heart* (Boston: Beacon Press, 1996). See also Corinne G. Dempsey, *The Goddess Lives in Upstate New York: Breaking Convention and Making a Home at a North American Hindu Temple* (New York: Oxford University Press, 2005); Diane Freedman and Olivia Frey, eds., *Autobiographical Writing across the Disciplines* (Durham, NC: Duke University Press, 2004); Deborah Holdstein and David Bleich, eds., *Personal Effects: The Social Character of Scholarly Writing* (Logan: Utah State University Press, 2001); Donald Trent Jacobs, *The Authentic Dissertation: Alternative Ways of Knowing, Research and Representation* (New York: Taylor and Francis, 2008); Dorrine Kondo, "Dissolution and Reconstitution of Self: Implications for Anthropological Epistemology," *Cultural Anthropology* 1.1 (1986): 74–88; Winona LaDuke, *Recovering the Sacred: The Power of Naming and Claiming* (Cambridge, MA: South End Press, 2005); Kirin Narayan, "How Native Is a Native Anthropologist?" *American Anthropologist* (New Series) 95.3 (1993): 671–86; Robert Nash, *Liberating Scholarly Writing: The Power of Personal Narrative* (New York: Teachers College Press, 2004); Jan Zlotnik Schmidt, ed., *Women/Writing/Teaching* (New York: State University of New York Press, 1998); Bronwyn T. Williams, ed., *Identity Papers* (Logan: Utah State University Press, 2006).

6. Samuel Pollard, *The Story of the Miao* (London: Henry Books, 1919); F. M. Savina, *Histoire de Miao* (1924; Hong Kong: Impr. de la Société des Missions-Étrangères, 1972). Quotation: Lue Vang and Judy Lewis, *Grandmother's Path, Grandfather's Way,* 2nd ed. (Rancho Cordova, CA: Vang and Lewis, 1990), iii, emphasis added.

7. William Robert Geddes, *Migrants of the Mountains: The Cultural Ecology of the Blue Miao (Hmong Njua) of Thailand* (Oxford: Clarendon Press, 1976). Quotation: Anne Fadiman, *The Spirit Catches You and You Fall Down: A Hmong Child, Her American Doctors and the Collision of Two Cultures* (New York: Farrar, Straus and Giroux, 1998), 17.

8. *Gran Torino,* DVD, directed by Clint Eastwood (Burbank, CA: Warner Bros. Pictures, 2008). Louisa Schein and Va-Megn Thoj, "*Gran Torino's* Boys and Men with Guns: Hmong Perspectives," *Hmong Studies Journal* 10 (2009): 1–52.

Sean Scallon, "Letter from the Upper Midwest: Diversity Bites," *Chronicle Magazine,* Feb. 1, 2005. Louisa Schein and Va-Megn Thoj, "Occult Racism: The Masking of Race in the Hmong Hunter Incident: A Dialogue between Anthropologist Louisa Schein and Filmmaker Va-Megn Thoj," *American Quarterly* 59.4 (2007): 1051–95.

Jessica McBride, "Cloak and Dagger," *Milwaukee Magazine,* Oct. 29, 2007, www.insidemilwaukee.com/Article/242011-CloakDagger (accessed Nov. 15, 2011); Anna Husarska, "Old Allies, Tagged 'Terrorist,'" *The Washington Post,* Dec. 16, 2006, www.washingtonpost.com/wp-dyn/content/article/2006/12/15/AR2006121501606.html (accessed Nov. 15, 2011). Erica Perez, "Provision of Patriot Act Treats Hmong as Terrorists," *Milwaukee Journal Sentinel,* Mar. 31, 2007, www.jsonline.com/news/milwaukee/29493854.html (accessed Nov. 15, 2011). Megan Twohey, "More Questions Than Answers," *Milwaukee Journal Sentinel,* Mar. 2, 2007; and "UW Professor Details Remarks," *Milwaukee Journal Sentinel,* Mar. 6, 2007. For a response to this controversy from scholars of Hmong American studies, see Dia Cha, Leena Her, Pao Lee, Ly Chong Tong Jalao, Louisa Schein, Chia Vang, Ma Vang, and Yang S. Xiong, "Perspectives: Knowledge, Authority and Hmong Invisibility," *Diverse Education,* Mar. 13, 2008, www.diverseeducation.com/artman/publish/printer_10828.shtml (accessed Nov. 15, 2011).

9. Yves Bertrais-Charrier, *Dictionnaire Hmong (Mèo Blanc)–Français* (Vientiane, Laos: Mission Catholique, distributed by the Cellar Book Shop, Detroit, 1964); Ernest E. Heimbach, *White Meo–English Dictionary* (Ithaca, NY: Cornell University Southeast Asia Program, 1969). Dwight Conquergood, "Fabricating Culture," in eds. Elizabeth C. Fine and Jean Haskell Speer, *Performance, Culture, and Identity* (Westport, CT: Praeger, 1992), 201–48; Sally Peterson, "Translating Experience and the Reading of a Story Cloth," *Journal of American Folklore* 101.99 (1988): 6–22. Paul Lewis and Elaine Lewis, "Hmong," in *Peoples of the Golden Triangle* (London: Thames and Hudson, 1984), 100–33; Sally Petersen, "Hmong Voices in Montana," *Journal of American Folklore,* 106.422 (1993): 468–75; Joanne Cubbs, "Hmong Art: Tradition and Change," in *Hmong Art: Tradition and Change* (Sheboygan, WI: John Michael Kohler Arts Center, 1986), 21–30.

10. For information on population statistics, see the Hmong Studies Internet Resource Center website (www.hmongstudies.org) for data compiled by Mark Pfeifer. Jacques Lemoine, "What Is the Actual Number of Hmong in the World?" *Hmong Studies Journal* 6 (2005): 1–8, provides information on Hmong population worldwide.

11. Benedict Anderson, *Imagined Communities: Reflections on the Origin and Spread of Nationalism* (New York: Verso, 1983).

12. Moua, *Bamboo Among the Oaks,* 6–7.

13. For recent research on Hmong and Hmong American literacy development, see John Duffy, *Writing from These Roots: Literacy in a Hmong-American Community* (Honolulu: University of Hawai'i Press, 2007).

14. Roger Daniels, *Coming to America,* 2nd ed. (New York: Harper Perennial, 2002); and Roger Daniels, *Guarding the Golden Door: American Immigration Policy and Immigrants since 1882* (New York: Hill and Wang, 2004); K. Tsianina Lomawaima and Teresa McCarty, *To Remain an Indian: Lessons in Democracy from a Century of Native American Education* (New York: Teachers College Press, 2006); Susan Forbes Martin, *A Nation of Immigrants* (New York: Cambridge University Press, 2010); Gary Okihiro, *Common Ground: Reimagining American History* (Princeton, NJ: Princeton University Press, 2001); and Gary Okihiro, *Margins and Mainstreams: Asians in American History and Culture* (Seattle: University of Washington Press,

1994); Alejandro Portes and Ruben Rumbau, *Immigrant America: A Portrait,* 3rd ed. (Berkeley: University of California Press, 2006); Ronald Takaki, *A Different Mirror: A History of Multicultural America,* rev. ed. (Boston: Back Bay, 2008); and Ronald Takaki, *A Larger Memory: A History of Our Diversity, With Voices* (Boston: Back Bay, 1998). Among the many acts of legislation attempting to define who can and cannot become an American citizen, five of the most important are the Naturalization Act of 1790, the Chinese Exclusion Act of 1882, the Quota Act of 1921, the National Origins Act of 1924, and the Immigration Act of 1965. U.S. Bureau of the Census, 2010 Census Data: 2010.census.gov/2010census/data/.

15. Stuart Hall, "Cultural Identity and Diaspora," in *Identity: Community, Culture, Difference,* ed. Jonathan Rutherford (London: Lawrence & Wishart, 1993), 222–37. Quotation: Bee Cha, "Being Hmong Is Not Enough," in ed. Mai Neng Moua, *Bamboo Among the Oaks,* 24, emphasis in original.

16. History: Paul Hillmer, *A People's History of the Hmong;* Gayle Morrison, *Sky Is Falling: An Oral History of the CIA's Evacuation of the Hmong from Laos* (Jefferson, NC: McFarland, 2007); Keith Quincy, *Harvesting Pa Chay's Wheat: The Hmong and America's Secret War in Laos* (Spokane: Eastern Washington University Press, 2000). Resettlement, adaptation, and identity: Nancy D. Donnelly, *Changing Lives of Refugee Hmong Women* (Seattle: University of Washington Press, 1997); Lilian Faderman and Ghia Xiong, *I Begin My Life All Over: The Hmong and the American Immigrant Experience* (Boston: Beacon Press, 1998); Cathleen Jo Faruque, *Migration of Hmong to the Midwestern United States* (Lanham, MD: University Press of America, 2002); Chia Youyee Vang, *Hmong in Minnesota* (St. Paul: Minnesota Historical Society Press, 2008). See also Sucheng Chan's work in note 2. Community life and cultural renewal: Julie Bomar-Keown, *Kinship Networks among Hmong-American Refugees* (El Paso, TX: LFB Scholarly Publishing, 2005); Jo Ann Koltyk, *New Pioneers in the Heartland: Hmong Life in Wisconsin* (Boston: Allyn and Bacon, 1997); Thao, *Mong Oral Tradition;* Gary Yia Lee and Nicholas Tapp, *Culture and Customs of the Hmong* (Santa Barbara, CA: Greenwood, 2010). Health care: Dia Cha, *Hmong American Concepts of Health* (New York: Taylor and Francis, 2003); Fadiman, *The Spirit Catches You.* Education and youth: Stacey J. Lee, *Up Against Whiteness: Race, School and Immigrant Youth* (New York: Teachers College Press, 2005); Bic Ngo, "Contesting Culture: The Perspectives of Hmong American Female Students on Early Marriage," *Anthropology and Education Quarterly* 33.2 (2002): 163–88. Myths, legends, and folktales: Charles Johnson and Se Yang, eds., *Myths, Legends and Folktales from the Hmong of Laos,* 2nd ed. (St. Paul, MN: Macalester College Linguistics Department, 1992).

Mark Pfeifer, *Hmong-Related Works, 1996–2006: An Annotated Bibliography* (Lanham, MD: Scarecrow Press, 2007). Nancy K. Herther, "Citation Analysis and Hmong Studies Publications: An Initial Examination," *Hmong Studies Journal* 10 (2010): 7–8.

17. Downing and Olney, *Hmong in the West*.

18. This view of enrollment is widely shared by people working in Hmong American studies. For their assistance in identifying Wisconsin enrollment trends, we thank two of our colleagues at the University of Wisconsin–Milwaukee: Dao Vang, Southeast Asian American Student Services coordinator, and Linda Huang, Administrative Program Manager in the College of Letters and Science. Preliminary data (unpublished) that we compiled in 2005 for four-year campuses in the University of Wisconsin System showed a steady rise in Hmong American undergraduate enrollment from the mid-1980s to the mid-2000s. In California, Professor Kou Yang (e-mail communication dated June 20, 2011) also has observed a significant increase in the number of Hmong American students in higher learning. Moreover, he notes that when he started teaching college courses in the late 1980s, the majority of Hmong American students were male and foreign born. In the last ten years, he has noticed a definite rise in the enrollment of Hmong American female students, most of whom are U.S. born. In his view, this trend could lead to an imbalance that should be of concern to the Hmong American community. Conversations with fellow educators at professional conferences such as those sponsored by Hmong National Development, Inc., Southeast Asian Resource Action Center (SEARAC), and the Center for Hmong Studies also have affirmed a continuing trend of increasing enrollment for Hmong American students.

19. Yang, *Hmong at the Turning Point*. Cha, *Hmong American Concepts;* Lo, *The Promised Land;* Thao, *Mong Oral Tradition;* Bruce Bliatout Thowpaou, *Hmong Sudden Expected Nocturnal Death Syndrome: A Cultural Study* (Portland, OR: Sparkle Publishing Enterprises, Inc., 1982); Vang, *Hmong in Minnesota* and *Hmong America;* Vang and Lewis, *Grandmother's Path*. On creative and literary work, see Moua, ed., *Bamboo Among the Oaks*. For autobiography, see Houa Vue Moua and Barbara Rolland, *Trail Through the Mists* (Eau Claire, WI: Vue and Rolland, 1994); Victor Neeejthoob Xiong, *From Refugees to Hmong Americans: Where in the World Do I Belong?* (Milwaukee, WI: PIP Printing, 2006); Yang, *The Latehomecomer*. And for examples of fiction, see Gary Yia Lee, *Dust of Life* (St. Paul, MN: Hmongland Publishing Company, 2004); Keith Quincy and See Vue, *Der: A True Story* (Marshall, WA: GPJ Books, 2007).

PART I

Identity and History

< 2 >

Searching for Sources of Hmong Identity in Multicultural America

VINCENT K. HER

The identity of an ethnic group is relatively stable with deep roots in family, culture, tradition, and history. Extensive research also has shown that politics, race, and intergroup interactions are all important considerations for individual and group identity formation. As Stuart Hall notes: "Cultural identities come from somewhere, have histories. But, like everything which is historical, they undergo constant transformation." For Hmong Americans, where should this *somewhere* in the development of their identity be located, what are the stories that constitute their *histories,* and what forces are influencing the *transformations* within their families and communities?[1]

As Hmong Americans situate themselves within the twenty-first century, what bonds them locally and globally and what links them to others in U.S. society? Being Hmong in America today is different radically from being Hmong in Laos or in the refugee camps of Thailand in the 1970s and 1980s. Yet, for those of us who are first-generation Hmong Americans, being Hmong in the United States continues to be influenced by our collective experiences in the other countries where we were born (and, in the case of the 1.5 generation, where we first were educated). Our lives have been altered by transnational migration. More significantly, our outlook has been nurtured by the ideology, beliefs, and lifeways of our adopted home country. People necessarily rethink their identities as they pick up new ideas, respond to contemporary challenges, and assess their contributions to society. The aim of this chapter is to explore identity formation within the context of transitions and changes accompanying Hmong adaptation to American society.

< 31 >

Experiential Approach to Identity

At a community conference in April 2011, an elder of the Vue clan stopped by at the conclusion of my workshop to introduce himself. After thanking me for the presentation, he forthrightly stated his disappointment at what I had *not* said. In his view, I should have been more explicit about the specific meaning of Hmong. "I know that you know what Hmong is," he said, "Tell the audience what you know. I wish you would *hais kom khov thiab muaj ceem tshaj ko.*" That is, I should "tell it as it is" rather than leave too much room for interpretation and questioning. This advice made me ponder once again questions central to my work in Hmong and Hmong American studies: What essential elements do people look for when defining what is Hmong? Also, do certain perspectives hold greater authority than others in portraying the changing lives of Hmong and Hmong Americans?

As a Hmong American educator, I have indeed developed my own perspective on what is Hmong and American; equally important, I recognize how productive it is for people—Hmong and non-Hmong, men and women, parents and children—to engage in discussion where different points of views on Hmong identity can be shared. Guiding my ongoing work in Hmong American studies is this goal to promote dialogue in families, communities, and schools on how Hmong have integrated into American society.

This writing is an experiential approach to exploring Hmong American identity. It is informed by the conviction that multiple entry points can lead to deeper understanding of the evolving meaning of what is Hmong, thereby contributing to scholarship on Hmong history, culture, and life experiences. Since I will include information that pushes the boundaries of ethnographic subjectivity, what follows is an understanding of Hmong American experience that is deliberately "situated." Here, I am embracing the concept of "self-inscription" as a means to link firsthand knowledge of what has happened in the recent past to broader understandings of community history and identity formation. I owe this inspiration to David Bleich, who writes: "Many of us want to speak more deeply from personal experience, to add this dimension to the habits of scholarly citation and critical interpretation. Our desire for self-inclusion has led to new genres of writing, new styles of knowledge." In this spirit, I include my family's story as a segue into history, to establish for this essay an important *somewhere* in

Hmong identity development. Although that point is not fixed, a Hmong American sense of place in the world and in human history has greatly been influenced by events of the 1960s and 1970s.[2]

Reenvisioning Community History through Firsthand Knowledge

Born at the start of the Secret War in Laos, I lived through its horrors as a child. I remember running away from Long Cheng in the dark with my mother and brother, as bombs and artilleries showered the base. After the Americans left, our family spent three harsh years, from 1976 to 1979, in the jungles of northern Laos, running, hiding, and evading death. To stay alive, we ate *qos ncoom* and *muas thiv,* types of wild tubers. During that time, I also experienced the terror of being chased by soldiers and shot at. I witnessed a friend die a slow, excruciating death when his abdomen was pierced by a piece of bomb shrapnel.[3]

Does firsthand knowledge of the past, told in the first person, hold value as history? This is a question of scholarship that has long been debated. In the West, history is widely perceived as a search for objective knowledge. Within its framework, a place has been reserved, by convention and tradition, for those who have made a highly valued difference to their community or country. Their achievements determine what society is to remember. In Hmong culture, every person's story, rich or poor, young or old, influential or unknown, is told. His or her life is recounted as community history during *zaaj qhuab ke,* or death initiation song. This traditional approach to remembering the past differs from the conventions of the West in that it is more inclusive. Every person deserves and is given a place in history.

In March 1979, our family arrived (with a group of about three hundred people) on the shores of the Mekong River as refugees of war. Under the cover of night, we crossed the Mekong into Thailand on the canoes of Thai smugglers. Early the next day, Thai border patrols confronted us as we marched, exhausted and starving, toward a main road just beyond the shoreline. After they had collected all of the weapons (M-16s, AK-47s, and B-40s) from the men, we were transported to a temporary shelter on the outskirts of Chiang Khan, a town in northern Thailand on the banks of the Mekong. From that location, Laos was just a stone's throw away. We could hear children shouting, babies crying, and roosters crowing from the other side. Thai officials reminded us that the border between Laos and Thailand runs directly through the middle of the Mekong River.

In my course "Refugees, Displaced Persons, and Transnational Communities," we discuss what it means to be a refugee; trace the history of refugee movement starting in the early twentieth century; and debate the politics and symbolism surrounding international borders, especially in terms of sovereignty, citizenship, and identity. On one side of the imagined line separating Laos and Thailand, Hmong were citizens unwanted; on the other, we were refugees unwanted. One country pushed us; the other accepted us, but only under strict conditions. After a month in Chiang Khan, we were relocated to Ban Vinai, where our family ended up in Center One, Quarter One, Building Six, Room Ten. Our room measured no bigger than twenty feet by thirty feet. For nine months, this single room became our home, or more aptly in my parents' words, a *chaw nraim ntxoo,* a shade from the sun. Yet, far reaching is the significance of each room to Hmong historical memory. Each building was a temporary shelter holding together Hmong lives fragmented by war, political conflict, and forced migration.[4]

In Ban Vinai, Hmong refugees did not hear of gold mountains, or frontier land awaiting settlement. Some held firm to hopes that there would be a future back in Laos; others left the camp as soon as they could in search of a new start abroad. Yet, not all who came to the United States grasped the full significance of their decisions. This is what Txhaj Xeeb, an elder of the Moua clan, said: "Everybody left so I simply followed. I didn't know what the future holds."[5]

New Beginnings in America

In the late 1970s to early 1980s, everything in this country was alien to Hmong refugees. What was routine for American citizens had yet to become customary to them. From teenagers to adults, people were full of nostalgia. Fresh on their minds were memories of home on the cloud-covered mountaintops of *Naaj Khasmav,* on the fertile slopes of *Phuaj Ee,* or in the scorching valleys of *Naaj Noi.* Physically they had left, but unshakable were people's feelings of *ncu teb ncu chaw,* attachment to places where they had made their lives. Home was over there and not yet over here. In the United States, Hmong appeared out of place as they struggled to transfer their village-based skills to a modern environment. Media outlets picked up their stories and began to question whether Hmong refugees could fit in and contribute substantially to the communities where they lived. Initially, Hmong themselves were not sure how to make this country their home. Hints of this can be found in their ritual text, as this example shows:

> Upon arriving in this country, I did not see cousins or relatives.
> What I saw were *nam Maab nam Suav* [strangers and foreigners].
> I am all alone.
> The knowledge I have brought over is no longer sufficient;
> What I have learned is now incompatible.
> . . .
> I abandoned all of my *kwvtij* [brothers and cousins] in the old
>   country.
> I had left behind all of my relatives.
> Reaching to the future, I find nothing to hang on to.
> Far beyond my reach lies the past.
> . . .
> Every time I sit down to a meal of *zaub tsuag* [plain boiled greens],
> I hear dirging so full of sorrow.
> Each dish of plain rice brings out more sadness and grief.
> Looking to the sky, I see stars scattered in full display;
> The night is a camouflage of colors.
> I have nothing with which to start a family.
> How shall I begin my life?
> Thinking about all of this has brought me many tears.
> Much of it has fallen, soaking my shirt, soaking my shirt.[6]

This *qeej* song conveys sentiments widely shared by Hmong refugees upon their arrival in this country. It shows their hesitations in a land where strange faces have yet to become familiar. Especially poignant was their sense of fragmentation, of being uprooted, making yearnings for family (*kwv tij*) and home (Laos) that much harder to tolerate. Although Hmong resettlement has been a subject of intense study, few have focused on the emotional elements of their transition to urban life. When people have told me about what was going through their hearts and minds during the first few years of life in this country, most have described that early period as *ua neej tsaus ntuj,* "to live a life in the dark." Other phrases used to articulate their feelings include *lwj sab,* "to be overwhelmed by the difficulties of life"; *nyuaj sab,* "to feel pressured by everyday concerns"; and *ntxhuv sab,* "to worry endlessly." All of these concepts point to the relentless, life-draining emotions involved in beginning a new life. As these sentiments and feelings are unveiled, we gain a better understanding of the hidden struggles at the heart of the Hmong immigrant experience.[7]

Reviving Hmong Culture

Rebuilding their lives in the Midwest was a daunting task for Hmong refugees. Their identities as Americans were to be shaped, in part, by their own choices. Some converted to Christianity. Others held on to Hmong traditional beliefs. Forced by necessity, this latter group came together, with husbands and wives as collaborators, to find ways to reconstitute Hmong culture in an urban setting. At the start, people congregated in family basements and living rooms to share their frustrations; to discuss what is and is not possible in American society; and to chart new paths for the future. These gatherings became the impetus behind the creation of self-help organizations including, for example, Shee Yee Community of Milwaukee.

Keeping their cultural heritage intact at a period when their lives were severely fragmented was a pressing concern facing Hmong refugees in the early 1980s. To revive Hmong culture, many practitioners volunteered to organize workshops to give people opportunities to acquire the skills necessary to carry out a specific rite, ritual, or ceremony. For example, at these mock sessions, people learned the intricate procedures of *zaaj qhuab ke* (death initiation song) and the key steps, from beginning to end, of performing *qeej tu sav* (*qeej* performance to open the funeral proceeding). Practitioners were strategic in their efforts. They understood that without trained individuals to take on these critical roles, a traditional funeral was all but impossible.

To ensure that the most essential components of Hmong culture—all of those elements that a community cannot do without—would be preserved, practitioners began to write down what they knew, including step-by-step instructions. Others recorded *zaaj xai* (songs of teachings in a funeral) and *nkauj* (songs accompanying *qeej* performances) on cassette tapes (some of which were later transcribed by their students and turned into manuscripts). Those who could not write pressed their sons and nephews, with great urgency, to write down their *txujci* (knowledge and teachings).

All of these early efforts to document Hmong culture also gave it a new life. Writing allowed the esoteric knowledge held by a select few to be shared with a wider audience of potential learners in the Hmong American community. More important, as text, that knowledge has been reorganized by practitioners to give it fresh meanings. Their actions clearly have suggested the need for scholars to reevaluate long-held assumptions in Hmong studies about Hmong culture being resistant to reexamination and change. Cultural change occurs when practitioners add new elements to their traditions or remove parts that have diminished in relevance.

Many well-respected practitioners today, from *mej koob* to *coj xai,* are individuals who have developed a thirst for knowledge by helping elders to record what has been passed down from generation to generation by a rich oral tradition. Through these purposeful interactions, young people have discovered their own ability to acquire and apply traditional knowledge. As their understanding of Hmong culture has grown, they have gained the confidence to engage their elders in considering how tradition can be adapted within the constraints of modern society. For example, could the repetitive parts of *zaaj qhuab ke* or *qeej tu sav* be streamlined to make its performance less time consuming? Concerns such as this have motivated Hmong Americans to fine-tune their tradition and keep it current with the changing realities of their lives.[8]

In addition to the collaboration between older and younger Hmong Americans, a significant development responsible for bringing permanent change to Hmong culture in the Midwest has concerned the status of women practitioners. For example, in Laos, a woman *txiv neeb* (shaman) commonly would refuse her seat at the table during the *ua tsaug* (thank you) ceremony when the men were acknowledging her help. By convention, her husband, who served as her assistant, would take her place. In the United States, people began to question this practice. Now Hmong Americans agree that she should be seated ahead of her husband and be accorded the same privileges as her male counterparts. Although small, this change shows how Hmong Americans are open to modern influences on their culture.

Within several years of their arrival, Hmong refugees began to put up *xwm kaab* (altars) in their homes. They held *nqee plig* ceremonies to celebrate the birth of their children. To ensure fresh starts to the New Year, they called on *txiv neeb* to perform *neeb kaab plig* (an annual cleansing ceremony). In addition, they revived many *noj tsab* (New Year) traditions, including *pe tsab*. This is when mothers and fathers take their sons and nephews from house to house to pay respects to grandparents, aunts, and uncles and to ask for their blessings. The revival of these traditional practices was vital to Hmong immigrants as they began their American lives. These family-oriented festivities provided the structure necessary for people to maintain continuity from Southeast Asia to the United States. They afforded opportunities for husbands and wives to renew their commitment to one another, to their children, and to their culture. Only with the stability in their families soundly assured were husbands and wives able to plan for the future, to turn a decisive corner in Hmong integration to modern society.[9]

Culture in Hmong American Identity

In the eyes of Hmong elders, cultural retention is key to the continued existence of Hmong identity. One of the lessons they try to impress on their children and grandchildren, even to the point of being unrelenting, is that Hmong should remember to *khaws Moob teej Moob tug,* or safeguard what is Hmong. For *qeej* players, the song below is a potent reminder of the link between tradition and cultural continuity.

> Follow the traditions of the ancestors.
> Learn the knowledge and skills of elders.
> What makes tradition important?
> How are the practices handed down significant?
>
> Tradition is knowledge
> Gifts of wisdom are the practices of the older generation.
> Knowing tradition makes one articulate.
> Learning the ways of the older generation renders one more
>   competent.
> For thousands of years, do not let the traditions of the ancestors
>   disappear;
> For centuries to come, keep the practices of previous generations
>   from fading away.

Tradition is knowledge of self, family, and society. It is identity rooted in the Hmong concept *puj ua tseg yawm ua ca*, or a way of life founded on the wisdom of the ancestors. When I asked an elder of the Xiong clan to explain the meaning of that Hmong phrase, this is how he articulated his answer: *"Tej laug txuj yog kev paub taab; tej laug ci yog kev paub cai."* That is, knowledge of the elders is depth of understanding; tradition is knowing the norms, conventions, and expectations of society. In his view, competency is the ability to grasp the implications of a culture's morals, values, and teachings in everyday life. To be articulate is to take what has been learned and put it to use to advance self, family, and community.

Whether a person chooses to be Hmong, American, or Hmong American, a cultural component is unquestionably mixed into her identity. In my view, practical knowledge of tradition is beneficial in several ways to Hmong Americans, especially young people. First, it allows them to evaluate for themselves the depth of creativity behind their culture, religion, and spirituality. Second, it provides them with the know-how necessary to capably fulfill obligations to family and extended families. Finally, it makes them more effective agents of change. I have learned that elders are much more inclined to listen to—and accept suggestions from—those who have acquired an informed understanding of Hmong culture.

In the United States, practitioners have been receptive to the idea that the rules of tradition should be reexamined and that the retaining walls of knowledge can be made more porous. In the Midwest, I am encouraged to see Hmong American girls breaking tradition to learn how to play *qeej*. Their courage has earned support and praise from other Hmong Americans, including well-respected *txiv qeej* (qeej players). More important, the performance of women at funerals is opening space for change in a sphere of power dominated by men and boys. Their contributions not only blur gender lines but also have become a source of debate among scholars of Hmong American studies, elders, and activists regarding how knowledge in a culture is created, put to use, and passed on. Amid newly acquired sensibilities, Hmong Americans have been pressed to reassess cultural norms that have long governed the roles and responsibilities of men and women. Through ongoing cultural adjustments, Hmong Americans are taking a concerted look at who they once were, how they have changed, and what they would like to become.

Hmong and the Story of America

In the Midwest, Hmong Americans have assumed their place in society as politicians, educators, assembly workers, welders, and health care professionals. Inseparably linked are their lives now to this multicultural nation. From Madison to Wausau, Green Bay to La Crosse, and Milwaukee to St. Paul, Hmong immigrants are continuing to build their lives as Americans. Their efforts have been motivated by a belief in the American dream that Hmong, too, can climb up the socioeconomic ladder as citizens of this country. While that dream has become a reality for some, I believe, as do most of my students, that the most important milestone in Hmong integration will be reached when their stories have been woven into the living memories of this nation.

This appears inevitable as Hmong Americans continue to search for meaning in their lives beyond the boundaries of their communities, taking their places in newly unfolding chapters of America's multicultural history. Across campuses in the Midwest, Hmong American college youth have demonstrated that they are more willing than older generations to speak out on issues of equality and equity affecting all Americans. For example, to make their presence visible and to form cross-ethnic alliances for change, they have organized annual conferences on topics ranging from racism and discrimination in public schools to global human rights. In addition, I have seen Hmong American students become exceptionally active on student senate and in university committees, gaining the skills and confidence necessary to collaborate with others in working for social justice. Finally, inspired by the formation of African American studies, Asian American studies, Latino/a American studies, and ethnic studies, Hmong American students have been leading the push on their campuses for more course offerings in Hmong American studies. By using their education to promote positive change, they are giving Hmong Americans a much more prominent voice in American society.

The road Hmong Americans have taken to get to where they are today has been a winding one, paved with stories of success and ongoing challenges. In the 1980s, Hmong entered the U.S. imagination as "backward" and "primitive" refugees who could not be assimilated. In the 1990s, they assumed the national spotlight in America's debate over integrated schools and immigration reform. The eyes of the nation were on Wausau,

Wisconsin, when its school boards attempted to integrate the school districts by busing students to schools outside of the area where they lived. The racial imbalance seen in many schools there was blamed on Hmong immigration. In the 2000s, issues of race and national security confronted the Hmong American community head on. Race became front and center when Chai Soua Vang, who is currently serving six consecutive life terms, killed six hunters in northern Wisconsin in 2004 following a verbal dispute over a tree stand. Three years later, those racial tensions resurfaced in the murder of Cha Vang in northeastern Wisconsin by a Caucasian hunter. Signed into law by President George W. Bush in 2006, the Patriot Act classified Hmong as "terrorists." Its impact on the Hmong American community became clear with the arrests of Vang Pao and eight others in 2007.[10]

History tells us that the experiences of Hmong Americans are not unique. Issues of race, immigration, and national origin have always been at the heart of the identity debate in American society. At one point in our nation's history, blood lineage was used to bolster racial divisions. Who was black was determined by the one-drop rule. A child during America's slavery years was to inherit the status of his or her mother. Mulatto children were considered black; some were enslaved by their own fathers. Moreover, between the 1780s and 1860s, an African American individual, under the U.S. Constitution, counted only as three-fifths of a person. In many states, miscegenation laws remained in the books until the 1960s. These institutional practices have left lingering effects on our national consciousness and the definition of who is an American.[11]

In principle, the United States is a nation of immigrants. Yet, at the practical level where policies are envisioned and enforced, the struggle for social justice and equality has been an ongoing fact of life. For example, many of our nation's immigration policies welcomed some and excluded others: the Naturalization Act of 1790 granted citizenship only to "free" whites; the Chinese Exclusion Act of 1882 restricted Chinese immigration to the United States for nearly sixty years; and the Quota Act of 1921 instituted an annual ceiling for immigrants of any nationality to a small percentage of the foreign-born persons of that nationality already in the United States. In each piece of legislation, racial preference was made explicit and legal. In addition, Americans considered the expansion of the country from east to west to be manifest destiny, a vision of nation building that did not respect the integrity of America's diverse groups.

A narrowly defined path to becoming American emerged as immigrants were expected to learn English, convert to Christianity, and become private property owners. Since the passage of the Immigration and Nationality Act of 1965, these expectations have been opened to broader interpretation in recognition of the United States as a destination country for immigrants from all over the world.[12]

In the unfolding narrative of the United States as an increasingly diverse nation, Hmong Americans hope to be recognized as full citizens who have made this country their home. Like other immigrant groups before them, Hmong refugees came to this country to save themselves, their culture, and their religion. Today, what it means to be Hmong and American is informed by a complex clan and interclan network, akin to Clifford Geertz's notion of "webs of significance." In a funeral, this aspect of Hmong life becomes especially apparent. Relatives on both sides of the deceased's family are asked to serve as role participants, or *hauv dlej hauv num*. The closer a person is to the deceased in that hierarchy of kinship relations, the more likely he or she is to accept a role. In that ritual context, the most meaningful relationships to a Hmong American are those dictated by *caaj ceg* (birth and lineage), *kwv tij* (clan and extended clans), and *neej tsaa* (interclan or marriage relationships). These bonds are lifelong, shaping individual priorities and commitments as much as, or even more than, other influences in modern society. Today, multiple expectations have converged, adding to the full meaning of what is Hmong and American.[13]

Conclusion

Using the lenses of history, culture, and the American immigrant experience, this chapter opens potential avenues for exploring Hmong American identity formation. Since 1975, the "somewhere" in Hmong identity development has taken root in the United States. For Hmong refugees, Laos was once home. For their children and grandchildren, it is only a distant place in their Hmong American story. Yet, across generations, Hmong Americans are bound to one another by what is happening in their families and communities; by ongoing debates in this country to clarify the grounds and rights of citizenship; and by global conflicts where Hmong have played key roles in U.S. and world history.

Hmong beginnings in this country were humble. From the 1970s until now, what it means to be Hmong and American has been informed by persistent efforts in families and communities to (re)build Hmong lives in the Midwest and across the United States. Such efforts have resulted in the deliberate restructuring of Hmong culture to make its traditions and practices consistent with a modern outlook. In light of these changes, "Hmong" no longer connotes, as it did for much of its history, a people circumscribed by geography or bounded by cultural absolutes. Signifying the name of a group, the power, elusiveness, and appeal of this word lie in its complex layers of history. While the origin of the term "Hmong" remains a source of disagreement, its contemporary American meaning has been broadened with each reinterpretation.[14]

NOTES

1. For debates on identity development and formation in the United States, especially in relationship to race, see Akeel Bilgrami, "Notes toward the Definition of Identity," *Daedalus* 135 (2006): 4–15; Karen A. Cerulo, "Identity Construction: New Issues, New Directions," *Annual Review of Sociology* 23 (1997): 385–409; Kenneth Prewitt, "Racial Classification in America: Where Do We Go From Here?" *Daedalus* 134 (2005): 5–17; Jimy M. Sanders, "Ethnic Boundaries and Identity in Plural Societies," *Annual Review of Sociology* 28 (2002): 327–57. For a discussion on stereotypes of Hmong people, see Mai Na Lee, "The Thousand-Year Myth: Construction and Characterization of Hmong," *Hmong Studies Journal* 2.1(1998): 1–23. Stuart Hall, "Cultural Identity and Diaspora," in ed. Jonathan Rutherford, *Identity: Community, Culture, Difference* (London: Lawrence & Wishart, 1993), 225.

2. Across disciplines, there is the realization that the norm of framing scholarship, of outsiders looking in, is only one of the ways to appreciate how people live their lives. In anthropology, scholars have responded to this shift in thinking by experimenting with approaches to include experiential, sensory, and bodily forms of knowing as central to the aims of research. I have been inspired by the extensive literature on this form of scholarship: Ruth Behar, *Translated Woman: Crossing the Border with Esperanza's Story* (Boston: Beacon Press, 1993); Arthur P. Bochner and Carolyn Ellis, eds., *Ethnographically Speaking: Autoethnography, Literature, and Aesthetics* (Walnut Creek, CA: AltaMira Press, 2002); Diane Freeman and Olivia Frey, eds., *Autobiographical Writing across the Disciplines: A Reader* (Durham, NC: Duke University Press, 2003); Paul Stoller, *Sensuous Scholarship* (Philadelphia: University of Pennsylvania Press, 1997); Barbara Tedlock, *The Beautiful and the Dangerous: Encounters with the Zuni Indians* (New York: Penguin Group, 1992).

Donna Haraway, "Situated Knowledge: The Science Question in Feminism and the Privilege of Partial Perspective," *Feminist Studies* 14.3 (1988): 575–99. David Bleich, "Finding the Right Word: Self-Inclusion and Self-Inscription," in eds. Freeman and Frey, *Autobiographical Writing across the Disciplines*, 41.

For those interested in developing a local, regional, and global understanding of the conflicts leading to the Vietnam War, see John H. Fifield, "The Thirty Years War in Indochina: A Conceptual Framework," *Asian Survey* 17 (1977): 857–79. To see how the Secret War in Laos changed Hmong lives, see W. E. Garrett, "The Hmong of Laos: No Place to Run," *National Geographic* 145.1 (1974): 78–111. For a review of the impact of the Vietnam War on the American consciousness, see also Howard Zinn, *A People's History of the United States: 1492–Present* (New York: HarperCollins Publishers, 2003), 469–501. A discussion of the constitutionality of the Vietnam War is provided by John Hart Ely, "The American War in Indochina, Part 2: The Unconstitutionality of the War They Didn't Tell Us About," *Stanford Law Review* 42 (1990): 1093–148.

3. For Hmong American accounts of their lives in Laos and the United States, see Sucheng Chan, *Hmong Means Free* (Philadelphia, PA: Templeton University Press, 1994); Wendy Mattison, Laotu Lo, and Thomas Scarseth, *Hmong Lives: From Laos to La Crosse* (La Crosse, WI: The Pump House, 1994). For a rare account of one of the battles between North Vietnamese troops and ethnic Laotian soldiers (most of whom were Hmong) for the control of Long Cheng, see William M. Leary, "The CIA and the Secret War in Laos: The Battle for Skyline Ridge, 1971–1972," *Journal of Military History* 59 (1995): 505–17.

A small group of Hmong remains in hiding in Laos. Their struggles, however, have received little U.S. and international attention. For more information, see Thomas Fuller, "Old U.S. Allies, Still Hiding in Laos," *New York Times*, Dec. 17, 2007; Tomas Van Houtryve, "The Forgotten Soldiers," *New York Times*, Dec. 16, 2007; Joshua Castellino, "The Hmong Struggle in Laos: Freedom Fighters or Terrorists?" *American Chronicle*, June 8, 2007.

4. For more on refugee life, see Dwight Conquergood, "Health Theatre in a Hmong Refugee Camp: Performance, Communication, and Culture," *TDR* 32 (1988): 174–208; Lillian Faderman and Ghia Xiong, *I Begin My Life Over: The Hmong and the American Immigrant Experience* (Boston: Beacon Press, 1998); Sally Peterson, "Translating Experience and the Reading of a Story Cloth," *Journal of American Folklore* 101.99 (1988): 6–22; Kao Kalia Yang, *The Latehomecomer: A Hmong Family Memoir* (Minneapolis, MN: Coffee House Press, 2008).

5. The reasons Hmong refugees did not want to come to the United States were complicated. Some insights into this issue have been offered by Keith Quincy, *Harvesting Pa Chay's Wheat: The Hmong and America's Secret War in Laos* (Spokane: Eastern Washington University Press, 2000).

Txhaj Xeeb's words in Hmong: *"Suav dlawg tuaj taag tes kuv ca le caum qaab xwb. Yeej tsi pum lub neej tom ntej."*

6. For further discussion of adjustment to American society, see Anne

Fadiman, *The Spirit Catches You and You Fall Down: A Hmong Child, Her American Doctors, and the Collision of Two Cultures* (New York: Noonday Press, 1997); see also Faderman and Xiong, *I Begin My Life Over.*

These names are of Hmong villages in the Muang Phuong district, a municipality just north of the city of Vangviang. Hmong Americans refer to people from this region as "Moob Moospheeb" (Hmong of Muang Phuong). Villages mentioned have since the 1970s been abandoned.

For recent examples of how Hmong continue to be viewed as unwelcome refugees, see Joe Guzzardi, "Hmong Wrong for America. America Wrong for Hmong," vdare.com, Aug. 1, 2003; Sean Scallon, "Letter from the Upper Midwest: Diversity Bites," *Chronicle Magazine*, Feb. 1, 2005.

7. Research by Joseph Westermeyer and his colleagues suggests that depression and anxiety were common among Hmong refugees. For example, see Joseph Westermeyer, John Neider, and Tou Fu Vang, "Acculturation and Mental Health: A Study of Hmong Refugees at 1.5 and 3.5 Years Postmigration," *Social Science & Medicine* 18.1 (1984): 87–93; Joseph Westermeyer, John Neider, and Allen Callies, "Psychosocial Adjustment of Hmong Refugees during Their First Decade in the United States: A Longitudinal Study," *Journal of Nervous and Mental Disease* 177.3 (1989): 132–39; and Joseph Westermeyer, "Prevention of Mental Disorder among Hmong Refugees in the U.S.: Lessons from the Period 1976–1986," *Social Science & Medicine* 25.8 (1987): 941–47.

8. A *mej koob* is a person with intricate knowledge of wedding ceremonies and wedding negotiations. In a wedding, one *mej koob* represents the groom's family and one represents the bride's family. They serve as intermediaries during the negotiation. Afterward, they also manage all of the ceremonial aspects of the proceedings. A *coj xai* is the individual hired by the family to deliver the songs of teaching (*qhuab kom*) and blessing (*foom kom*) in a funeral to the children and grandchildren of the deceased.

9. For information on Hmong village life in Laos and Thailand, see Robert Cooper, *Hmong: A Guide to Traditional Lifestyles* (Singapore: Times Edition, 1998).

10. For controversies surrounding the immigration debate and Hmong Americans, see Roy Beck, "The Ordeal of Immigration in Wausau," *Atlantic Monthly*, Apr. 1, 1994, 84–97. For press coverage of the incident, see Bob Kelleher, "Hunter Kills Six, Wounds Two after Tree-Stand Dispute," Minnesota Public Radio, Nov. 22, 2004; Brandt Williams and Bob Kelleher, "Man Arrested for Deer-Stand Shooting Says He Was Fired on First; Hmong Leaders Condemn Shooting," Minnesota Public Radio, Nov. 23, 2004; *Associated Press,* "Man Who Shot Hunters Found Guilty of Homicide," MSNBC, Sept. 5, 2005; Catherine Donaldson-Evans, Jane Roh and the Associated Press, "Arrest Made in Wisconsin Hunting Massacre," Fox News, Nov. 22, 2004.

This incident is discussed by Robert Gutsche, Jr., "In Northern Wisconsin, Death of Immigrant Fuels Tensions," *Washington Post*, Jan. 16, 2007; Andreas Jurewitsch,

"Cha Vang Laid to Rest in Saint Paul," *Hmong Times,* Feb. 1, 2007; Associated Press, "Wisconsin Hunter Gets 69 Years in Slaying," *USA Today,* Nov. 28, 2007; Robert Imrie, "Hmong Outdoors Club in Wisconsin Aims to Ease Racial Tensions," *USA Today,* Apr. 25, 2008. For information on this issue, see Amanda Perez, "Patriot Act Classifies Hmong as Terrorists," ABCNews, Feb. 18, 2007; Erica Perez, "Provision of Patriot Act Treats Hmong as Terrorists: Many Barred from Immigrating, Work," *Milwaukee Journal Sentinel,* Mar. 31, 2007; Anna Husarska, "Old Allies, Tagged 'Terrorist,'" *Washington Post,* Dec. 16, 2006. For developments leading to the arrest of General Vang Pao and others in June 2007, see Jessica McBride, "Cloak and Dagger," *Milwaukee Magazine,* Oct. 29, 2007. For a historical perspective, see Roger Warner, "The Strange New Life of an Old Secret War," www.youtube.com/watch?v=iqRJwy69mG4 (accessed June 16, 2011).

11. Ian Hacking, "Why Race Still Matters," *Daedalus* 134 (2005): 103–16; see note 1 above for additional readings relevant to this discussion. David Hollinger, "The One Drop Rule and the One Hate Rule," *Daedalus* 134 (2005): 19–28. After Reconstruction (1865–77), many states passed miscegenation laws to prevent race mixing. Many of these laws remained in effect until the 1960s. Some of this information can be found on the Jim Crow website, www.pbs.org/wnet/jimcrow/maps.html (accessed June 20, 2011).

12. Julius W. Pratt, "The Origin of Manifest Destiny," *The American Historical Review* 32.4 (1927): 795–98. Roger Cushing Aiken, "Paintings of Manifest Destiny: Mapping the Nation," *American Art* 14.3 (2000): 78–89; Matthew Baigell, "Territory, Race, Religion: Images of Manifest Destiny," *Smithsonian Studies in American Art* 4.3/4 (1990): 2–21. Ronald Takaki, *A Different Mirror: A History of Multicultural America* (Boston: Little, Brown and Company, 1993).

13. Clifford Geertz, *Interpretation of Cultures* (New York: Basic Books, 1973), 5. Regarding funerals, I am referring to the funeral traditions of a community who originated from the Muang Phuong (Moos Pheeb) region of Laos (see explanation in note 6). As my research focuses on their funeral practices, I have limited insights into the lives of Hmong Christians. For scholarly perspectives on Hmong Christian life, see Lisa L. Capps, "Change and Continuity in the Medical Culture of the Hmong in Kansas City," *Medical Anthropology Quarterly* (New Series) 8.2 (1994): 161–77; Daphne N. Winland, "Christianity and Community: Conversion and Adaptation among Hmong Refugee Women," *Canadian Journal of Sociology* 19.1 (1994): 21–45. For developments related to Hmong Catholic burials in the United States, see Joe Orso, "New Book Helps Hmong Catholics Prepare for Mass of Christian Burial," *La Crosse Tribune,* Jan. 14, 2007.

14. An informative account of Hmong adaptation to U.S. life is provided by Kou Yang, "The Hmong in America: Twenty-Five Years after the U.S. Secret War in Laos," *Journal of Asian American Studies* 4.2 (2001): 165–74.

< 3 >

Homeland Narratives and Hmong Americans in Wisconsin

JEREMY HEIN

A casual glance at a Wisconsin map reveals towns named Denmark, Holland, Norway, and Poland. This landscape is a reminder that immigrants in Wisconsin have pondered the meaning of homelands for a long time. From the mid-1800s to the early 1900s, European immigrants brought diversity when they came to work in mines, lumber camps, wheat fields, cow barns, and factories. For example, in the 1840s and 1850s, thousands of German, Dutch, and Irish immigrants settled in Sheboygan, Wisconsin.

The first Hmong family arrived in 1976, and the city is now home to more than twenty-seven hundred Hmong Americans. After overcoming initial public resistance, a multiracial committee obtained city approval for a Lao, Hmong, and American Veterans Memorial. Dedicated in 2006, a circle of polished black granite blocks displays a map of Southeast Asia and recounts the story of Hmong involvement in the Vietnam War, their flight from Laos, and resettlement in the United States.[1]

Yet, Wisconsin's European veneer can hinder an accurate understanding of the American immigrant experience. Some place names are not authentic. Railroad owners gave grand titles to tiny depots—such as Milan—as a marketing strategy. A real estate investor in Krakow, Wisconsin, "named the village in honor of the ancient capital of Poland, because he wanted to entice Polish emigrants to settle here." Names such as Germantown imply that homeland means national origin and thus the name of a country.[2]

The Hmong, however, are a stateless people in the mountains of southern China and Southeast Asia who began a global diaspora after 1975. In *Hmong America,* Chia Youyee Vang points out that Hmong Americans define homeland in multiple ways "rather than solely in relation to a shared

< 47 >

physical homeland." Yet, in order to participate in the dominant national-origins discourse, Hmong Americans are forced to cite Laos as their "homeland." They are not the only people in the United States whose conception of homeland challenges European American discourse. The ancestry of many African Americans reaches back into the history of the slave trade, making national origin difficult to determine. Native Americans' conception of homeland is closely linked to sovereignty on reservations, not distant countries. To better understand the many meanings of homeland that now intersect in the United States, this chapter investigates how Hmong Americans answer a question they are commonly asked by non-Hmong: "If you're from Laos, why aren't you Lao?"[3]

A Nation of Nations?

In 1855, the poet Walt Whitman coined the phrase "a nation of nations" to describe a unique characteristic of American society: most of its people can identify ancestors born in another part of the world. President John F. Kennedy's book *A Nation of Immigrants*, published in 1958 when he was still a senator, helped cement the idea in American popular culture that everybody comes from somewhere. Commonsense understandings of "somewhere," however, are greatly influenced by the discourse of European Americans. They usually name one or more countries in Europe to identify the homeland of their immigrant ancestors.[4]

For example, I think of myself as German American. My father emigrated from Germany to the United States with his parents, brother, and sister in 1939. My mother's grandparents also came to the United States from Germany in the late 1800s. Although I was born in New York City, I have lived in Wisconsin since 1989, and its numerous Germanic qualities help me feel at home. These cultural comforts range from tongue-twister surnames such as Schlegelmilch and Leinenkugel to the veneration of Oktoberfest and an orderly efficiency that I did not experience on the East Coast but immediately recognized when I visited my father's hometown of Freiburg with him and my family in 2001.

Of course, connecting Germany and Wisconsin's German American-isms to create a sense of home(land) is a social construction validated by popular culture. Most nineteenth- and early-twentieth-century European immigrants did not have a strong sense of nationality. Instead, they usually identified with their local, not national, origins. In Wisconsin these immigrants frequently gave their new hometowns the names of well-known cities—Hamburg, London, Oslo, Paris, and Stockholm—but also obscure hamlets, such as Altdorf, Krok, Oostburg, and Patzau. Similarly, European immigrants often defined their homeland as their region—not country—of origin. Wisconsin, therefore, has place names such as Caledonia (Scotland), Cambria (Wales), Friesland (the Netherlands), and Schleswig (Germany). Only through revisionist hindsight has European American discourse homogenized peasants and agricultural day laborers into discrete national-origin groups. Some Hmong Americans believe a similar process of homogenization has also been imposed on them, such as the blurring of differences between the Hmong and Mong linguistic groups.[5]

The ease with which European Americans selectively work country names into their social identities is an important but often overlooked form of white privilege. The modern world system comprising nation-states is largely an artifact of European colonization and decolonization. For example, I am still uncertain when Laos actually became a "country." Paul Hillmer's definitive book, *A People's History of the Hmong*, notes that "Laos was proclaimed a constitutional monarchy with a national assembly in May 1947." *The New Oxford American Dictionary* states that Laos "became independent in 1949." But according to Sucheng Chan, editor of *Hmong Means Free*, "the French granted Laos full independence in October 1953."[6]

Whatever the date, the boundaries of present-day Laos first took shape in 1893. That year France forced Thailand to grant it all territory east of the Mekong River. This acquisition completed the formation of French Indochina, which began with the capture of the southern Vietnamese city of Saigon in 1861. "Countries," however, are formed primarily by politics rather than geography. In 1904 and again in 1907, France pressured Thailand to cede some land west of the Mekong River, the natural border between the countries. This narrow salient is still part of Laos, although it temporarily reverted back to Thailand when Japan took control of Southeast Asia during World War II.[7]

While most European Americans are comfortable with the dominant national-origins discourse, for Hmong American refugees and their descendants it is simplistic at best and offensive at worst. Questions that may appear benign to non-Hmong—such as "What is your nationality?" and "Where are your ancestors from?"—are problematic when posed to

Hmong Americans whose heritage is that of a stateless people. In response to this world-map paradigm for talking about ancestry, Hmong Americans use a narrative to convey the complex meanings of "homeland" to non-Hmong.

Name or Narrative?

Because Hmong people arrived in Laos through a nineteenth-century diaspora from China, their relationship to an ancestral homeland is much more intricate than that of most European Americans. As a result, Hmong Americans tell a story, not just name the country Laos, to articulate what homeland means to them. I can empathize with this challenge. My own familial story is actually much more complex than simply saying "German." I am Jewish, and my father and his family left Nazi Germany in 1936: he was fifteen years old. By then, Jews had already been stripped of their German citizenship. Anti-Semitic violence on a large scale began the next year.

The Hein family first resettled in Italy, but in less than three years anti-Semitism again forced them to emigrate, this time to the United States. At the U.S. consulate in Naples, immigration officials purposely put barriers in their path. Consequently, my grandfather arrived first (February 1939), followed by my grandmother and their three children (April 1939). World War II started less than five months later. On June 6, 1944, my father landed on Omaha beach, one of about one hundred fifty thousand allied soldiers taking part in the D-Day invasion of Nazi-occupied France. Wounded that night, he was awarded a Purple Heart. By the time he returned to civilian life in the United States in October 1945, the Nazis had killed more than six million European Jews. Several of his relatives were among them, but his paternal aunt, age fifty-eight, survived a concentration camp. To say "German American" does not convey the complex social identities I have as a Jew whose ancestors were pushed by Roman armies from what is now Israel to what is now Germany. When I talk with Hmong Americans, I appreciate the complexity of their ethnic and homeland identities.

As part of research for my book *Ethnic Origins,* I conducted semistructured face-to-face interviews in English with Hmong American refugees in Wisconsin: six in Milwaukee and seven in Eau Claire. Knowledgeable coethnic research assistants in each city selected informants based on the following guidelines: participants had to be age eighteen or over and foreign born; could not come from the assistant's household or immediate kin; and could not be current employees of an ethnic association. This last condition was intended to keep the study focused on the viewpoints of community members other than organizational representatives. The team also used quota sampling to ensure demographic variation among informants by clan as well as by sex, ethnicity, urban locale, age, and employment (see Appendix A). Researchers assigned the participants a Hmong or American pseudonym corresponding to the real name they gave the coethnic research assistant who organized the interview.[8]

A considerable literature sheds light on the meanings of homeland for Hmong Americans when they converse among themselves. Hmong Americans frequently ask each other where they lived in Laos to gauge possible family connections through marriage and clan affiliations originating in those places. Through these questions, members of families and communities elicit information about customs and traditions that are vital for cultural continuity and reclamation. Intergroup communication about homelands in a multicultural society, however, remains understudied. Therefore, I asked my informants, "How do you explain who the Hmong are to non-Hmong who don't know about your group?"[9]

As a European American, I felt this question to be ethnographically appropriate. It created a collaborative learning process that encouraged participants to think of me as a peer rather than a social scientist. For example, when I interviewed Ying in his Milwaukee grocery store, I sat in a dilapidated comfy chair next to a huge pile of twenty-five- and fifty-pound bags of rice. Ying pulled over a foldout chair. Customers frequented the aisles near us, his children came by a few times, and workers occasionally asked him questions. Nonetheless, Ying gave me his complete attention. He was extremely animated and never flinched from criticizing white people who had mistreated him. As I left, he told me to get in touch with him when my book came out, so he could read it. Then he gave me a bottle of water and a can of guava juice. I almost always felt this level of rapport with the Hmong Americans I interviewed.

Homeland as Intergenerational Story

In Eau Claire, a teacher's aide named Chou offered only a one-sentence response to my interview question, but it provides a brilliant summary of the story Hmong Americans convey to non-Hmong: "I say that the Hmong migrated from China to Laos and then to the United States because of the Vietnam War." Chou's statement contains three narrative elements: diaspora, war, and refugee. Most of the Hmong Americans I talked with invoke one or more of these themes in the homeland story they tell other Americans.

The first motif in Hmong Americans' homeland stories concerns the diaspora from China. Yer, a college student in Milwaukee, described a common scenario of meeting other students for the first time:

> When they say, "Where are you from?" I say, "I don't really have a country, but I'm from Laos." That's what I tell them. When I tell them that they say, "Oh, you're from Laos, but how come you're Hmong?" Chinese, Lao, Hmong look similar. I just say my grand, grandparents came from China, so that's how we ended up there.

Teng, a factory worker in Eau Claire, has developed a similar narrative: "I say I am not Chinese, not Vietnamese, I'm not Lao. I'm Hmong from Laos. I lived in Laos, but I have information from my grandparents and great-grandparents. I know how the Hmong got from China to Laos."

The second motif I found in Hmong Americans' homeland narratives for non-Hmong concerns military conflict and political violence. Many participants used the word "war" or "Vietnam war" to name this part of their homeland story. Although the general public may seem to regard the Vietnam War as long ago and far away, Hmong Americans perennially address its repercussions because it is so central to their meaning of homeland. You, a teacher's aide in Eau Claire, responded to my question, "What do you tell other Americans when you need to explain who the Hmong are?" by stating,

> You should ask my husband about that. I can do a little bit of that. I say that the Hmong are a group of people from Southeast Asia. They moved here because of the war. In 1975 our leader, General Vang Pao, moved out of Laos. We didn't have a leader, so we couldn't live there. We had to follow our leader to this country.

You's intriguing phrase "I can do a little bit of that" implies that the history of the Vietnam War has become a narrative deeply embedded in the consciousness of the Hmong American community. I can simply say "Nazis" or "Holocaust" to provide a one-word synopsis of my relationship with my father's German homeland. Hmong Americans, however, often feel pressured to educate non-Hmong about the details of U.S. foreign and military policy during the Vietnam War. This burden is conveyed by Chong, a social service worker in Eau Claire:

> Even though we've been here 22 years, something like that, some of those people, they are not isolated, but they must be real busy because they don't know. They are still asking, "What is your nationality? How did you come to the United States? What was the reason? Did you come by passport or a sponsor?" The reason we came here is because the CIA [kept] fighting in Laos. Otherwise we would have no reason to come here. If you want to know more, search in the library. That's what I say, "Go to the library."

Robert, a manager at a retail store in Eau Claire, is a practiced raconteur who can immediately deliver a complex narrative on the topic of Hmong history. College-educated and often called upon to explain who Hmong are, he gives this lecture:

> Whenever I meet Caucasian people, they wonder, you know, at first, they want to know who are you, why are you here. Most of the time it's "Who are you? Chinese, Hmong, Vietnamese, Korean? Where are you from?" Those are the questions asked the first time you meet. I tell them a little bit of history, that the Hmong originally came from Laos because of the war. They got involved in the war to help Americans and afterwards couldn't stay and had to flee. That's why they are here. The Hmong are one of the tribal groups in Laos. They say, "You are from Laos? How come you don't speak Lao?" I say, "There are so many ethnic groups in Laos. The Hmong live in a certain part. They have their own religion, language, own food, techniques for farming, own name. But they were under the government in Laos. It's the same as this country: black Americans, whites, Native Americans, Mexicans who still speak Spanish. In Laos it's the same thing. The Hmong were a minority, they still practiced religious traditions,

whatever, all under control of the government." Then they say: "Okay, now I know. The Lao people were the majority. The Lao language was official."

As Robert indicated, the refugee experience is the final motif of the story many Hmong Americans deploy to participate in the European American national-origins discourse. Although it is important to avoid conveying a "perpetual refugee" image of Hmong Americans, forced migration remains very significant for the social identities of the first and 1.5 generations. In Milwaukee, Yer explains the meaning of that experience to him:

> "Refugee" means people who don't have a real place to stay. Hmong are all over the world—Laos, Vietnam, United States— they have no special place to stay. For example, when I say, "I'm Hmong," other students say, "Where are you from?" So I say, "Laos." "Are you Lao?" Some people say that [because] they don't know about the Hmong, so I say "refugee." So I do use that for the Hmong. There was a refugee camp, a small place for people to come to, Hmong and other people. I stayed there.

In Eau Claire, You recalled similar conversations with non-Hmong. When they ask about her place of origin and how she came to the United States, You condenses her experiences into one word:

> If I say "refugee," they already know I haven't lived here for a long time, that I'm from a different country, a different group of people. There's never been a person who asks me and then doesn't understand what a refugee is. The Hmong often say, "We are refugees." One time at school I was translating in a classroom with Hmong kids. The teacher asked what "refugee" means and all the Hmong kids said, "Yeah, that's us."

Chong also thinks the term "refugee" is not always imposed on the Hmong. As part of everyday Hmong vocabulary, the word *thoj nam* is linked to memories of the Vietnam War. According to Chong: "In our own Hmong language, we still say *thoj nam* [to refer to] 'refugee.' When we talk for our own, it's not negative . . . It means not the Hmong in Thailand, Vietnam, China. In Hmong, *thoj nam* means 'refugee people.'" Researchers refer to this perspective on social identity as emic discourse, that is, a discourse grounded in the experiences of community members.

As the speakers above suggest, the asymmetry between the name of their ethnic group and the name of their country of origin challenges Hmong Americans when articulating the meaning of homeland to non-Hmong. Rather than simply naming a country, as a German American or Irish American could do when discussing ancestry, Hmong Americans relay a narrative linking diaspora, war, and forced migration as refugees.

Other Southeast Asian Americans face a different quandary over homeland national identity. Unlike Hmong refugees, Cambodian refugees came from an established nation-state. They look with pride on the powerful kingdom of Angkor (circa AD 800–1431) and its monumental stone temples. One of these—Angkor Wat—is the largest religious structure in the world and an emblem on Cambodia's flag. Yet, like Laos, Cambodia is not a well-known country. Cambodian Americans, therefore, experience an inconsistency between the rich culture and history of their homeland and its obscurity for the general American public.[10]

Vietnamese Americans also differ from Hmong Americans in having a nation-state homeland. They take great pride in Vietnam's thousand-year history as an independent country. The epic Vietnamese resistance to China includes the Trung sisters' revolt in AD 39, independence in 939, repelling two Mongol invasions in the 1280s, and then a final war of independence in 1427. In contrast to the country names of Laos and Cambodia, Vietnam is well known to the American public. Unfortunately, the name often has negative connotations due to the lingering divisiveness of the Vietnam War.[11]

Cambodian Americans and Vietnamese Americans, however, are similar to Hmong Americans in one respect: their homeland identities are shaped by the intense civil wars during the 1960s and 1970s that left millions of compatriots dead. The interethnic dimension of this conflict is particularly salient for Hmong refugees. A major motivation for them to fight against the Pathet Lao and North Vietnamese troops was to protect their mountain villages in Xieng Khouang province. Since Hmong fought the war on three fronts—civil, regional, and international—their homeland narratives often have more references to recent political conflict in Southeast Asia than those of Vietnamese and Cambodian refugees.[12]

Insights

As a sociologist, German Jewish American, and friend of the Hmong American community, I am still in the process of investigating the many layers of meaning in homeland narratives. Yet, one thing is clear to me about American society. The era of supposed cultural homogenization when there was comparatively little immigration (1940s–60s) was actually a historical anomaly. From the 1840s to the 1930s and again since the 1970s, large segments of the society are immigrants and their children struggle to feel at home in multicultural America. Place names that begin with "New" are evidence, and there are many in Wisconsin: New Amsterdam, New Cassel, New Denmark, New Franken, New Glarus, New Holstein, and New Munster. These and other "News" in the United States suggest that American society renews itself when people from other places come here to make a home.

But the homeland is not entirely left behind. As in the experience of earlier immigrants from Europe, "homeland" has deep ecological meanings for Hmong Americans. In describing her grief at having "lost our homeland," a Hmong elder mentions missing "the farms, the forests, the trees." Similarly, a Hmong American youth wrote, "To imagine Laos, picture a mountain." One reason Hmong refugees stayed in Wisconsin after resettlement, or moved there after initial resettlement elsewhere, is that opportunities for traditional subsistence activities such as gardening, foraging, and hunting evoked "memories of the home country."[13]

Nineteenth-century European immigrants would have empathized with these sentiments. They often named places in Wisconsin after the geography of their homeland, such as a small port on the Mississippi: "In 1868 Italian settlers thought it resembled Genoa, Italy because of its hills and rivers." Wisconsin also has towns named Rhine, Mosel, and Glen Haven. The history of European and Hmong Americans suggests that establishing a relationship to the land is essential for people to imagine their new surroundings as "home." In this respect, both groups take after the first settlers in the state, the Anishinaabe, who named it *Wees-kon-san,* or "gathering of the waters."[14]

Appendix A: Informants Interviewed (1998–99)

NAME	SEX	CITY	AGE	ACTIVITY
Cher	Female	Milwaukee	37	Public school teacher
Chong	Male	Eau Claire	37	Social service worker
Chou	Female	Eau Claire	35	Teacher's aide
Ka	Female	Milwaukee	18	College student
Kelly	Female	Milwaukee	31	Public school teacher
Mee	Female	Eau Claire	22	College student
Nao	Male	Eau Claire	21	Sales representative
Robert	Male	Eau Claire	31	Retail store manager
Sy	Male	Milwaukee	34	Church pastor
Teng	Male	Eau Claire	36	Factory worker
Yer	Male	Milwaukee	19	College student
Ying	Male	Milwaukee	34	Grocery store owner
You	Female	Eau Claire	20	Teacher's aide

NOTES

1. *Hmong Times,* "Sheboygan Lakefront: Site for 'Secret War' Memorial," Oct. 16, 2003.

2. Robert Gard and L. G. Sorden, *The Romance of Wisconsin Place Names* (New York: October House, 1968), 66.

3. Chia Youyee Vang, *Hmong America: Reconstructing Community in Diaspora* (Urbana: University of Illinois Press, 2010), 6.

4. John F. Kennedy, *A Nation of Immigrants* (1958; New York: Harper and Row, 1986).

5. Josef Barton, *Peasants and Strangers: Italians, Rumanians, and Slovaks in an American City, 1890–1950* (Cambridge, MA: Harvard University Press, 1975); Ewa Morawska, *For Bread with Butter: Life-Worlds of East Central Europeans in Johnstown, Pennsylvania, 1890–1940* (Cambridge, MA: Cambridge University Press, 1985). Gard and Sorden, *Wisconsin Place Names.* Paoze Thao, "Cultural Transition and Adjustment: The Experiences of the Mong in the United States," in ed. Huping Ling, *Emerging Voices: Experiences of Underrepresented Asian Americans* (Piscataway, NJ: Rutgers University Press, 2008), 34–51.

6. Paul Hillmer, *A People's History of the Hmong* (St. Paul: Minnesota Historical Society Press, 2010), 58. *The New Oxford American Dictionary* (New York: Oxford University Press, 2001), 958. Sucheng Chan, ed., *Hmong Means Free: Life in Laos and America* (Philadelphia, PA: Temple University Press, 1994), 21.

7. Chan, *Hmong Means Free.*

8. Jeremy Hein, *Ethnic Origins: The Adaptation of Cambodian and Hmong Refugees in Four American Cities* (New York: Russell Sage Foundation, 2006).

9. Lillian Faderman, *I Begin My Life All Over: The Hmong and the American Immigrant Experience* (Boston: Beacon Press, 1998); Mai Neng Moua, ed., *Bamboo Among the Oaks: Contemporary Writing by Hmong Americans* (St. Paul: Minnesota Historical Society Press, 2002); Jennifer L. O'Donoghue and D'Ann Lesch, *We Are the Freedom People: Sharing Our Stories, Creating a Vibrant America* (St. Cloud, MN: Sentinel Printing Company, 1999); Yer J. Thao, *The Mong Oral Tradition: Cultural Memory in the Absence of Written Language* (Jefferson, NC: McFarland, 2006); Kao Kalia Yang, *The Latehomecomer: A Hmong Family Memoir* (Minneapolis, MN: Coffee House Press, 2008).

10. Usha Welaratna, *Beyond the Killing Fields: Voices of Nine Cambodian Survivors in America* (Palo Alto, CA: Stanford University Press, 1993).

11. Sucheng Chan, ed., *The Vietnamese American 1.5 Generation: Stories of War, Revolution, Flight, and New Beginnings* (Philadelphia, PA: Temple University Press, 2006).

12. Hein, *Ethnic Origins.*

13. O'Donoghue and Lesch, *Freedom People,* 34, 157. Jo Ann Koltyk, *New Pioneers in the Heartland: Hmong Life in Wisconsin* (Boston: Allyn and Bacon, 1998), 111.

14. Gard and Sorden, *Wisconsin Place Names,* 46, 141.

< 4 >

From War to Resettlement

How Hmong Have Become Americans

KEITH QUINCY

My Introduction to and Immersion in Hmong Life

Thirty-two years ago, a Hmong student took my introductory university course in government. When he did poorly on the first exam, he came to me worried. His English was halting, so I asked if he knew another language. "French," he said. I dropped into French and learned after a few pointed questions that he had a good grasp of the material. My questions on the test were at fault because they were not clear enough. While I worked to hone my question-writing skills, I had him take the rest of the tests in my office, going over the questions with him until I was satisfied that he understood what I was asking. He was very bright and did well.

Meeting weekly in my office for the exams, we got to know each other. I told him about my background and asked about his. I saw immediately that his story was more interesting than mine. I knew something about Southeast Asia, yet I had never heard of "Hmong." When I asked about his life and his people's history, he told me over many sessions what he knew. After he reached a point when his barrel of knowledge was empty, he asked if I might write a book about their journey from China to Southeast Asia and then to the United States. He thought Americans should be told about their story. Because he wanted to know more himself, he kept prodding until I gave in. It was a daunting task. As the first American to make the attempt, I knew I would make mistakes. Yet I was determined to put the book in his hands.

Long before the book was finished, my friendship with my student had drawn me into the Hmong American community. To help Hmong immigrants, I translated birth records and death certificates (from French to English) required by the INS. I helped write requests for federal and state

< 59 >

grants to fund programs for Hmong refugees. My wife and I sponsored four families. Hmong friends helped me with a community garden on my little ranch. The women taught me proper Hmong farming. Each year we had bumper harvests. Gradually and happily, the life of my family became entwined with other Hmong families.

I mourned Hmong American deaths, celebrated births, and was there when children graduated from grade school through college. Recently I was given the place of an elder in a naming ceremony: a great honor. Three times I have gone to the hospital for operations. Each time shamans watched over me to make sure my soul did not wander.

I had not asked for the ceremonies. Shamans performed them on their own out of kindness and respect. I learned after one operation that the shaman was kept busy. When I came around in recovery, the anesthesiologist, a friend, confided that at one point in the operation there had been an alarming problem. Yet, to his puzzlement, the problem had suddenly and unaccountably resolved itself—at a time when I knew the shaman was watching over my soul.

What follows is my own history of Hmong involvement in the Vietnam War and my reflections on Hmong life in the United States after the war. Here I am continuing a lifelong project of delving into the dynamic interrelationship of identity, history, and culture among people who have over thirty-some years become my teachers as well as my friends.

A Violent Time

The twentieth century gave us two world wars, a war in Korea, and the Vietnam War. Already in the first decade of the twenty-first century, the United States fought long-term wars in Iraq and Afghanistan. The world seems to be becoming more bloody, not less. Yet, as difficult as it might be to believe, the world is becoming less violent.

Anthropologists tell us armed conflict was more common in the past. The farther back we go, the more of it there was. When humans were more commonly organized into tribes, the chance of dying a violent death was twenty times greater than it is today. With these odds, the carnage of the twentieth century would not have been one hundred million killed, but two billion.[1]

We get an inkling of the violence of earlier times from the history of Laos, Cambodia, and Vietnam. In the nine centuries before the French began their conquest of Indochina, there were sixty-two "significant wars and invasion on the territories of present-day Cambodia, Laos, and Vietnam." That is an average of roughly seven wars per century or a little more than two wars per generation. By this measure, the twentieth century was relatively tame.[2]

Hmong people have been no strangers to violence. They once had their own kingdom in China on a swath of territory that straddled present-day Guangxi, Hunan, Hubei, and Henan provinces. Chinese armies destroyed the kingdom and decimated the population. Hmong people who survived scattered into the highlands of Yunnan and Guizhou, where they became known as montagnards.

Life was hard, but at least it was relatively safe. The highlands held nothing of value to the Chinese, who remained mostly in the lowlands. After four centuries, however, the Chinese armies were back on the offensive, slogging up the mountain trails with road-building crews in tow. Their aim was to take command of the highlands occupied by Hmong villagers and construct roads to Burma, creating a gateway for trade with all of Southeast Asia. To feed soldiers and the road crews, the Chinese government gave the best land to Chinese farmers. Moreover, to pay for the enterprise, taxes on Hmong farmers kept on rising.

Over the next two hundred years, Chinese history refers to repeated Hmong uprisings, sometimes as many as one rebellion every year. Finally, in 1854 the Chinese committed the soldiers necessary to obliterate Hmong troops. For twenty years they fought back ferociously. However, their numbers dwindled not only from battle deaths but also because thousands fled China to the mountains of Vietnam and Laos.

Hmong and the French

While Hmong straggled across the border, the French were busy taking command of Laos and Vietnam. It was not long before the two groups collided. In Laos, Hmong rose up against the French in 1896, protesting high taxes. The French wisely decided to involve Hmong leaders in future decisions, ruling by consensus instead of force. But in Vietnam the French allowed the native authorities—highland Thai—to govern the Hmong populace. Thai rule was brutal. Hmong had already rebelled against them in the messianic uprising of 1862, inspired by a leader promising a return to the glory days of the past through the creation of an independent Hmong kingdom. The messianism did not go away. Instead it emerged again in 1910, and yet again in 1919, this time led by Pa Chay Vue.[3]

The Hmong had never developed a written language. Yet, Pa Chay miraculously created a Hmong script on his own, which he taught to his followers. Pa Chay performed spectacular feats of magic and convinced followers and fellow villagers that he could talk directly to heaven. Believing that Pa Chay had been sent by God to liberate them, people set aside their clan differences and transferred their loyalty to him.

Pa Chay's rebellion would eventually include Laotian Hmong. The fighting lasted nearly three years and in its final stages shifted to Laos. The French won only by sending nearly all of their colonial troops against Pa Chay. Though the French defeated Pa Chay, the Hmong had demonstrated their power when aroused. The French saw that it was better to have them as an ally than an enemy. The policy of cooperating with key Hmong leaders, established earlier in Laos, was now intensified.

Hmong cooperation would prove critical for the success of France's narcotics trade. The only colonial enterprise that proved profitable for the French was the sale of opium. Until World War II, the French purchased the drug from India. However, this source was cut off when Japan occupied Indochina. Hmong in the highlands grew opium, but not enough to replace sixty tons imported from India. The chief of the Ly clan, Touby Lyfoung, persuaded Hmong farmers to grow all the opium the French needed. The French were so grateful that in 1946 they pressured the king of Laos to grant Hmong political autonomy, with Touby as their governor. Hmong people would at last have their kingdom.[4]

Yet, Touby refused the offer for three reasons. First, to run a bureaucracy for an entire province, he would need competent staff to write reports, keep records, and write birth and death certificates—all in Lao. He knew only two other Hmong in Laos who were fluent in written Lao, so he would not have enough staff for the task. Second, clan politics could not be ignored because Hmong identified with their clan first and foremost. They turned to fellow clansmen when in need and did not fully trust members of other clans, who always would put their own clan's interests above everything else. Only messianic leaders like Pa Chay had been able to transcend clan loyalty and unite the Hmong as a people. Touby was not a messiah. He had no link to heaven. He was only an adept politician. In Hmong eyes, he did not deserve to be their king. Should he try to rule over all the Hmong, he realized, he would be viewed as a usurper. Hmong would grumble and blame him for everything that went wrong; in fact, the Lo clan had already begun challenging his authority. Assuming the mantle of king would tip the scales in their favor, and he would eventually be deposed.

Third, Touby was no fool. He knew Ho Chi Minh would soon be sending his soldiers into Laos. The invasion would come through Hmong territory, where roads linked Laos to North Vietnam. Were he to become the ruler of the region, it would be his responsibility to raise a Hmong army to confront the invaders. Hmong people would perish in large numbers. He would quickly become unpopular with his own people. Ultimately, the clans would abandon him.[5]

Therefore, Touby refused Hmong autonomy and settled for a compromise: when the French forced Laotians to admit Hmong into Laos's national assembly, Touby became a cabinet minister. The Hmong were not autonomous, but they became a force in national politics. They would keep their power as long as the French remained in Indochina. Touby had linked the fate of his people to the destiny of an imperial state. He could not foresee that France would eventually leave Laos.

After Japan's defeat, the French were determined to reclaim their authority over the colony, but Ho Chi Minh stood in their way. The war had left much of the world in ruins; only the United States emerged from the conflict richer and stronger. It would take two decades for the economies of Europe to recover. Meanwhile, Europe's poverty forced its countries to abandon their colonies in Asia and Africa, releasing nearly a quarter of the world's population from colonial rule. Indochina was an exception. France held on only because the United States paid the bills. However, after nine years of fighting the communists and no victory, French voters ran out of patience. When legionnaires were humiliated at Dien Bien Phu, antiwar riots broke out in Paris. At last, French politicians ordered the soldiers home.

Hmong and the CIA

American troops replaced French legionnaires not only in Vietnam but also in Laos. It was a critical period in Laos. The national government was on the edge of collapse. Communist guerrillas fought at full tilt trying to take over the country. The United States gave the Laotians the best equipment and training. Yet, even when led by American Special Forces, Laotians preferred to retreat rather than fight. When North Vietnam sent more troops to tilt the balance for a communist victory, instead of meeting the challenge, Lao generals lingered in the capital where it was safe.

If it were not for the Geneva Accords of 1962, the United States would likely have committed more troops in Laos, as it had done in Vietnam, and Americanized the war. But the Geneva Accords required all foreign troops to leave Laos. Continued U.S. military operations in Laos would have to be in secret. The specialist in such affairs was the Central Intelligence Agency. In fact, a CIA operation in Thailand was just winding down and searching for a new job. Agents rushed to Laos to get the lay of the land. What they found was a Hmong officer and fighter in the Lao army named Vang Pao. The CIA offered Vang Pao the command of an army of his own, with Hmong instead of Lao recruits. The CIA would train, supply, and pay for this Hmong army. Vang Pao agreed.

The CIA had high expectations of Vang Pao. They were impressed and gratified when he exceeded all hopes and became perhaps the greatest general in his nation's history.

The CIA plan was for the Hmong army to slow the advance of the Vietnamese. Helicopters would make Hmong airmobile. They could attack and withdraw anytime and anywhere. Eventually, the CIA diverted jets and bombers from Vietnam to back up the Hmong in Laos. The air assault was unrelenting: more bombs were dropped in Laos (which is the size of Idaho) than in all of World War II. The air support enabled Hmong guerrillas to decimate tens of thousands of North Vietnamese.

These casualties, plus those inflicted in earlier campaigns, resulted in an incredible number of enemy killed. There is no official count, but my own estimate from battle reports puts the number of North Vietnamese casualties from 1962 to 1972 at between one hundred thousand and one hundred fifty thousand. This would account for 17 to 25 percent of all North Vietnamese Army battle deaths during the war, inflicted by a Hmong army only two percent of the size of American forces. In my view, the Hmong army was America's most lethal weapon.

Hmong people paid a horrible price for these victories. Had the Secret

War gone on much longer, few Hmong men between the ages of fourteen and fifty would have remained to sire the next generation. In the mountains lay thousands of Hmong men buried beneath stone cairn. No one saw it at the time, but the Secret War began to mutate into a conflict that threatened their survival.

By 1970, twelve- and thirteen-year-old Hmong boys were replacing their fathers, uncles, and older brothers killed in battle: "The boys were no taller than their rifles. They disappeared inside their uniforms, and walked out of their boots when they marched." Their CIA instructors were hard men but had no stomach for sending children to war. The larger issue was the survival of the Hmong as a people. What saved these boys, and future Hmong generations, was the CIA's decision to use Thai troops to replace Hmong killed in action.[6]

How this happened would perhaps seem believable only to a Hmong. Henry Kissinger did not want Thai soldiers in Laos. He had been banned from the Oval Office for a week for having angered Nixon by giving him false figures about operations in Laos. When Nixon repeated the numbers to reporters, he was savaged in the press for his errors. From then on, Kissinger vowed to keep Laos out of the news. He had established a secret committee, the Special Actions Group, which met regularly in the Situation Room. The committee included the top staff of the State Department, Joint Chiefs, CIA, and National Security Council. When CIA agents in Laos requested permission to recruit Thai soldiers to replace Hmong boys, Kissinger panicked.

What if reporters found out? The United States and Thailand had a special agreement called Project Taksin. The essence of the plan was that if the North Vietnamese Army ever swept over Laos, it would trigger joint operations between U.S. and Thai forces to fight back. Kissinger feared if reporters discovered a sudden rush of Thai troops into Laos, they might think Taksin was under way. Stories would likely begin to appear in newspapers that the Vietnam War was on the edge of swallowing all of Southeast Asia. Then Kissinger would again be locked out of the Oval Office.

During a week of daily and sometimes twice-daily meetings, Kissinger persuaded the members of the Special Actions Group to oppose sending Thai soldiers. They drafted a letter informing Laos's prime minister that no Thai troops would be sent. When Kissinger showed the letter to Nixon, the president approved it. How could he not? It had the endorsement of the top brass of the CIA, the State Department, Defense, and the National Security Council.

Satisfied that the issue was settled, Kissinger caught a plane for France to spend the weekend in secret talks with his North Vietnamese counterpart, Lê Dúc Tho. But when he returned on Monday and met with the president, Nixon announced he was going to send the Thai troops. There was no changing his mind.[7]

What had happened over the weekend? It was a total mystery to Kissinger. What he did not know was that while he was away in France, Hmong shamans had asked their helper spirits to persuade Nixon to send the Thai. Vang Pao's main base at Long Cheng was under siege and about to fall. Only the Thai could save it. Had the spirits reached Nixon and changed his mind? A Hmong person would not find this inconceivable.[8]

Not only did Nixon send enough Thai to save Long Cheng. To Kissinger's bewilderment, Nixon kept delivering more Thai soldiers until there were enough to send every Hmong boy in uniform home. By 1972, Thai replacements had become half of the secret army. Even more Hmong soldiers were spared when Vang Pao used the remaining Hmong battalions only for crucial battles.

Looking back, how was Vang Pao able to draw the Hmong into a war that cost so many Hmong lives? While Touby had rejected the offer of Hmong autonomy, Vang Pao accepted it. He was given complete authority over the Hmong region of Laos, encompassing Xieng Khouang and Sam Neua provinces. Though Vang Pao was charismatic, he was not a messiah figure. Therefore, he had to rule as Touby had done, as a skillful politician. The main problem was dealing with the clans. Vang Pao knew this well:

> [F]rom the time of their migration from China, the Hmong have always considered the clan as paramount. Everyone respects only his clan and everyone gravitates only to his [clan] leader since there had long been a break in the Hmong leadership structure. The problem is that he has no confidence [in a leader from another clan].[9]

Realizing it was necessary to secure the support of clan leaders for the war effort, Vang Pao appointed them to high military and civilian posts. All of these positions came with salaries, if not actual duties. At one point

Vang Pao was creating so many new officer positions that the American ambassador, Charles Whitehouse, complained that the Hmong army was "very top-heavy, with almost more majors than privates." Many years after the war, Vang Pao was quite open about the process: "I tossed leadership titles to everyone. Whatever [title] they wanted, I would make recommendations to the King who would just sign [giving his seal of approval]. Whatever Hmong wanted they got so it was not hard [to maintain their loyalty] at all."[10]

Yet, Vang Pao longed to cut the Gordian knot of clan politics. In the past, only messianic leaders had been able to lead Hmong people as Hmong and not as members of this or that clan. Could a Hmong *politician* accomplish this? Vang Pao wanted to try. The war had displaced thousands from their villages and homes. The United States provided relief. Vang Pao would have accepted it under any conditions because he felt responsible for his people. But he had options. It was in his power to shape the relief effort so that it created a direct link between himself and the Hmong unmediated by clan leadership. Nearly a third of the Hmong lived in USAID refugee camps providing free rice, schools, and medical care. In their view, these benefits came from Vang Pao, not clan leaders. It was he who was helping them directly to survive.

Vang Pao also encouraged Hmong to think of themselves as Laotian citizens, to broaden their loyalties and thereby weaken clan power. In village schools, children were being taught to read and write Lao. The king visited Vang Pao's headquarters at Long Cheng to tell Hmong people they were bona fide citizens of Laos. CIA agents and refugee aid workers constantly preached to Hmong that they were citizens of the Lao nation. One CIA agent, Vinton Lawrence, thought he saw progress because "Hmong were on their way to being successfully assimilated into the larger Laotian scene." But another American who worked on the project, Ernie Kuhn, was more circumspect. While "there was this constant effort to tell them that they were part of one country," Kuhn had no idea if they believed this, or even understood it. The prevailing view of Hmong individuals I interviewed for the book *Harvesting Pa Chay's Wheat* was that the Laotian state and its political apparatus was corrupt and hostile to the interests of Hmong people.[11]

Vang Pao also apparently tried to dilute the influence of clans by creating substitutes for their services. Clans settled personal disputes internally or, if they involved other clans, by negotiations between clans. Hmong were not always satisfied with the results but had nowhere else to turn. Vang Pao created a court system that bypassed the clans; he set up courts in major settlements and an appellate court at his headquarters at Long Cheng. Hmong unhappy with clan decisions could turn to these courts for an independent hearing. The courts were so popular that their dockets were crowded from the start. Most cases were torts: disputes over debts and damages—personal and property. But the courts had no enforcement power and decisions handed down relied on clans for enforcement, which often did not happen.[12]

In the end, Vang Pao had to rely on patronage to clan leaders to get the support he needed from Hmong to fight the war. The money for this came from his patron: Washington, and mostly the CIA. No scholar has a better grasp of this than Mai Na M. Lee. If a Hmong politician is to be successful, he must have the support of the clans. And to gain their support, he must use patronage. On his own, he does not have the resources. But with an external patron, such as the French with Touby or the Americans with Vang Pao, the patronage can flow. Lee informs us this source of power is fraught with problems. The politician must serve two masters, the external patron and the clan leaders. If the external patron asks too much of Hmong, clan leaders might abandon the politician or seek to remove him from power.[13]

The other problem is that the external patron may vanish. France abandoned Laos, as did the United States. When the French left Laos, Touby's days as the preeminent Hmong leader were numbered. Once the Americans, and their deep pockets, were gone, Vang Pao had little patronage to dole out. For a time after the CIA left, he channeled funds from USAID relief programs to fund patronage, but by 1975 this money was also gone (the agency closed shop in Laos in 1975). Without the Americans, Vang could not continue the war. Nor is it likely, given the sacrifices already endured, that Hmong would have continued to contribute to the cause.

On May 14, 1975, Vang Pao accepted the CIA's offer to fly him to safety in Thailand. The destination was Namphong, an abandoned air base near Udorn. The CIA also airlifted twenty-five hundred Hmong to join Vang Pao at Namphong. Two cargo planes and a ten-passenger Pilatus Porter flew six round trips. The first Hmong to go were Vang Pao's family, his top officers and their families, and clan notables. The next to follow were those with enough bribe money to buy a place on a plane: "One wealthy widow had no difficulty booking passage for her family. She came with three large chests of silver, each so heavy it took several men to hoist them onto the plane." After this it was every man for himself. As one woman recalled, "There are too many people! I hold the hands of my children, and when we get close to the airplane, my husband just *pushes* the children into the plane. I try to crawl in from the side of the ramp, but it is too hard for me. Finally my husband *pushes* me through that small space. We all squeeze onto the airplane." So many people clambered to get aboard the cargo planes that often the crews could not close the ramps for takeoff. To get people away from the plane, the crews dumped duffle bags full of Lao kip onto the tarmac. As Hmong scurried to gather up the kip, the crew closed the ramp and the pilots gunned the engines. Propeller wash sent the kip aloft. Realizing what had just happened, the abandoned Hmong wept amid a confetti of money.[14]

In short order, the communists took over the country. Hmong people were herded into concentration camps, their property seized, and their movements monitored. Tax collectors took half of all harvests as payment in kind. Starvation spread. Some Hmong ate roots to supplement their diet. Many others tried to escape to Thailand. Not only was the escape hazardous—communist soldiers often shot Hmong on the open road— crossing the Mekong was often a death sentence. Hmong children had been taught by their mothers to never enter deep water because evil river spirits pulled swimmers down. Growing up with this dread, few Hmong learned to swim. When their makeshift bamboo rafts came apart in rapids, Hmong refugees splashed and gasped and drowned.[15]

Refugees in Thailand

The first Hmong refugees to reach Thailand were taken by border police to Nong Khai. As the crow flies, the camp was directly across the Mekong from Vientiane, the political capital of Laos. The camp was a mixture of Lao and Hmong, divided into separate sections. Newcomers were given plastic sheeting to use as cover against the rain. They had to make their own shelters from whatever was handy, usually resulting in no more than a lean-to fashioned from branches, with plastic sheeting lashed to the branches with twine for a roof. The food was vegetable gruel; from time to time, bits of meat were tossed in. It was starvation rations. For a real meal, the refugees had to buy food from vendors who set up stands next to the camp. To get money for the food, Hmong sold their valuables—silver jewelry if they had any.[16]

It was a bad time to be a refugee, not just in Thailand but also anywhere in the world. Since 1950, the policy of the agency responsible for refugees, the United Nations High Commissioner for Refugees (UNHCR), was to provide refugees humanitarian aid, asylum when necessary, and resettlement in third countries. The UNHCR did not force refugees to repatriate. This policy changed in 1971. In that year the civil war between Pakistan and East Pakistan created ten million East Pakistani refugees in India. The Indian government did not have the funds to provide camps and provisions for the refugees. When it turned to the United Nations for help, the UNHCR had at its disposal $70 million in voluntary contributions from member nations. It quickly ran through this money. It was much cheaper to repatriate the refugees. Repatriation cost $10.7 million, considerably less than the price tag for humanitarian aid and within UNHCR's budget constraints.[17]

The India experience caused the UN agency to change its policy. Making grim necessity a virtue, repatriation became the UNHCR's overriding goal. The incident did not burnish UNHCR's image. In the agency's official history, the Indian relief effort is not mentioned. Even the principal scholars of UNHCR fail to give any space in their narrative to this crucial incident in the agency's history.[18]

Hmong refugees experienced the first phase of this policy: make camp life so miserable that refugees might be persuaded to repatriate. When Nong Khai was full, other camps were established for Hmong. Eventually, the main camp for Hmong was at Ban Vinai. At the start, the camp was austere. But with pressure from the United States, bolstered by increased aid to Thailand, the camp improved. Eventually, refugees set up schools, markets, and Hmong businesses. By 1989, the camp had "one of the highest living standards of any refugee camp in Southeast Asia."[19]

Washington may have abandoned the Hmong in Laos, but it did its best to help Hmong refugees. Congress repeatedly amended its immigration policy to permit larger numbers of Southeast Asian refugees to settle in the United States. Eventually, a million would get in. To help Hmong at the camp resettle to the United States, Washington sent special teams to interview applicants and prepare the necessary documents to insure everything was in order. Yet, many Hmong refused to apply. Vang Pao needed them for guerilla raids into Laos. Even though the raids would not bring about the overthrow of the communist regime, the guerrillas were essential to Vang Pao's attempt to transplant Hmong politics to the United States.[20]

Transplanting Hmong Politics to America

In 1975, the CIA moved Vang Pao into a four-hundred-thousand-dollar mountain ranch in Montana. The agency paid a hefty amount down to keep the mortgage payments low. Washington also gave Vang Pao a pension of thirty-five thousand dollars a year. In that year, only a few hundred Hmong had followed Vang Pao to the United States, but in 1976, thousands arrived. Vang Pao kept tabs on every family, putting them in contact with other Hmong who had resettled. He crisscrossed America, visiting Hmong wherever they were. In 1977, the largest Hmong community in the United States was in Santa Ana, California. Toward the end of that year, Vang Pao went to Santa Ana to organize Lao Family Community (LFC); funding for refugee self-help groups came from both the state and federal governments.

When California awarded LFC a large grant, federal money soon followed and Vang Pao had an external patron again. He left his Montana ranch, relocated to Santa Ana, and quickly went to work setting up LFC organizations in every sizable Hmong community in the United States. To head the organizations, Vang Pao selected from the educated Hmong of the younger generation. They were responsible to him, not to clan elders.

Clan leaders began to complain about being left out of decision making. To appease them, Vang Pao needed to establish a dependable system for sustaining his support base in the United States. His plan was two pronged: send the order to his followers in Ban Vinai to organize a guerrilla force, and create *Neo Hom* in America to solicit funds from Hmong immigrants to support the guerrillas. Soon the organization was receiving $160,000 a month. From 1987 to 1988, *Neo Hom* also became a bank for Hmong deposits; of the $400,000 to $500,000 deposited, no interest was ever paid and the principal disappeared. Vang Pao was able to use the money from these sources to fund positions (mostly without official duties) in *Neo Hom* for clan leaders and former officers and bureaucrats. He also made payments to camp officials, who appointed Hmong of his choosing to run much of camp life. Vang Pao could count on them to provide the guerrillas needed for cross-border raids. To make sure there were enough Hmong in the camp to staff the guerrilla units, camp officials also persuaded many Hmong not to apply for resettlement.[21]

Vang Pao told American Hmong that the communist regime would soon fall and that Hmong could return to reclaim their provinces. People believed that future positions for officials and Hmong officers would be held for them by a fee paid to *Neo Hom;* by 1988, their payments raised the amount in *Neo Hom*'s coffers to nine million dollars. However, in 1990, the Civil Rights Bureau of California's Department of Social Services discovered LFCs in the state had been forcing refugees to contribute to *Neo Hom* as a condition for receiving aid. One Hmong went to jail. The state stopped funding the LFCs. Across the country, LFCs severed all relations with Vang Pao's parent LFC in Santa Ana. Vang Pao's political machine was falling apart. Yet, he would not step down as a leader.

In 1997, America had honored the Hmong sacrifice in the Vietnam War with a tiny memorial out of the way in the National Cemetery. It is a simple block of granite with a bronze plaque that reads:

Dedicated to the U.S. Secret Army in the Kingdom of Laos 1961–1973
In memory of the Hmong and Lao combat veterans and their
American advisors who served freedom's cause in Southeast Asia.
Their patriotic valor and loyalty in the defense of liberty and
democracy will never be forgotten.

Vang Pao promoted other memorials, not only for the pride of Hmong people but also to keep the war alive in the minds of Hmong and to kindle hope for a return to Laos. The community erected a second memorial in 2005 in Fresno, California. It is a larger-than-life bronze statue depicting two Hmong guerillas saving a downed American pilot. On their own, Hmong in Wisconsin, many of them veterans, created a third war memorial. Dedicated in 2006, it stands in a lovely park beside Lake Michigan in Sheboygan. The monument is a circular wall of polished stone panels bearing the engraved names of some of the fallen. There is also a narrative of the war and an etched map of Southeast Asia.

The memorials had their effect. Yet, however much Vang Pao strove to create a sense of unity that eclipsed clan—and to link it to his leadership—clan loyalty still thrived. He had promoted a national celebration of the Hmong New Year to foster a sense of Hmong as one people, but any feeling of sheer togetherness competed with Hmong differences. Hmongness was filtered by clan. Despite the festivities enjoyed by everyone, identity was in the details, in the different ways each clan performed the rituals associated with the New Year festival. Once back home and away from the yearly celebration, Hmong felt the intense impact of local rituals. At funerals and weddings, each clan performed the rituals according to its own cross-generational practices.

Not even the LFCs were immune to the influence of clan. Created to establish a direct link between Hmong and Vang Pao, the LFCs soon had the opposite effect. The young leaders that Vang Pao had selected to direct the LFCs across the nation quickly discovered that they could not deliver job training or financial aid to Hmong without the consensus of the clan leaders in their community. In the minds of Hmong who were helped, the aid bore the fingerprints of their clan as well as of Vang Pao.

Not one to give up, Vang Pao devised another way to diminish the influence of the clans. In 2005, he distributed a thirty-one-page pamphlet entitled "Hmong Traditional Culture Procedural Guide," which prescribes a uniform code for Hmong rites and rituals. One of the rules caps bride-prices (traditional dowries) at five thousand dollars. Customarily, this figure is determined by negotiations between clan elders, which can take days or even weeks. The bride's worth to her natal family and future family need not be the sole topic. Since Hmong view marriage between members of the same clan as incest, the parties to the negotiations always represent different clans. Financial settlements between clans for past misdeeds, such as unpaid debts or situations causing loss of face, are on the table for discussion. Capping the bride-price at five thousand dollars derails the open-ended nature of these negotiations, thereby limiting the ability of the clans to keep the peace. To Vang Pao's disappointment, clan elders did not entirely accept the rules, and for the most part the clans do not follow them.

In 2007, Washington turned on Vang Pao and indicted him for conspiring to overthrow the government of Laos. It was a symbolic act to grab headlines for being tough on terrorism. In fact, for more than a decade after the war, Washington had financed through back channels guerrilla raids in Laos. With Washington's approval, Vang Pao had been involved; if there was a crime, Washington was complicit. No proof existed that Vang

Pao had been planning to do anything illegal. The evidence was so scant that in September 2009, Washington dropped all charges. A little more than a year later, Vang Pao was dead. Washington neglected to bury him as a war hero in Arlington National Cemetery. Twenty-eight foreign nationals have received this honor; the latest was an Iraqi Air Force pilot, buried with full honors in Arlington in 2005. One could argue that Vang Pao was America's most valuable asset in the Vietnam War and was deserving of the same honor.[22]

Vang Pao's arrest and incarceration exposed cracks in the unity of America's Hmong. When asked their views by reporters, many Hmong people admitted that they no longer wanted to return to Laos. America was their country now. They felt that Hmong should not waste any more time thinking about Laos; instead, they should concentrate on improving their lot in America.[23]

In the end, Vang Pao did not win the battle to bypass the clans and represent the Hmong as one people. In any case, it was an impossible task. If the past is any guide, only a messiah figure like the charismatic Pa Chay, who rallied Hmong from all the clans to fight the French, can achieve this.[24]

What It Means to Be Hmong for First and Second Generations

How much have Hmong assimilated to American life and culture? A common measure of assimilation is the degree to which an immigrant group mirrors the average American in income, occupation, education, and rates of intermarriage. By this standard, Michael Barone finds the Irish have taken the longest to assimilate, nearly 120 years, while the Italians took eighty years. Even though they were destitute upon arrival, the Jews took only sixty years. Moreover, in only forty years, many Asian immigrants not only matched but also surpassed the general population in income and education. What set the Jews, Chinese, Japanese, and Koreans apart from other immigrant groups was their determination to establish and work in their own businesses, even when they faced severe restrictions on where they could live and what they could own. Another major factor was their commitment to education, which remained strong even in impoverished circumstances.[25]

By measures of income, occupation, education, and intermarriage, Hmong Americans lag far behind the general population and seem on a pace to match the slow assimilation of the Irish and Italians. Most of the

Hmong people who arrived in the United States had been struggling to survive for years. The war made them refugees in Laos; the communists made them refugees in Thailand. When they arrived in the United States, the first generation seemed to consider the American welfare system a kind of military pension for helping in the war. However, even though the first generation attached no stigma to welfare, it was clear to many that welfare dependency was not a way to get ahead in America. While supporting their families on minimal monthly welfare payments, Hmong fathers and mothers tried their best to acquire language and job skills necessary to once again become self-sufficient, but the obstacles were formidable.

Yet, every year more Hmong Americans become professionals and earn advanced degrees. The rate of their progress seems exponential instead of arithmetic. For example, Hmong American students in Montana's Upward Bound summer program have performed much better than other Upward Bound students. The program gives six weeks of enriched instruction in math, science, and English to prepare high school students for college. Seventy percent of the Hmong American students in the program go on to earn degrees or are currently enrolled in college. No other ethnic group, including poor white students, has done so well. While anecdotal, this is evidence that Hmong Americans may be poised to turn things around and catch up.[26]

Another significant meaning of assimilation is the degree to which an immigrant group adopts the general values of the larger society as its own. This is commonly thought to be a zero-sum game. The more a group assimilates, the less it retains its own culture. Native language is the typical example: "The immigrant generation makes some progress but remains dominant in their native tongue, the second generation is bilingual, and the third generation speaks English only." Obviously, bilingualism is not zero sum. Both languages are used. Is it possible that many immigrant values, including bilingualism, survive despite assimilation?[27]

Paul Johnson reminds us that the Jews are the rare example of "a totally assimilated community which still retained its Jewish consciousness." It is instructive that Jews hesitated to embrace the last piece of assimilation—intermarriage. It was not until the 1990s that they matched the general population in this respect. The reason this last piece did not easily fall into place was the fear that intermarriage would dilute their Jewish identity. Yet this has not happened, so intermarriage is no longer feared as before. Hmong

Americans, however, have some way to go before this fear loosens its grip. Unlike other Asian Americans, whose intermarriage rates range from 30 to 60 percent, Hmong Americans still marry mostly within their ethnicity.

Yet, in other respects evidence indicates that Hmong Americans, especially the new generation, will likely close the gap between themselves and the general population in the areas of education, occupation, and income. Also, because of the influence of their clans, even as they become increasingly at home with the civic culture of America, like the Jews they will retain their unique ethnic identity.[28]

The stubborn independence of the clans and the intensity of clan loyalty that so nettled Vang Pao are not a Hmong weakness but strength. The clans are the depositories of Hmong culture and its conduit. The clans are where Hmong culture is expressed full strength and transmitted across generations. Clans also filter this culture, for each clan puts its own stamp on rituals and practices. In this sense, Hmong culture is like a language with many dialects. Each clan has its dialect, yet they all speak the same language.

Hmong clans are also impressively adaptable. In the past, clansmen scattered by war and living apart for generations discovered when they finally reunited that they were now different in many ways. Instead of demanding uniformity, they simply divided into subclans. From then on, allegiance was to the subclan—essentially creating two separate clans. Disputes within a clan can lead to the same result; the dissenters become a subclan and restrict their allegiance to it.

This process enables Hmong people to adapt to new situations, to be different and yet remain Hmong. Such organization, despite its decentralized nature, has remarkable staying power. It is able to preserve a culture indefinitely, even in the face of a determined effort to destroy it. Significantly, at the core of American civic values is the same fierce determination to govern one's own life that is so typically Hmong. The Hmong independent spirit is typically American.[29]

Changing Lives of Hmong Americans Today

The four Hmong families that my wife and I sponsored began their American lives in Spokane. When many of the Hmong in Spokane left for California, Minnesota, and Wisconsin in the late 1980s, two of these families joined the exodus. At New Year festivals, funerals, and weddings, there were reunions, where I learned from clansmen how they were faring. Among the first generation, there was bad news and good. One wife left her husband when he married a second young wife in Thailand. But the head of one family became a computer programmer and earned a good living, while another launched several short-lived small businesses. Many of the wives earned as much as or more than their husbands. This troubled the husbands, though it was not a great loss of face since they still ran the affairs of the family, and with enterprising sons the families soon left welfare far behind.

The sons and daughters of the second generation excelled in school, and all entered professions. There was one tragedy, however. A teenager died suddenly and mysteriously; he took a nap one afternoon and never woke up (a case of Sudden Unexpected Death Syndrome). As a boy, he was a delight, always active, always curious. Often he sat on my lap as I told him fairy tales. I can still see his happy face and bright eyes. It was a very sad funeral.

Members of the second generation have become success stories by American standards, yet they have not lost their Hmong identity. Their links to their family and clan are as strong as ever. They seek the counsel of their fathers and clan elders on important decisions. When they are sick, they consult doctors but also use Hmong remedies, and if the matter is truly serious, they consult a shaman. The spirits good and bad that populate the Hmong universe are as real to them as they were for their parents and grandparents. As hard as they might try, they cannot excise those spirits from their imagination.

Hmong people have been my friends and companions for more than twenty years. One of my dearest friends is a Hmong man. I spend more time with him than any other person, except my wife. His children are like my own, and I am fiercely proud of them. I go to more soccer games than I can count, and my voice turns raspy by the end of the season from all the cheering.

Recently, at a Hmong American family gathering, there were eighteen Hmong people and my wife and myself. There was the usual storytelling and playful verbal pokes, some directed at me. The next day, a young man from the party looked at me and said, "You are different now." I asked what he meant. He thought. "You are comfortable." It was a wonderful compliment.

NOTES

1. Stephen Pinker, "A History of Violence," *The New Republic*, Mar. 19, 2007, 3.

2. Arthur Dommen, *The Indochinese Experience of the French and Americans: Nationalism and Communism in Cambodia, Laos, and Vietnam* (Bloomington: Indiana University Press, 2001), 1.

3. Mai Na M. Lee, "The Dream of the Hmong Kingdom: Resistance, Collaboration, and Legitimacy Under French Colonialism (1893–1955)" (PhD diss., University of Wisconsin, 2005), 45–77.

4. Keith Quincy, *Hmong: History of a People*, 2nd ed. (Spokane: Eastern Washington University Press, 1995), 149–50.

5. Lee, "The Dream of the Hmong Kingdom," 323.

6. See Vue and Keith Quincy, *Der: A True Story* (Marshall, WA: GPJ Books, 2007), 60.

7. Henry Kissinger, *White House Years* (Boston: Little, Brown & Company, 1979), 448–57; Richard Reeve, *President Nixon: Alone in the White House* (New York: Simon & Schuster, 2001), 177–79; Department of State, *Foreign Relations of the United States, 1969–1976* (Washington, DC: Government Printing Office, 2006), declassified minutes of the Special Actions Group (WSAG), Sept. 2, 1969 to Mar. 27, 1970.

8. Vue and Quincy, *Der: A True Story*, 68.

9. Lee, "The Dream of the Hmong Kingdom," 348.

10. Kenneth Conboy and James Morrison, *Shadow War: The CIA's Secret War in Laos* (Boulder, CO: Paladin Press, 1995), 410. Lee, "The Dream of the Hmong Kingdom," 349.

11. Roger Warner, *Backfire* (New York: Simon & Schuster, 1995), 117, 178. Ernest Kunh, interviewed by Arthur Dommen, *Foreign Affairs Oral History Collection*, Georgetown University Library, Mar. 25–26, 1995.

12. Vue and Quincy, *Der: A True Story*, 60, 92.

13. Lee, "The Dream of the Hmong Kingdom," 353–54.

14. Keith Quincy, *Harvesting Pa Chay's Wheat: The Hmong and America's Secret War in Laos* (Spokane: Eastern Washington University Press, 2000), 363. Gayle Morrison, *Sky Is Falling: An Oral History of the CIA's Evacuation of the Hmong from Laos* (Jefferson, NC: McFarland & Company, Inc., 1999), 152. Vue and Quincy, *Der: A True Story*, 100.

15. Quincy, *Harvesting Pa Chay's Wheat*, 428.

16. Vue and Quincy, *Der: A True Story*, 105–10.

17. United Nations High Commissioner for Refugees (UNHCR), *The State of the World's Refugees: Fifty Years of Humanitarian Action* (Oxford: Oxford University Press, 2000), 65. UNHCR, "Report on the South Asian Subcontinent Repatriation Operation," Jan. 1, 1975, 2.

18. Gil Loescher, Alexander Betts, and James Milner, *The United Nations High Commissioner for Refugees: The Politics and Practices of Refugee Protection into the Twenty-First Century* (New York: Routledge, 2008).

19. Courtland Robinson, "Laotian Refugees in Thailand: The Thai and U.S. Response, 1975 to 1988," in eds. Joseph Zasloff and Leonard Unger, *Laos: Beyond the Revolution* (New York: St. Martin's Press, 1991), 226.

20. Lynellyn Long, *Ban Vinai: The Refugee Camp* (New York: Columbia University Press, 1993), 186.

21. Quincy, *Harvesting Pa Chay's Wheat,* 451.

22. Quincy, *Harvesting Pa Chay's Wheat,* 436–38.

23. Monica Davey, "Arrest Uncovers Divide in Hmong-Americans," *New York Times,* June 14, 2007, www.nytimes.com/2007/06/14/us/14hmong.html (accessed Nov. 15, 2011).

24. Quincy, *Harvesting Pa Chay's Wheat,* 31–40; Lee, "The Dream of the Hmong Kingdom," 78–94, 118–32, 177–82, 338.

25. Thomas Sowell, *Ethnic America: A History* (New York: Basic Books, 1981), 286.

26. David Andrew Keightley, "A New Life in Montana: The Laotians—Their History, Culture and American Journey" (master's thesis, University of Montana, 2010), 48.

27. Mary Waters and Thomás Jiménez, "Assessing Immigrant Assimilation: New Empirical and Theoretical Challenges," *Annual Review of Sociology,* Apr. 7, 2005, 110.

28. Paul Johnson, *A History of the Jews* (New York: Harper & Row, 1987), 568. Barone, *The New Americans,* 247. C. N. Le, "Interracial Dating and Marriage," *Asian Nation,* June 2, 2011, www.Asian-Nation.org/interracial.shtml (accessed Nov. 15, 2011).

29. Ori Brafman and Rod Backstrom, *The Starfish and the Spider: The Unstoppable Power of Leaderless Organizations* (New York: Portfolio, 2006), 95.

< 5 >

The Spirit of Enterprise and the Emergence of Hmong and Hmong American Identities

Reflections of a Hmong Anthropologist

GARY YIA LEE

Being Hmong is having many identities, starting at birth and continuing throughout life. Sometimes these identities are clear-cut, but often they clash with each other. As we mature, most of us learn, although it is not easy, to navigate through this maze of confusing self-images. We just accept it as part of our life, of belonging to a minority living on the margin, and of having to accommodate the demands of majority groups we live with. For a Hmong, even one's birth order puts a difference on one's identity: the firstborn is expected to lead and to bear more family responsibilities. Moreover, one's Hmong identity is determined by whether one is a boy or a girl. A boy's placenta is traditionally buried at the base of the central post of the house: he is expected to uphold the family line and assume the spiritual role by observing all religious rituals and making offerings to family ancestors. A girl's placenta is buried under the bed in her parents' bedroom: a girl has fewer responsibilities in ritual performance and ancestral reverence. She is expected to *ua neej nrog qhua,* to "marry out of the clan."

After marriage and a few children, a married Hmong man is given his *npe laus,* "adult name," by his parents-in-law and will be referred to by that name for the rest of his life. A married woman will also be known by her husband's name, such as *Niam Tooj* (Tong's wife), almost suppressing her own name given at birth. Moreover, being born into a particular clan also sets a Hmong's identity for life. The name of the clan one belongs to is also one's family name, whether it is Moua, Vang, Yang, Xiong, Chang, Lo, Lee, or any of eleven others. For those from Laos and Thailand, another determining factor is the subdivision into which one is born: White Hmong or Blue Mong. Many older Hmong also reckon their identities on the basis of which village or region they come from.

< 81 >

However, in the context of transnational migration and international politics, self-identity becomes more complicated. If a person is a refugee or the child of a refugee, new layers are added to his or her identity. It is no wonder that many young Hmong in the United States and elsewhere are confused about who they are. If a Hmong American teenager is asked, "Where are you from?" her answer could be as simple as Sheboygan, Wisconsin; or depending on the depth of her knowledge, it could stretch farther back into the past and around the globe. Moreover, if she were to visit relatives in Laos, would she be seen as a Hmong, or a Hmong from America, or an American? If she goes to China or Vietnam, would she be called Hmong, Miao, or Meo? All of these are possibilities in her self-image as a Hmong American living in the twenty-first century.

Many of the trends and transformations I have witnessed over the past twenty-five years reflect not only the complexity but also the flexibility of Hmong and Hmong Americans as they align their culture and identity with their social and political environment. What is crucial is that new cultural features continue to evolve with a new self-image that has enormously raised Hmong consciousness about where they have been, where they are now, and where they are heading.

My Life and Identities

I was the firstborn son for my parents, a bouncing boy coming to earth around the New Year of 1949. At birth, I failed to cry out like other babies, so my father put me under a wok and hit it with a spoon. The noise made me scream in fright, and thus I was named *Yia*, a Hmong word for wok. This is a common name for Hmong boys and girls.

Early in my life, I knew only war. It shaped my destiny and ability to struggle for survival. I was only a month old when my parents had to abandon everything in Ban Houei Kouang (Fib Khab) near the Vietnamese border, where we were living with other Hmong relatives. A Hmong leader on the communist Pathet Lao side came with his men, burned our houses down, and confiscated all our possessions because we belonged to the Lee clan, supporters of Touby Lyfoung, their rival on the French side. For safety, we moved to Xieng Khouang city, where my father worked as a militiaman. When the Vietminh invaded in 1953, we hid for many months in the jungle with other military families. In 1954, the French were defeated in Dien Bien Phu and left Indochina. My parents enrolled me in the provincial primary school the following year with my older sister. Ten other Hmong students attended school with us, including some who traveled from nearby villages and others who were local. Each day, my sister and I made a ten-mile round-trip journey on foot, lunch packs on our backs, from our village of Tham Kat to school. After two years, my parents decided the walk was too much for me, so we moved to the city, where we stayed until I was accepted by the provincial high school, College de Xieng Khouang. Because Laos had been under French influence since 1893, all levels of education were taught in French.

Even before Laos became independent, Hmong knew the value of formal schooling, and a few parents sent their children to school in Xieng Khouang city or other district areas with primary schools. For example, in the 1930s, in the village of Nong Het, Touby Lyfoung's father had the foresight to hire a private tutor to teach him and his two brothers, Toulia and Tougeu. They would go on to become the first Hmong to complete high school in Vietnam and would later work for the French in Laos. Likewise, my father always valued education and gave me all the necessary support, including numerous books and a bicycle, a rare gift in those days. His parents died while he was still young; his older brother, Xeng, was left to take care of my father and a younger brother. An itinerant trader, Uncle Xeng, who died in his twenties, recognized that Hmong children needed education.

In 1942, Uncle Xeng sent my father to Muang Gnanh for his primary studies. Three years later, my father was one of the few Hmong who could read and write in Lao, and he was later given the position of *tasseng* (canton chief) for Tham Thao. Working closely with Uncle Touby, he knew education was the only way to get ahead in life, so he enrolled my siblings and me in school once we moved to Xieng Khouang city. However, as a soldier and policeman, my father was not always home, so it was left to my mother to make sure that I studied hard. As the oldest son, I had to plow the rice field and do the heavy work when my father was not home. While grazing the family buffalo and horses, I would read a book or do my homework. I loved reading stories, but there were no libraries or bookshops, so I bought Thai folktales, written in poetic rhymes, from a local Thai man. Having taught myself Thai, I would read these epic tales aloud with voracity, sometimes singing them in Lao *mor lam* opera style in the meadow to my animals and myself.

Education in Laos and Australia

In 1961, the year I entered high school, Xieng Khouang was overrun by Kong Le's Neutralist troops. Because my father was a policeman with the right-wing faction under which Vang Pao's troops also served, my family fled south with them to Pa Dong, which was attacked three months later. When we were evacuated to Vientiane, I joined Hmong students from across the country who were moving there to do secondary studies. In 1962, at least thirty young Hmong, including myself, enrolled in the Lycee de Vientiane, and another twenty in Dong Dok Teachers' College. Previously, less than half a dozen had gone this far in the Lao educational system due to the high cost of living in the Lao capital and the lack of other opportunities for Hmong there. Thus, even in wartime, the desire for education remained strong among Hmong people.

In 1963, my family safely returned to Pha Khao, Vang Pao's headquarters, leaving me in Vientiane to study. To help meet my expenses and to feed my four brothers and two sisters, my mother and older sister sold small goods at the local market and nearby villages. Like other parents, my mother wanted to see me finish my studies and had grand hopes for me to pursue higher education in France or the United States and then return home to a good government position. I continued to read, spending nearly all of my pocket money on Western classic novels from the only French bookshop in Vientiane. Like other students, I was very poor. Two teachers, Monsieur Robert Loche and Madame Renee Souvannavong, gave me clothes, took me to their homes, and provided extra coaching in French and Latin. When I was studying too hard and ended up in the hospital for three months in 1963, they visited me. Even after 1975, when she had returned to France, Madame Souvannavong continued to write to me with advice and news.

Through my education, I came to see life beyond Hmong villages in the highlands. However, my thinking was so colonized that I believed France was the center of world civilization. My goal was to go there for higher education. Acting on my own rebellious impulses, I started to use foreign knowledge to question my Hmong origin and beliefs. Moreover, I explored other options for my Hmong identity by delving into Buddhism, Catholicism, and Baha'i. Yet I was not happy because "the real me" remained elusive.

In 1965, a postcard from a cousin in Australia changed my life. Reading his description of that beautiful country, I decided to enter a scholarship competition to study there. Winning the Colombo Plan scholarship opened the door to a new opportunity and chapter in my life. After finishing senior high school in Australia, I completed a bachelor's degree and a master's degree in social work, specializing in community development and refugee resettlement. Each vacation, I went back to visit my family in Laos, where people continued to suffer from the war. Many school friends who had enlisted were dead. In the tens of thousands, civilians were displaced from their villages. There was no prospect for peace.

Having grown up during wartime and having seen so many people suffer, I planned to help them in any way possible to get back on their feet when peace should come. One of my main influences was Uncle Touby, who asked the Lao government to continue giving me a scholarship so I could stay in Australia to do my master's studies. Even while suffering from the daily humiliations at a so-called re-education camp in Sam Neua where he was taken after the war, he wrote messages urging me to return to Laos and serve the country. In 1978, he died from a gunshot to the heart after defying a camp guard. Like other high-ranking inmates, he was buried without a funeral, without a proper grave. For me, Uncle Touby remains a great Hmong leader, a true hero and a lifetime inspiration.

In 1975, I started my PhD studies in anthropology at the University of Sydney under Professor William Geddes. He had just completed a book on the Hmong of Thailand in which he referred to them as "Miao." When I was critical of that term, he suggested that I should become a researcher since I would be able to write from a Hmong perspective. In doing so, he validated the possibility that a Hmong scholar could offer a valuable alternative perspective on Hmong history and culture. He not only accepted me as a PhD student but also helped find funding for my studies. A great influence in my life, he taught me to be methodical in my search for answers. His interest in cross-cultural research was evident in his efforts to help establish the Tribal Research Centre in Chiangmai and his many visits to Hmong refugee camps in Thailand. With great enthusiasm, I read everything in the anthropological literature on the Hmong.[1]

While waiting for the graduation ceremony for my master's degree in 1975, I heard news that my mother, brothers, and their families were at Ban Namphong, Thailand, with twenty-five thousand other Hmong refugees.

Without any family remaining in Laos, I decided to apply for asylum in Australia, which the government soon granted. When Hmong refugee friends and relatives in Thailand asked for help, I sent the Australian Immigration Department a list of families interested in resettlement. I believed this was the least I could do for other Hmong made homeless by war. In 1976, my mother, four brothers, and their families arrived in Sydney with the first group of 260 refugees from Laos. The government housed them temporarily in government accommodation, and I visited them regularly in between my studies. By now, I had acquired an academic knowledge of Hmong lives that I realized was very limited. Having been away from other Hmong for most of my life, I had lost touch with Hmong culture and tradition and thus had lost track of who I was. With my mother and brothers safely in Australia, I became motivated to visit Hmong in the villages and refugee camps of Thailand. By learning about their Hmong ways of life, I hoped to find myself.

A Real Hmong Life

In 1976, I began fieldwork for my PhD at the Tribal Research Centre in Chiangmai, Thailand. My research site was the village of Khun Wang, a White Hmong settlement with twenty-one households participating in a United Nations opium replacement project. After ten years in Australia, meeting Hmong in Thailand was a turning point in my search for identity. What impressed me most was their hospitality. As a newly married couple, my wife and I appreciated the graciousness of people who always invited us to eat with them after our initial introduction. Recognizing us as fellow Hmong, many local people spent long hours telling us about their villages and their work.

Once we were established, village women would visit my wife to do embroideries, chatting away the hours, while I interviewed the men and measured their farms. At the Hmong settlements of Mae Wak and Khun Klang, I attended weddings and funerals, recording their proceedings and learning about them in depth. To understand farming through the seasons, I helped to clear the fields, plant crops, weed, harvest, winnow rice (*yuj nplej*), and grind corn. Most important, I came to understand Hmong religion and shamanism through participant observation and personal immersion in some of the rituals. I taped all the funeral reed pipe music (*qeej tuag*) and the blessing funeral chant (*txiv xaiv*), asking questions about their meanings and procedures. At Khun Wang and later in Australia, through my father, who is a shaman, I returned to Hmong religion and spiritual practices. Much of this life-changing experience was later used in my autobiographical novel *Dust of Life*.[2]

From this new knowledge, my life direction became much clearer as I finally found my real ethnic identity based on both tangible and intangible cultural markers that I could see or was keenly aware of. I began to see every Hmong ritual as having proper procedures with logical explanations, including guiding the soul of a dead person to thank household guardians; to revisit and honor all the places essential to his or her survival in the past; to retrieve the placenta from his or her birth location to use as an afterlife garment (*tsho tsuj tsho npuag*) for the dead before his or her journey to the ancestors in the afterworld; and ultimately to undergo reincarnation. The journey to the ancestors may be frightening in places, but it has the happy destination of reunion with them. Those who commit suicide or who die without a proper funeral may stay in limbo, but there is no hell (Hmong have no word for it). Above all, Hmong religion is aimed at the living, to protect them here and now and not after death, to unite members for mutual support. Thus, at Hmong funerals, it is common to see how extended families across generations come together not only to fulfill their social obligations but also to affirm their deep connection across time, space, and the upheavals of history. Large amounts of food may be consumed at great cost, but no expense is spared so long as kinship ties can be maintained through the inclusion of all kin members in ceremonies and the renewal of social bonds with their presence.

An Unfolding Journey

In 1978, I returned to Australia after sixteen months of doing fieldwork and learning to be Hmong at Khun Wang. After completing my PhD in 1981, I worked with Indochinese refugees in Australia. In 1983, I was invited to give a talk in the United States on Hmong refugee resettlement in Australia. On that trip, I talked with many newly arrived Hmong families in California and the Midwest regarding their concerns about welfare assistance, difficulties learning English, and limited job opportunities. Hmong leaders and workers and those who had been in the country longer were all eager to lend a hand in the resettlement of new arrivals. The government, church groups, and many Hmong mutual assistance associations provided refugee services. Everywhere I went, I found abundant evidence of Hmong Americans taking initiatives to be self-sufficient. Wherever they started new lives, whether as farmers or assembly line workers, they were making the new country their own.

During my return trips to the United States in the 1990s, I recognized that in Hmong American families, traditional roles were certainly in flux; some were even reversed. For example, children were finding it fairly easy to learn to speak English and assimilate into mainstream culture, while their parents were still speaking Hmong and feeling uncertain about their place in American society. Speaking different languages, sometimes parents and children were following different cultural values, widening the generational gap between them. Moreover, when wives found employment while their husbands were still searching for jobs, traditional family structure became even more difficult to maintain as wives instead of husbands became providers. Another shift in traditional roles could be seen in attitudes toward the first generation. On the one hand, whether they spoke English or not, elders remained highly visible and respected as carriers of tradition and customs. Potentially their wealth of knowledge was a resource that their children and grandchildren could depend on for guidance in their lives. However, younger generations sometimes resisted asking for advice from their elders because they were more influenced by American culture. More at ease in navigating their way in American society, they felt entitled to their independence and often rejected elders' values that seemed to have become irrelevant to modern urban life.

As with my life, the journey of Hmong Americans continues to be full of unexpected twists and turns. It is a story of becoming, of learning to leave their rural subsistence farming life behind and become city dwellers, to see themselves as global citizens. In 2006, I was invited to be the first scholar-in-residence at the Center for Hmong Studies at Concordia University in St. Paul, Minnesota. In 2008, the university awarded me an honorary doctorate. As I sat on the podium waiting to receive this degree, I could not help but wonder what I had accomplished and what my true identity is: Hmong, Lao Hmong, Australian, Hmong Australian or Australian Hmong, a member of the Hmong global nation, or all of them. I realized that although in my mind I have many identities, I am and will always be Hmong at the core through my birth, my physical appearance, and the culture I have embraced.

Compared to what I saw in 1983 and 1985, when anxiety and fear of the future were widespread among first-generation Hmong Americans, the individuals I met in 2006 and 2008 were of a different kind: confident, politically engaged, socially committed, and forward looking. Since their resettlement around the world, what have Hmong immigrants achieved and where are we now with our culture and identity as a people? To me, they have achieved much in the space of thirty years. They have now built a solid foundation for their new life in America, which will help to fulfill their dreams well into the future.

Global Exchanges and Hmong Identity Production

Hmong are now well informed about their multiple global identities, including Chinese Miao, Vietnamese Hmong, Lao Hmong, Australian Hmong, French Hmong, and Canadian and U.S. Hmong. As anthropologist Louisa Schein points out, contradictions and disagreements allow Hmong opportunities to engage in "identity exchanges" and "identity production." When Hmong from America visit their coethnic "Miao" in China, they are bewildered by the fact that large segments of the Miao population do not speak Hmong nor do they have customs and myths pointing to a shared cultural and ancestral origin. Yet, Hmong American visitors usually identify themselves as Miao with their hosts. On the other hand, when Miao from China visit Hmong communities in America, they refer to themselves as Hmong. This switching of identity affiliation by both groups is based not on a common culture and language but on a "general notion of fraternity as well as more particularized bonds of kinship and marriage alliance," leading to mutual obligation. This experience of "identity production" arises out of social, economic, and political expediency, carved from "not only linguistic and cultural dimensions, but also political and economic strategies . . . a multidimensional and potent transnationality that is constructed precisely out of the entangling of the cultural with the economic and the political."[3]

From my point of view, decisively positive results accrue from the Hmong and Hmong Americans' ongoing search to explore identity possibilities, to experiment with different versions, and to mix them from a variety of source countries in the hope of finding the best possible model—as Hmong women have done with their costumes. For people of Hmong descent, exposure to a bewildering diversity of cultures and identities across ethnic groups has become a constructive force, allowing them to borrow desirable cultural features from other groups while recuperating and reinterpreting their own culture and self-identity. This new identity can reflect a new transnational group image, a public representation made possible largely by modern communication and travel.

Furthermore, Hmong Americans are movers and shakers in forging Hmong identities around the world. As the biggest group of Hmong living in a highly industrialized Western country, they have shown that they can lead Hmong in other countries in the spirit of enterprise and political initiatives. Increasingly since the late 1990s, Hmong Americans have become frequent visitors to their fellow residents of other countries. In these transnational travels, they provide friends and relatives with financial assistance; in addition, they contribute to community projects, such as supplying books for libraries in Laos or computers for remote village schools in China. Speaking out against discrimination and political persecutions, they have acted as a representative voice on human rights issues. Through the Internet and Hmong American radio stations, magazines, and newspapers, they provide information and news on current situations of Hmong in the United States and elsewhere in the world. As observed in 2008, through their cultural groups, they send their talented young dancers, artists, and singers to Laos and Thailand to give dazzling performances in front of local Hmong audiences, including officials and dignitaries. Student associations and community organizations have been active in promoting cross-cultural exchange between Hmong in the United States and other places. When Miao professionals and businesspeople come from China, Hmong Americans welcome them by providing interpreters, arranging sightseeing tours, and hosting them in their homes with much drinking and feasting. Likewise, when U.S. Hmong visitors go to China, the same bonding and hospitality occur.

These myriad activities have elevated the status of Hmong Americans as leaders in business, culture, politics, and education. Others around the world have come to perceive them as champions in fostering friendship and solidarity; advocates in local and international politics, especially in persuading the United Nations and other bodies to address Hmong issues;

and broadcasters of Hmong voices around the world. In other words, the international Hmong community has come to see Hmong Americans as their representatives on the world stage. While Hmong in other countries continue to work through their respective and government channels, they assume their local identity as Lao Hmong, Chinese Hmong, or Thai Hmong, but now they know they are part of another identity, the transnational global Hmong community. Thus, the role of Hmong Americans is similar to that of the U.S. government in pushing for the rights of oppressed people around the globe.

Emergence of Hmong American Entrepreneurial Spirit

In my perspective, the political and economic system of the United States has contributed positively to Hmong ability to take the initiative in achieving entrepreneurial success. With freedom and opportunities come incentives to compete and do well. This is one of the outstanding Hmong traits in life: desire to compete (*sib twv*), to excel and improve one's living conditions (*sib twv ua neej*). This is critical at every life stage. Hmong people are not happy with remaining at the same spot. Traditionally, when moving villages, they wanted to find better pastures and more fertile farming land, so they could make a secure living and accumulate wealth. In the U.S. capitalist economy, some Hmong have especially thrived by following this age-old migration but now from one city to another, from one life stage to the next in search of better opportunities.

Living in a capitalist economy with private ownership of the means of production and personal profit as main incentives, Hmong appear to have readily adopted free enterprise based on minimal government intervention and an open market. Few Hmong liked the socialist economy in Laos, where they had to work under cooperatives, return half of the goods they produced to the government, and, before the 1920s, pay colonial tax in the form of opium and silver coins to French authorities. Now in the United States, citizenship includes the obligation and benefits of paying income taxes, which support public education and other services.

In the late 1970s and early 1980s, when Hmong refugees were urgently trying to rebuild their lives, they accepted any jobs they could find, most of which were unskilled. Exceptions were individuals who worked as translators, teacher's aides, or welfare service workers dealing with Hmong refugees. In 1983, when I first visited the United States, this was the situation. As former soldiers and subsistence farmers, Hmong refugees did not have the business acumen or capital to start their own businesses. Yet, during my research in 1985, I was surprised to see that the Hmong of Merced, California, were already running two thriving grocery shops and a pig farm. Their Hmong neighbors in Fresno were working in their own market gardens, growing vegetables for sale in farmers' markets across the state, from Los Angeles to San Jose. Some were even engaging in commercial agricultural activities, selling to large wholesale distributors. At that time, except for a few who had accumulated enough money to buy their own small farms, most Hmong were leasing land from other people.

Because most Hmong were used to agricultural work in Laos, it is not surprising that many wanted to return to an area in which they had knowledge and expertise. Yet, what they were doing was not subsistence farming but commercial enterprise, something few of them had undertaken before. Skills required for this venture were far ranging, including bookkeeping, negotiating with buyers, and keeping up with new product development. Initially, many had been able to cope with these requirements with the assistance of their fast-learning children. They later learned to handle these situations themselves through practical experiences. Although many Hmong families still engage in market gardening today, most in the 1980s found it to be a difficult way of making a long-term living.[4]

During my most recent stay in the United States from 2006 to 2008, I could see clearly how far Hmong Americans have progressed. Across the country, I was astounded to discover this successful diversification into many areas of businesses. Most of them still cater largely to Hmong consumers, but this high rate of participation as service providers within the U.S. economy is to be admired. In Detroit, for example, many Chinese restaurants and takeout businesses are operated by Hmong Americans. Similar developments can be seen in the Twin Cities of Minnesota, including grocery stores and specialty shops. Two Hmong flea markets have opened in St. Paul and attract thousands of shoppers per week, including out-of-state and overseas visitors. Based on one estimate, they bring in four to five million dollars a week to stall holders and operators. In addition, many Hmong are real estate agents, financial planners and lenders, accountants, lawyers, doctors, and chiropractors. A Hmong American presence in these latter fields is especially noteworthy in Minnesota and Wisconsin.[5]

Cultural Innovations in the United States

Hmong cultural development has been made richer, more complex and interesting, through the innovations of young Hmong Americans who have added new music and dances to their repertoires. Every year, groups of young Hmong American men and women compete at Hmong New Year festivals and other venues to showcase their creativity and originality. Many elements in their dances are inspired by cultures other than their own, including Indian, Chinese, Lao, and Thai. Yet, their performances have retained stylistic qualities unique to Hmong people through improvisation and clever use of Hmong costumes. Furthermore, Hmong culture has been transformed through visits by Hmong Americans to Laos, Thailand, or China to join New Year celebrations or sight-see to get a taste of the diversity of Hmong people and cultures around the world. Even a quick trip to the Hmong flea markets in St. Paul can be just as eye-opening regarding how Hmong identity has been redefined in the current global environment of rapid exchanges of information, ideas, and material cultures. To look at displays of Hmong traditional herbal medicine, handmade embroideries, ethnic costumes from the homeland, and publications on the Hmong worldwide is to contemplate the evolving and elusive nature of what is "Hmong" itself.

Hmong spirit of enterprise is most amply manifested by the many ways in which Hmong Americans have tried to "package" their cultural heritage for personal use as well as for commercial consumption. In response to radical changes to their family and community life, many filmmakers are capturing and preserving on film Hmong traditions and cultural practices. Countless music videos, feature films, and video documentaries are now available in Hmong. Made each year by enterprising Hmong American individuals and Hmong American media companies, these creative productions are intended mainly for Hmong consumers in the United States and other Western countries as a way to reflect on where they have been and where they are now. Themes in the amateur productions range from rock music and martial arts action to documentaries on Hmong life in Thailand, Laos, and China. In addition, Thai, Korean, Indian, and Chinese films have been dubbed in Hmong for older viewers, thus expanding their cultural horizons and global awareness.

Along with Hmong self-image or identity, Hmong culture has undergone much change during the last thirty years. Even Hmong language has been affected. Many young people, no matter where they live, are no longer fluent in their parents' tongue. While some have tried steadfastly to maintain their culture, others are embracing modernity by adopting ideas and practices from the mainstream culture in which they live. In the United States, one symbol of change is that costumes—once unique markers of ethnic identity, such as the distinct clothing of White Hmong and Blue Mong—are now used interchangeably by all Hmong groups.

At the same time, Hmong Americans are careful to maintain cultural skills and practices that many Hmong believe to be essential to their identity across generations. In fact, parents encourage their children to take lessons in playing *qeej,* practicing songs and funeral chants, performing dances, learning needlework, and developing Hmong language fluency (including reading and writing as well as speaking). Mutual assistance associations in many cities offer after-school cultural programs. The Hmong Culture Center in St. Paul and similar organizations in other cities have served as excellent venues for these learning activities. Equally important, young people are acquiring invaluable cultural knowledge from older generations. For example, they are learning ritual chants and songs from their grandfathers, fathers, and uncles and, subsequently, taking part in funerals to gain hands-on experiences in honing their skills.

Since the mid-1990s, the Internet has contributed to the enrichment of Hmong culture and intellectual development. Hundreds of websites on Hmong history, culture, and other issues of concern are now available. Hmong people today are able to enjoy reading and writing in their own language by recomposing and disseminating cultural information through books and other communication media, including television, radio broadcasts, and newspapers.

Being and Becoming in New Places

In my view, three traits have enabled Hmong Americans to take great steps forward in the United States. First, they have capably dealt with great hardship, political persecution, and racial discrimination. While subjected to centuries of domination by other ethnic groups, including Chinese, French, Japanese, and Lao, they have strengthened their self-sufficiency and mutual support systems. During times of war, Hmong people were driven by the need to survive. They had to be ready to live a life on the run, to accumulate food reserves to feed their families from one day to the next, and to build makeshift shelters with whatever tools they had. Discontent with the refugee camps' meager United Nations food assistance, they went outside to work for local Thai farmers for wages, no matter how small the pay and how risky the undertaking. To this day, Hmong people understand how important it is to make the most out of a good opportunity, whether a fertile piece of farmland or a profitable market. Wherever they settle, they need to feel that they can help themselves; they can make use of their own two hands to feed their families. After the destruction of their entire way of life in Laos, Hmong people were intent on establishing families, clans, and community that would endure in a new land. To regain pride in themselves, they wanted to control their own fate.

The second main trait for Hmong Americans is that a person belongs not only to a family but also to an extended family network. One has obligations to reach beyond oneself, to family members and others in need, and to contribute to American society as a full citizen. Mutual dependence is expected and mutual support provided. For this reason, a family in the United States feels obligated to help relatives left behind in refugee camps of Thailand or villages of Laos.

Finally, a major trait contributing to Hmong American progress during the last thirty years is that they have learned from the success of other people; they continually try to apply ideas they have become familiar with in urban America. At a 1998 Hmong National Development conference presentation, I expressed hope that Hmong people would learn to be in relationships with other people and to open themselves to new experiences so that they can discover new ideas and work with other groups for mutual benefits. I am glad to see that many have now taken up this challenge. They have done this not only through formal education but also through the contacts they have in their everyday life, at work, at school, through the media, and across the fence with their neighbors. Over time, Hmong Americans have gradually developed networking skills that enable them to advance and contribute as much as they can to American society.[6]

Conclusion

Because Hmong people everywhere are changing, they may no longer view as important the possession of an "authentic" Hmong cultural identity. Will the spirit of enterprise, which has been essential to Hmong American economic, social, and cultural development up to this time, continue at the same pace of transformation? Considering that they used to be soldiers and subsistence farmers in the hills of Laos, away from urban centers and formal education, they have done very well for themselves in their new country. Greater changes lie ahead, but there is much for Hmong Americans to look forward to, including even more economic and educational advancement.

Culture is the main area of concern as more and more of the younger generation become assimilated and adopt the values and practices of mainstream society, and as members of the first generation pass away and leave their ideas behind to be revitalized and made relevant to the lives of future generations. A new Hmong identity, with its full range of nuances and subtleties, will no doubt emerge as young people become more and more integrated into a multicultural society with an international outlook. As yet, it is difficult to predict what this identity will be. For now, Hmong people have become a transnational community without borders. They have formed a global identity encompassing many subgroups, traditional markers, and dialects, woven into the many layers of national and international images of themselves as Hmong and American.

As Rabbi Kushner observes, "When you are young, you admire people who are smart and strive to be like them, to use them as role models. And that is good. But as you grow older you admire people who are kind. In our youth, we do things for ourselves but in our maturity, we do things mostly for other people." As my life journey has revealed, the acceptance of a multilayered set of self-concepts can make each of us a richer and more capable human being. As exemplified by the experience of Hmong and Hmong Americans, self-acceptance, along with respect for others, is a rewarding path to building a healthy global family.[7]

NOTES

1. William Geddes, *Migrants of the Mountains: The Cultural Ecology of the Blue Miao (Hmong Njua) of Thailand* (Oxford: Clarendon, 1976).

2. Gary Yia Lee, *Dust of Life* (St. Paul, MN: Hmongland Publishing, 2004).

3. Louisa Schein, "Hmong/Miao Transnationality: Identity Beyond Culture," in eds. Nicholas Tapp, Jean Michaud, Christian Culas, and Gary Yia Lee, *Hmong/Miao in Asia* (Chiangmai: Silkworm Books, 2004), 273, 274, 278.

4. Timothy Dunnigan, Douglas P. Olney, Miles A. McNall, and Marline A. Spring, "Hmong," in ed. David Haines, *Case Studies in Diversity: Refugees in America in the 1990s* (Westport, CT: Praeger, 1997), 155–56.

5. Lee Pao Xiong, e-mail message to author, Sept. 30, 2007.

6. Gary Yia Lee, "Hmong Living Their Dreams—Then and Now," closing keynote address, Fourth Annual Hmong National Conference, Apr. 16–18, 1998, Denver, CO. Available at www.garyyialee.com.

7. Rabbi Harold Kushner, *Living a Life That Matters* (London: Pan Books, 2001), 5.

PART II

Family Challenges and Community Transitions

< 6 >

The Good Hmong Girl Eats Raw *Laab*

KA VANG

In this chapter, I will examine social and cultural implications of "a good Hmong girl" by addressing these questions: What does it mean to be a good Hmong girl or a bad Hmong girl? Who defines the good Hmong girl? Who practices it and enforces the rules? Moreover, what are the rewards and consequences for the Hmong girl and her family if she is not a good Hmong girl? Finally, would Hmong culture be diminished if there were no more good Hmong girls left?

The kitchen is buzzing with the sounds of plates being stacked, forks and spoons being polished, and ladles scooping soup made with mustard greens and freshly slaughtered pork into bowls. Gao Nou releases a warm puff of breath onto the back of a spoon, making it moist so she can polish it. On the back of the spotless spoon, the young girl sees the reflection of women behaving like bees, each with a sense of purpose and determination. Her mother, who is hosting the *ua neeb* feast, shouts at her, "Just don't stand there! Be a good Hmong girl and start setting the table. The men are hungry."

Gao Nou nods obediently as she silently contemplates the idea of a good Hmong girl. Lately, her mother has been directing the phrase at her, beginning and ending each sentence with "good Hmong girl":

"Make sure you have dinner ready by the time your father and I get home from work because that is what good Hmong girls do!"

"Good Hmong girls do not talk on the phone with boys. It makes them appear loose!"

"If you want to be a good Hmong girl and have a good Hmong life, then do not comb your hair when it is wet after dark because you will not find a man to love you."

"Good Hmong girls do not stay after school to play volleyball. There are men lurking in the gym and hallways who will suck your sweet nectar dry so you are no longer a fresh flower!"

< 101 >

"Gao Nou!" yells her mother, snapping her out of her daydream. "Your younger sister is already setting the table for the men; make sure you remember to serve both the raw *laab* and the cooked *laab*." Once again Gao Nou nods obediently. She loves raw beef *laab* and cannot wait to savor the gritty rice powder, hot peppers, cilantro, and green onions mixed into the minced beef and chopped tripe. *Cooked laab holds back the flavors of the dish,* Gao Nou thinks to herself as she slowly and diligently scoops the raw *laab* onto plates to be put on the table. Three metal folding tables are set end-to-end so as to make one long table with fifty chairs intrusively pushed against it. As though Aunt Blia and her daughters have sonar telling them the *laab* is ready, the women appear out of nowhere and gather the *laab* plates to set on the table. But no one can see the cheap, pressed wooden tops underneath the plastic table cover that has been taped tightly underneath. Her mother hisses, "You are moving too slowly! Aunt Blia's good daughters have already set the table."

Her mother is right. The table is set with steaming jasmine rice, mustard greens and pork belly soup, chicken and bamboo soup, crispy fried pork, raw and cooked *laab,* and stir-fried mustard greens and hot pepper sauce. The elder men and married men sit at the table. A raisin-faced shaman sits next to Gao Nou's father at the center of the table. Before the *ua neeb* meal can begin, her father, brothers, and uncles together thank the shaman for his services for her younger brother who had been ill. The men *pe* to show their gratitude. To *pe,* they bow their heads, swinging their clasped hands toward the shaman while reciting words of appreciation before kowtowing onto their knees. Following these formalities, the father chooses two men to oversee the toasting and feasting, considered the culmination of a communal gathering that begins with the arrival of the *txiv neeb* in the early hours of the morning. Such lengthy preparations testify to the commitment of Hmong American women to their families.

For important ceremonies, such as a *neeb khu* (a performance considered essential by Hmong Americans following a serious illness), two to four rounds of alcohol (served in two-, four-, or six-ounce wine glasses depending on the preference of the father and the two men overseeing the toasting) are typically poured before their meal is over. At the onset of the first round, people at the table are instructed to begin eating. The toasting at this time lasts twenty-five to forty-five minutes, depending on how quickly everyone drinks. The men make conversation as they feast on the dishes. While all of this is taking place, Gao Nou's heart sinks at the knowledge that there will be no more raw *laab* left by the time it is the women's turn to eat. Her family is traditional; therefore, the men eat before the women. All the women stand silently and submissively waiting to refill the diminishing dishes on the table. Gao Nou wants to break free from the chains of being a good Hmong girl, run up to the table and push her father and the shaman aside, and scoff down the plate of raw *laab* in front of them. She does no such thing; instead she is the good Hmong girl and serves the last of the raw *laab* to a drunken uncle from Madison whose crimson face tells her he will not be driving back right after the feast. When he abruptly leaps out of his chair and vomits on his way to the bathroom, her father laughs and says, "Gao Nou will clean it up." Gao Nou obeys her father and gets on her hands and knees with a cloth to clean up vomited *laab* on the carpet.

Gao Nou is a good friend of mine, and I use her story as an entry point to examine the good Hmong girl concept. When it was time for the women to eat, Gao Nou had completely lost her appetite; besides, there was no more raw *laab*. In front of her, a gnawed fried pork rib with her uncle's crooked teeth marks reminded her that she was eating the men's leftovers. Both the chicken and pork soups were now cold, and the once-green mustard leaves floating in the soup appeared stale and brown. She wanted to shout at her parents and the guests that she was not a good Hmong girl, she was just plain hungry!

In my view, while the ritual of men eating first and women eating second has changed somewhat since Hmong resettled in the United States, these changes do not demonstrate equality between the genders. For example, with some families, at religious feasts such as shaman ceremonies or wedding rituals, the men sit at the formal table while an informal table is set up for the women. I acknowledge this is a sign of progress, but I remain disturbed when the formal men's table is larger and set with the better food and silverware. If the men's dishes need replenishing, do they still receive the best part of the food? I am tired of sitting at the women's table, gnawing on the little meat on a chicken neck while an uncle chews a hearty piece of chicken breast.[1]

Gao Nou is not the only woman I know who struggles with the responsibilities and constraints that Hmong society puts on her to be a good

Hmong girl. As I composed this essay, my own experience as a Hmong woman formed an insider's perspective on traditions and values influencing Hmong family life. In fact, at various times in my life, I have been both a good and a bad Hmong girl. I am a good Hmong girl because I cleaned, cooked (I can kill and pluck a chicken by myself), took care of my younger siblings, graduated from college with a bachelor's degree, became a notable published writer, and established myself as a cross-cultural teacher and professional. Working in higher education and active in the community, I am aware of my family's history and the larger Hmong history and culture, and I have immense Hmong pride. However, I am also a bad Hmong girl because I do not always listen to my parents; I have been known to wake up late for our family's *ua neeb* ceremonies; in my teens I ran away from home and was involved with gang activities; I was arrested several times in my youth; I am divorced from an Asian man and now married to a Caucasian man. I do not believe in these standards of being good or bad, mostly created by our Hmong male-dominated culture. However, I accept that these are the parameters of what is considered to be good and bad in defining a Hmong girl.

Who Defines the Good Hmong Girl?

In my point of view, the role of the good Hmong girl has been historically and is still currently defined by Hmong men. Hmong society is patriarchal and patrilineal. The men who have made the rules for Hmong society also have made the rules for Hmong women. As I researched the traditional roles of Hmong women, I found limited material on the topic. However, there was extensive material on Hmong men's roles. According to numerous researchers, for example, the boy will carry both the family name and family tradition, including spiritual practices. This is important because family is the heart of the Hmong community; it defines everything from our social interaction to our funeral rituals.

As William Geddes reports, "The role expectations of sons and daughters are symbolized by the places where their placentas are buried at birth," including the burial of a boy's placenta at the base of the central post of the house and the girl's under her parents' bed. According to Gary Yia Lee in "The Shaping of Traditions: Agriculture and Hmong Society," this custom stems from the Hmong belief that the central post holds the house structure as well as the household spirits and religious symbols. Not only do boys have obligations to maintain the lineage and spiritual tradition of the family, but also they are raised to be lifelong authority figures. As Kou Yang has documented, from childhood to old age, Hmong men assume many superior roles and are perceived by family and society to be the breadwinners, protectors, leaders, and pillars of the family. As Yang also points out, men are regarded as important and intelligent. Because they are viewed as the eventual pillars of the family, boys receive special attention, love, and care, and they may be given more privileges, including opportunities to venture beyond their family circles and acquire leadership skills.[2]

Women have responsibilities in a traditional Hmong household that are valued by an agrarian community; however, none of those responsibilities transfer to equality and power for them. These include clearing land, an activity of particular importance for upland farmers; collecting thatch, bamboo, and other housing materials; planting and weeding staple crops; harvesting and threshing rice; pounding rice; feeding livestock; gardening; fetching firewood; and foraging for wild vegetables. Traditionally, a good Hmong girl also is a hard worker who can cook, clean, work the fields, bear children (the majority of them boys) with relative ease, behave obediently to her father and husband and his family, smile sweetly at strangers, and greet guests to her home with a genuine smile, even if she does not like the guests at all.[3]

Not only in the past but often in the present, she never stays in her room if she is unmarried; instead, she sits silently in the living room, waiting to be called upon to do the dishes. If she is married, she never stays in her room; instead, she sits silently in the living room, waiting for her in-laws to call upon her to wash the dishes or sweep the floor. Of course, she is a virgin until she is married, a spring flower whose sweetness and nectar have been untouched by the birds and bees. Did I mention a traditional good Hmong girl can also kill a chicken without any help? Gao Nou's mother made sure she learned how to do it, tsking, "If you don't know how to slaughter and clean a chicken by yourself, your in-laws will send you back! Then who would want to marry you?"

Gao Nou learned how to pull both wings back behind the chicken and tie them into a knot with one hand while holding the wriggling claws together with the other hand. Then she tucks the claws between the knotted wings, while with her free hand she plucks the feathers from the elongated chicken throat. With a quick slice across the chicken's throat, blood gushes out of the opening into a bowl catching the warm liquid that will be made into blood chicken salad later. Gao Nou is careful that none of the feathers from the thrashing bird get into the bowl as the chicken struggles and shakes for life. She also remembers to hold the bottom of the chicken away from the bowl as the chicken releases its last waste, signifying that it is dead and ready to be cleaned. Years later as Gao Nou divorces, she remembers her mother's chicken slaughtering lessons and how chickens had nothing to do with her divorce, only her husband's infidelity and physical abuse.

Gao Nou, who was born in Laos and came to this country when she was five years old, grew up with a strict definition of a good Hmong girl, but new terms were added to the old. For example, in addition to everything that was expected of her mother and grandmother, she was also to earn only As in school, attend college, complete her degree, and obtain a high-paying job. Never mind that Gao Nou was torn between two cultures, American and Hmong, which have two conflicting sets of rules and expectations for her. Through mass media and social networks, the American culture tells Gao Nou that she is not a good American girl unless she has blonde hair and a model-thin figure, wears trendy designer-brand clothes, and dates popular boys from school. In order to feel like Gao Nou belongs in America, she has to rebel against the good Hmong girl. Acts of rebellion such as staying after school to play sports, going to see movies with friends, and coloring black hair blonde can brand a Hmong girl forever with the label of a bad Hmong girl, bringing shame to herself and her family.

Hmong women are caught in this trap, seeing the temptation of freedom and opportunities that American life has to offer them. If they pursue these opportunities, they set themselves up for resentment and shame from the Hmong American community. This leads me to investigate who enforces the rules of the good Hmong girl. More specifically, why would a woman be hurt, and who would hurt her if she does not live up to the good Hmong girl ideal?

Who Keeps the Good Hmong Girl in Her Place?

In my eyes, Moua, a fellow writer, is a good Hmong girl. She never dyed her hair blonde. She was never involved in gangs. She never used drugs. She was a virgin until she got married. She got As in all her classes from kindergarten to twelfth grade. She even watched wrestling with her father, translating the spit-laden tirades of Hulk Hogan and Randy Macho Man Savage for him because he spoke not a word of English but understood that good and evil exist in the ring. She was the complete opposite of Gao Nou.

"Moua, you are the perfect model of a good Hmong girl!" I exclaimed during lunch at our favorite Vietnamese restaurant as I explained my research for this chapter.

"No, I am not," she countered.

"But you did everything right."

"You're wrong because I didn't do everything right—I was lazy."

Moua, a self-proclaimed Hmong nerd, was more interested in playing Mario Brothers on Nintendo than vacuuming the family room. In fact, one evening when she was twelve years old and diligently being Mario—flipping and kicking crabs from the New York sewer to rescue Princess Peach—her older brother Sue arrived to visit her parents. A few minutes earlier, her younger brother, Jim, a ten-year-old Howard Hughes neat freak, had started vacuuming the family room. Her older brother immediately turned off the Nintendo and berated Moua for allowing Jim, a man, to do women's work. For the next four hours, Moua's older brother huffed and puffed about Moua being a bad Hmong girl because she was lazy.

"She doesn't know her place in the house," he ranted. "Jim shouldn't be vacuuming! It's Moua's job as the daughter!"

"But I like vacuuming," offered Jim, who gave Moua a weak smile for support.

Sue was a good ten years older than Moua, and in his Hmong world, men and women had defined roles that were being blurred by Jim's vacuuming. He made his parents feel terrible about not enforcing the gender roles for their young children who were raised in America.

"Sue, it won't happen again," his father said softly, wanting to get back to his pretaped wrestling match.

"You are not good Hmong parents if you allow your children to behave like this! What would the world say if they came into your house and saw your son cleaning while your lazy daughter plays videos?"

Not waiting for their answer, he continued, "They would think we were a bad family. No one will respect us. We will have no face!"

In Moua's case, her brother was the enforcer of the good Hmong girl definition. He was disrespectful to his parents because he felt they no longer valued traditional Hmong gender roles. Because his father did not act as the man of the house, Sue decided that he would be. He used fear of being disgraced to keep his parents in line, to make sure they enforced the gender rules for Moua and Jim. For Hmong people, the family's good name and the respect that comes with it is everything. The family's name is the foundation on which people build community. Your family's reputation is how people know to treat you well or poorly, if you are invited to their homes for feasts, if people pretend not to see you at the market, if your sons and daughters marry well, if people visit you in the hospital when you are ill, if people attend your funeral, and the list goes on. When you have a bad Hmong girl in your family, your standing in the community is diminished.

I can understand why men are the police of the good Hmong girl, but I have never understood why women are as well. While she was growing up, Gao Nou's harshest judges, reminding her of her duties as a good Hmong girl, were her mother, older sisters, aunts, grandmothers, mother-in-law, and Hmong girlfriends.

After she ran away from home when she was thirteen, Gao Nou's mother beat her with a broom while her father looked on. Her mother's words hurt more than the blows: "You are a prostitute now! Who will want to marry you? You are not worthy to be your father's daughter!" Gao Nou had no intention of ever getting married, and she still was a virgin. However, instead of defending herself, she took the beating that she believed a bad Hmong girl deserved. Afterward, when her father had gone to bed, her mother clarified why she was the one holding the broom: "Your father thinks it's my fault. He said I am a bad wife and mother and that is why you are not a good Hmong girl."

When she told her mother-in-law that she was leaving her husband because he had begun to beat her in the last month or so, the elder woman proudly said, "Ger's father has beaten me black and blue for the last thirty years, but I never left him because I am a good Hmong woman. One time he kicked so hard, like they do in the kung-fu movies, that his footprint was on my belly for a month, but I never left him because I am a good wife and mother. Just bear with it and stomach the pain. You'll get used to it as I did."

Gao Nou shook her head in disbelief at the old woman who spent most of her time in the corner of the living room stitching *paj ntaub*. That day she had embroidered traditional Hmong clothes for Gao Nou and Ger's never-to-be-born children. "Do you like the needlepoint?" the old woman asked, as her wrinkled hands proudly showed off her latest work to Gao Nou. It was the back collar for a traditional Hmong baby girl jacket. The mother-in-law added, "Your daughters will need Hmong clothes even if they wear American clothes." *I don't want to have daughters,* Gao Nou thought, *at least not with your son and not with you as the grandmother.* Gao Nou left her husband that day and became a divorcée, a bad Hmong girl.

History has shown that sometimes community members who are oppressed tend to oppress each other. After all, the easy targets are those who are already weak. Women who are victimized sometimes collude with their oppressors because, like Gao Nou's mother, they want to be regarded as good Hmong women even when they know that expectation is unfair. Older Hmong women also may be policers because after being forced to be good Hmong girls, they do not see why younger Hmong women should be given the choice to be anything else. Lastly, I think some women are enforcers because they truly believe they are doing their daughters a favor by forcing them into subservience. By teaching their daughters to be docile women who can endure anything, older women believe they are setting younger women up for a life of prosperity and happiness.

Would Hmong Culture Be Diminished If Good Hmong Girls Disappeared?

In the Hmong community, rigid gender roles are laid out for men and women by the larger community. Women play the subservient role as the good Hmong girl, while the men are in power. If women were to stop playing the good Hmong girl role, where would this leave the men? Like old-fashioned ships, they would be left without a lighthouse, without equipment to tell them shore from sea, to ensure their safe return to land. The men would be culturally lost at sea. Dominance is intoxicating for men: the right to eat first, play without being branded promiscuous, marry as many wives as they want, and divorce and remarry without consequences. Why would men give up power? Why would they ever let go of the good Hmong girl concept? It is in their best interest to keep the concept of the good Hmong girl alive and thriving so they can retain their power.

The only way for the good Hmong girl concept to change is if women decide to stop colluding with men to oppress other women. Hmong women have to stop being enforcers of the good Hmong girl role. They have to rec-ognize that there are respectable roles for their daughters that go beyond being a good Hmong girl. I also have to acknowledge that not all Hmong men are obsessed with power and force their sisters and daughters to be good Hmong girls, but in my experience, exceptions are few.

In the hearts of Hmong people is an unspoken fear that Hmong cul-ture will be diminished somehow if women are no longer good Hmong girls. I think the fear is unfounded and ridiculous. History is on my side. Hmong culture will not be devalued if women have more rights; instead, it will flourish. Despite oppression from Hmong males, Hmong women have made progress. Because they have emerged as doctors, lawyers, edu-cators, business owners, artists, and elected officials, Hmong Americans have seen an improvement in their quality of life. Women such as Gao Nou and Moua, who rebelled against the good Hmong girl role, have enriched their lives and also our lives. Gao Nou is a teacher and community activist fighting for the rights of all Hmong people, while Moua, a writer, creates beautiful art of our community that will last generations.

Gao Nou and Moua have flourished, according to my viewpoint, despite the limitations put upon them by the good Hmong girl concept. However, I know that some in the Hmong community would think that Gao Nou and Moua are both failures. Why? Because Gao Nou is divorced and has no marriage prospects, while Moua is happily married but still childless in her early thirties. However, I admire both women for carving out their own identities and fulfilling their dreams.

Hmong culture and gender roles certainly will change if the current good Hmong girl concept is eliminated. Yet, I believe Hmong culture will change for the better because half of the Hmong population, the women, will be allowed to flourish and contribute fully to the intellectual and spiri-tual growth of Hmong people. Then the new "good Hmong girl" concept will accurately reflect and celebrate the contributions of Hmong women. It will no longer represent archaic and unrealistic moral and social stan-dards for women to achieve.

Privately in Hmong households, husbands and wives do eat together, a situation raising the following questions: Can gender equality be found in a couple's home when they eat together? If gender equality is evident in a couple's home, is it lost when they go to a feast where the husband eats first and the best of dishes while his wife serves him? I am inclined to believe that if gender equality does not exist in public, then it cannot exist in private either.

Gao Nou, Moua, and I deserve to be at the table with the Hmong men, eating at the same time, feasting on the same warm, delicious food, instead of being invisible bodies waiting to refill dishes, waiting for the leftovers. My suggestion is that women and men must come together and eat together. Cooperation and respect between genders are needed to hold onto the best of our culture. Indeed, I am not asking that traditions associated with feasts or ceremonies such as *neeb khu* be altered in order to accommodate women at the eating table. At traditional events, men and woman can and should continue to observe gender roles that demonstrate mutual respect. However, outdated eating practices need to end. In modern society, the only barrier preventing men and women from eating at the same time is the prevalent attitude that men are superior in status and therefore deserve better treatment.

In my view, eating together would represent true equality between men and women and signal progress for women's rights. It represents the integration of a new value into Hmong culture for women. However, if other Hmong women and I are not invited to the men's table, then we will just have to create our own women's table and the men will have to refill their own dishes. But I think it is much wiser for both men and women to eat together.

NOTES

1. Dia Cha, "Hmong and Lao Refugee Women: Reflections of a Hmong-American Woman Anthropologist," *Hmong Studies Journal* 6 (2005): 1–35. Cha notes that it is the cultural norm for men to eat first and women to eat later: "As witness to this fact, it is possible to cite several instances of Hmong holiday feasts in which the author was invited to take part. By custom, it is the men who eat first at such affairs. Only after the men have finished are the women—who do most of the food preparation—permitted to dine, and most of the time there is very little food left. During the aforementioned feasts, however, the author was asked to dine *with* the men, often as the only woman sitting among them. Despite the author's efforts to encourage other women present to join in, they refused; the men, not surprisingly, made no move to encourage them to do so" (24).

2. William R. Geddes, *Migrants of the Mountains: The Cultural Ecology of the Blue Miao of Thailand* (New York: Oxford University Press, 1976), 53. Gary Yia Lee, "The Shaping of Traditions: Agriculture and Hmong Society," *Hmong Studies Journal* 6 (2005): 18. For additional discussion on Hmong identity development, see also Gary Yia Lee, "Diaspora and the Predicament of Origins: Interrogating Hmong Postcolonial History and Identity," *Hmong Studies Journal* 8 (2007): 1–25. Kou Yang, "Hmong Men's Adaptation to Life in the United States," *Hmong Studies Journal* 1.2 (Spring 1997): 2.

3. Cha, "Hmong and Lao Refugee Women," 10.

< 7 >

"There are no GLBT Hmong people"

Hmong American Young Adults Navigating Culture and Sexuality

BIC NGO

> The people who weren't accepting just repeated the myth that
> Hmong people have about GLBT people. For example, that there
> are no GLBT Hmong people and that it was only when we came to
> the U.S. that we learned from the white people how to be GLBT.
>
> *Ong*

My involvement with the Hmong American community began in the late
1990s with an employment position at a Hmong social service agency. In
my day-to-day interactions with coworkers and participants in our youth
and adult education programs, I learned about the social and cultural
contexts of the lives of Hmong Americans. My immersion in the Hmong
American community was also facilitated by my participation in home visits, donation drives for new refugees, soccer and volleyball tournaments,
and Hmong New Year celebrations.

This engagement with the Hmong American community highlighted
for me the central role of gender in the lives of Hmong American women
and men. Issues related to gender role expectations, early marriage, and
the implications for education and aspirations were frequent themes of
conversation at work. The news media reflected this concern in another
way, with stories about domestic violence and underage marriage in the
Hmong American community. These stories frequently emphasized perspectives on and practices of gender issues as related to the assumed traditional values and customs of Hmong culture. Yet, my conversations with
Hmong American youth and adults belied such easy explanations; they
pointed instead to struggles over gender identity within social relations.

In recent years, research has demonstrated the salience of gender in the
experiences of Hmong American youth and adults. For example, researchers have illuminated the experiences of Hmong American women who

< 113 >

choose education over marriage; the social stigma young married women experience from non-Hmong peers and teachers; and practices of masculinity among Hmong American youth which have resulted in antischool behaviors. Along with these researchers, my own work has examined the role of gender in the educational experiences of Hmong American students.[1]

Despite these important contributions toward understanding cultural transitions within the Hmong American community, Hmong Americans are still characterized as traditional and patriarchal. More than thirty-five years after Hmong refugees began to arrive in the United States, news stories still cast Hmong culture as singularly traditional and backward. For example, in 2005 a Minneapolis *Star Tribune* article highlighting Hmong American gang violence asserted that a Hmong American female rape victim did not report the assault because "she feared her culture would require her to marry one of her attackers to save her reputation." The journalists argued that struggles between Hmong American youth and parents were due to irreconcilable differences between Hmong and American cultures: "The problem comes in mixing Hmong traditions with American culture. While Hmong refugees are struggling to survive in a culture foreign to them, their children are adapting more quickly and disobeying what they see as their parents' antiquated rules."[2]

In a similar vein, a *Fresno Bee* special series called attention to several suicides among Hmong teenagers and underscored the tensions between Hmong parents and youth. In one of eight stories, the journalist explicated the circumstances behind the suicide of a Hmong lesbian couple. According to the reporter, the "lesbian couple committed suicide together, knowing their love would never be accepted by their families or the Hmong community, which strictly forbids homosexual relationships." Once again, Hmong culture and identity are portrayed as irreconcilably traditional and suspended in time.[3]

In different ways, both of these news stories make sense of the experiences of Hmong American youth and adults through an understanding of the clash between Hmong and American cultures. Here, the cultural implications surrounding sexual assault and the suicides among gay teenagers are sensationalized as events that only occur in Hmong families. Such stories also ignore the multiple generations, perspectives, and complexities in the Hmong American community. They obscure experiences of struggle that signify cultural transformation.

In addition to the propensity to portray Hmong culture as unitary and static, we still lack knowledge about the multiple ways that Hmong Americans are transforming gender and sexuality. In particular, we do not know about the experiences of gay, lesbian, bisexual, and transgendered (GLBT) Hmong Americans. Indeed, with few exceptions, little research has covered the experiences of GLBT Asian Americans and no research has been published about GLBT Hmong Americans. The few studies on GLBT Asian American students reveal that at school, students face racism, homophobia, and heterosexism. At home, relationships between GLBT youth and parents are imbued with fear and conflict. As Joan Varney cogently observes, "In Asian communities where heterosexuality is assumed and in queer communities that are predominately White, queer Asian American youth have often felt as if they do not quite fit."[4]

This chapter seeks to explicate the ways that Hmong Americans are changing what it means to be Hmong women and men in their families and communities. It provides an understanding of the experiences of gay and lesbian Hmong individuals in their early to mid-twenties. The stories I share highlight experiences of alienation and conflict with parents and Hmong community members. At the same time, I illuminate the ways that Hmong parents, who at first disowned their children, became strong supporters over time. My research offers critical insights into the lives and experiences of Hmong GLBT youth. It advances our knowledge base on GLBT Asian Americans in general and GLBT Hmong Americans in particular. Further, and more important, my work highlights the way that Hmong culture and identity are not a static "given" but are sites of change and disagreement.

Research Background

Data for this chapter were collected as a part of a larger ethnographic study on the role of culture and culture change in the educational experiences of Hmong American youth and families. From June 2006 to October 2008, I conducted research with Hmong American community leaders, parents, young adults, and high school students in a major metropolitan area with the world's largest urban Hmong population. The data I collected included field notes from participant-observations at various community sites and events (e.g., Hmong New Year), cultural artifacts (e.g., community newspapers), and in-depth, semi-structured interviews.

In this chapter, I primarily draw on my research with Hmong American young adults who were allies of or identified as gay, lesbian, bisexual, or transgendered people. I connected with a total of ten participants through word of mouth and with the assistance of an organization for Hmong GLBT youth. Here, I present data from my interviews with one bisexual woman and two gay men whom I call Ong, Brian, and Tougeu.

Ong

Ong was born in Minnesota in 1982. Her parents were born in Laos and came to the United States in 1979. At the time of my study, she was twenty-five years old with eleven siblings ranging in age from sixteen to their early thirties. When Ong was in middle school, her older sisters married and moved out of the house. At this time, she took on responsibilities of cooking meals, doing household chores, and taking care of her seven younger brothers and sisters.

Ong started to question her sexuality during high school but admitted that, at the time, she "didn't have a word for it." It was not until her first year at a small, liberal arts college that she started to meet "different types of people" and "the world got bigger." In college, especially in sociology classes, she was introduced to readings and GLBT classmates who provided opportunities for "a lot of conversations and questions, and raised explicitly sexual orientation in class." It was during her first year in college that she came out to her best friend. Soon after, she came out to the rest of her group of Hmong friends. Her best friend was "very accepting" of the news; nevertheless, Ong had difficulty talking about her sexual orientation: "Even though I was learning a lot about the GLBT community and myself, I didn't really have a word. I hadn't really claimed a label. So I guess I kept thinking I was a lesbian. And I couldn't say lesbian to her, but she knew what I was saying."

Brian

Brian was born in 1981 in California, in a city just south of Sacramento. When he was twelve years old, his family moved to Charlotte, North Carolina. He lived there until 2006, when he relocated in order to become involved with a Hmong GLBT organization. During the time of the study,

Brian was twenty-six years old. His siblings included five brothers and one sister, ages fifteen to thirty.

Brian has known for most of his life that he is gay because "girl things," including fashion, fascinate him. He remembers that even as a child he "would come out of the closet with [his] mom's clothes on or with her shoes on." More significantly, his attraction to males rather than females goes back to when he was only "two or three." In fact, Brian cannot remember a time when he did not feel gay; in his words, "I think I knew all my life." In part, Brian also knew because people made fun of him: "Growing up, everybody would always make fun, 'Oh, you're a girl.'" Once in high school, friends and family started to ask him, "Oh, Brian, are you gay? Do you have a girlfriend?" Consistently, his response was, "No, I am not gay and I do have a girlfriend." In high school, his closest friends included one lesbian and two gay Latino Americans who were all out to their families. He attributed this difference to the "conservative" nature of Asian and Hmong communities: "I don't want to quote the Hispanic culture. I guess they're more accepting of the GLBT community than the Asian communities . . . Being Hmong, they're very conservative. They came out to their parents like flying colors. And here I was, I'm hiding myself, not telling my parents."

Tougeu

Tougeu was born in a refugee camp in Thailand and came to the United States in 1986 with his family. At twenty-five, Tougeu was the oldest of six children. At the time of the study, his brothers and sisters were seventeen to twenty-four years old. When Tougeu was nine, he took on the responsibility of looking after his siblings while his parents were working at the family restaurant.

At a young age, Tougeu knew he was gay. While his parents were away at work, one activity he and his siblings liked was playing house. The role of the mother was his preference: "Every time we'd play house I would always want to be the mother. I would always wear my mom's bra. I'd put on her bra . . . and pretend that my siblings were my kids." During high school, he was conscious of his attraction to men. Due to the stigma attached to homosexuality, he remained closeted and even turned to his Christian faith to help him change: "Throughout the whole time I just felt like, God, I don't want to be gay. If you can help me, I don't want to be gay." Speaking about the isolation he felt during his childhood and adolescence, Tougeu said, "I'd never met anyone who was gay at that time, so I was alone by myself trying to figure out what's right, what's wrong, the straight life and the gay life . . . I actually never knew that there were gay books, or there were articles on gay issues."

All the participants in the study believed that knowledge about the existence of GLBT Hmong Americans would have made a difference in their lives. My interest in investigating the multiple dimensions of what it means to be Hmong American resonated with their realities. By and large, the participants wanted to share their stories as GLBT Hmong Americans and complicate what it means to be Hmong. This is important for educating the larger public and the Hmong American community as well. According to Ong, increasing the visibility and conversation about GLBT Hmong Americans is central to changing the attitudes of the Hmong American community. In her own words, "[A] large part in why the GLBT community remains hidden for so long in the Hmong community is because people refuse to talk about it."

My interviews with Ong, Brian, and Tougeu focused on their experiences growing up as GLBT Hmong Americans, their "coming out" experiences, and the reactions of their families and community to their sexuality. The interviews were all audiotaped and transcribed. The interview transcripts were then coded, using qualitative software designed for organizing qualitative data. I coded the data by ideas that emerged from the interviews. These ideas provided the themes for deeper analysis and interpretation. In this chapter I focus on three themes: (1) reactions to the sexual orientation of participants; (2) pressures to conform to heteronormative expectations; and (3) support from friends and family.[5]

Similar to other qualitative studies, my research is not designed to include a large sample that is randomly selected. Moreover, it does not seek to generalize from a sample of the population of Hmong GLBT youth. Instead, by focusing on a small number of participants, I hope to illuminate the details and contexts of the lives of Hmong GLBT youth. This is critically important given the current dearth in research on the identity negotiations of the Hmong American GLBT community. Unfortunately, my research did not include interviews with the parents of Hmong GLBT youth. In large part, this was due to the sensitivity of the topic, language barriers, and other issues of access.

My research is informed by perspectives and commitments that are particular to my worldview and experiences. As an educational researcher, I seek to better understand the social and cultural contexts of the education of Southeast Asian American students. My research examines the ways in which race, gender, class, and other dimensions of identity affect educational experiences and outcomes. This allows me to learn about the lives of immigrant students, the practices of schools, and the implications for critical multicultural education.[6]

Personal dimensions also influence my work. My extensive engagement with Hmong American youth and adults has provided me with opportunities for personal interactions that have deepened not only my scholarship but also my bond with the Hmong American community. Hmong American students, parents, and community members opened their world to me in a variety of ways. They invited me into their homes, to social gatherings, and to small and large community events. I accompanied students to New Year celebrations, participated in graduation picnics, attended hip-hop music performances, and contributed to community listening forums at the request of nonprofit leaders. Through these and other interactions, I learned about the complexity of Hmong American identity, the richness of Hmong American social relations, and the generosity of community members.

To be sure, my work with the Hmong American community has allowed me to better understand their experiences in U.S. schools and society. Furthermore, it has provided me with a deeper understanding of my own life. As a 1.5-generation Vietnamese American, my experiences as a refugee of the Vietnam War are similar to those of the participants and families involved in my study. We share a history of coming to the United States as refugees. Yet, in contrast to the participants in my study—whose lives were enmeshed with those of relatives and the larger Hmong American community—I grew up having little contact with my extended family and other Vietnamese Americans. As a result, my experience and understanding of what it means to be Asian American is in many ways different from that of my Hmong participants. For example, while gatherings of extended families were a central part of their lives as Hmong Americans, I have had very little contact with relatives outside of my immediate family. While the social relationships of my participants involve numerous Hmong Americans, my social networks include no Vietnamese Americans and very few Asian Americans. Overall, in this study, my personal as well as professional background shapes my research perspective.

In the following section, I share the responses of friends and family to the GLBT identities of Tougeu, Brian, and Ong. Next, I illustrate the difficulties my participants faced as they navigated gender and sexuality as members of a close-knit ethnic community. Then I reveal the support that exists in their everyday lives. Lastly, I discuss the implications of the experiences of Hmong GLBT youth for understanding Hmong culture and identity and for addressing the needs of GLBT Hmong Americans.

Reactions to GLBT Identity

The GLBT young adults in my study came out to their parents and families in a variety of ways. Some voluntarily shared their sexual orientation, while others were forced to disclose their sexuality in confrontations.

In 2004, Tougeu wrote an article for a local Hmong newspaper in which he came out to the Hmong community. He wanted to share his thoughts as a way to connect with other Hmong GLBT individuals. As Tougeu acknowledged, "When I wrote the article, I didn't think about what's coming my way. All I thought about was I felt like I'm the only one and I wanted to see who's out there that feels the way I feel." However, soon after the article was published, his parents read it and confronted him. Although Tougeu was astonished that his parents saw the article, he admitted that he wrote it. His parents reacted with disbelief. According to Tougeu, his mom asked, "Why did you write that? Why did you write that you're gay when I know that you're not gay?" Similarly, his dad asserted, "Whoever wrote this, let's get it straight and go talk to them."

Once Tougeu convinced his parents that he was indeed the person who wrote the article, they responded with anger. Their remarks emphasized the implications of his sexual orientation for the family:

> He said that it's an embarrassment for me to write that. She said that by writing that, no one's gonna marry my brothers and my sisters. And they're never gonna find a husband and a wife because everyone is gonna think that it's a disease within the family. And

if you marry their side of the family, their kids are gonna have it, become like me.

Tougeu's parents were concerned about the standing of the family in the Hmong community. In this tight-knit community, where a family's reputation often carries great import, Tougeu's gay identity had implications for his family. His parents, for example, believed that his homosexuality would be viewed negatively by others as "a disease within the family" and thus be detrimental to the family name and the marital prospects of his siblings.[7]

Since Tougeu was exceptionally close to his mother, he especially struggled with her response to his sexuality. Her reactions included the assertion "that if she knew that [Tougeu] was going to be gay, then she could've let [him] die when [he] was little" rather than continually taking care of him when he was sick as a baby. Tougeu's accounts of his family's initial struggles underscored the way his sexual orientation affected his relationship with his mother:

> When they first found out, for the first few weeks they took me to my uncle's house . . . We were at the dinner table and my uncle was there and my dad was there and my grandma was there, my mom's mom. [My mom] was pulling my hair, she was spitting at me, she was hitting me, and she was crying at the same time when she did that 'cause she hurt so much . . . When she did that, she just told me to go kill myself and don't come back. My grandma had to stop my mom from hitting me and pulling my hair. I just sat there and I was just crying and didn't talk back to her, didn't do anything. I just sat there and just let her do whatever she needs to do. After that I just felt like I didn't belong.

Tougeu's explanation makes clear the anguish and pain for him and his family. This was a turning point in their relationship. As he painfully admitted, "After that I just felt like I didn't belong." In the years that followed, Tougeu's parents and some of his cousins and uncles shunned him. They stopped talking to him and walked away from him at family gatherings. Indeed, Tougeu recognizes how the men in his (extended) family "don't acknowledge me as a male anymore." Although he continued to live and work with his parents because they needed help with the family restaurant, his mother refused to speak to him directly, communicating with him only through his siblings.

For Brian, fear of censure was a primary reason for hiding his sexuality. In remarks similar to those in the mainstream press, Brian described the Hmong community as "conservative" and "traditional": "I knew that the Hmong community was going to not accept a gay person in their community. That's why I've been in the closet for so long even though I knew I was gay ever since I can remember." According to Brian, coming out to his family was possible because of his parents' divorce in 2003. As he explained, homosexuality and divorce were similarly prohibited in the Hmong community: "I finally came out of the closet when my parents had a divorce. They were going through their divorce and in the Hmong culture, it's taboo to have a divorce. And it's also taboo to be gay . . . I'm like, 'If my parents are going through a divorce, which is a taboo, then let me come out.'"

Brian came out to his mother by introducing her to his boyfriend. Despite their shared "taboo" behaviors, his mother did not react well to the news. Similar to Tougeu's experience with his parents, Brian and his mother did not talk for a month, although they "lived in the same house, under the same roof." He went out of his way to avoid his mother by going to work early in the morning, pretending to work overtime, and coming home late at night just to sleep. This was especially difficult for both of them because they had a very close relationship. After a month, their bond prevailed. According to Brian, his mom told him, "I understand where you guys are coming from, and I don't want to break that relationship that we have." In large part, Brian felt that his mother was able to be accepting because from a young age he acted in ways that were more characteristically "feminine." He described their relationship, "She always knew that I was not a boy, but a girl in a kind of sense. But she never understood the word 'gay.'" Rather than conforming to masculine behaviors, Brian remembers being "very flamboyant growing up" and doing "girly stuff." During his childhood and adolescence, Brian and his mother believed he was more like a girl than a boy. In their view of Hmong culture, "all the girls cook and clean and they take care of the house and that's what I did."

In Ong's case, coming out to her family members was more of a subtle and gradual process. It began with Ong sharing her sexuality with her mother and sisters in a joking manner: "The way that I came out to my sisters and my mom actually was because we joke around with my mom." Although she had a few shorter conversations with her mother and sisters afterward, their response was not volatile. Ong's sisters were immediately accepting, while her mom "took it really hard, I think." While Ong's relationship with her mother did not change after she shared her bisexuality, her mother "still hopes that [she] will settle down with a nice Hmong man." According to Ong, her mother wanted her to marry a Hmong man so much that "it wouldn't matter if he was gay."

The quiet manner in which Ong's mom received the news of her bisexuality was also reflected in her father's response: "I don't talk to my dad about it. But I'm sure he knows because my mom and him talk about everything. So I'm sure he knows. He just doesn't say anything." Ong attributed this silence to the dynamics of their relationship, which she considered to be common between Hmong fathers and daughters:

> And not that I expect him to because I'm a daughter, he's a father, and there's this weird you're-not-supposed-to-go-there kind of thing . . . With my dad—and I sense maybe with other Hmong daughters' dads—that he doesn't want to see me as, I don't know, a sexual person, I suppose. And when people talk about GLBT people, the first thing they think about is that you know GLBT means that this person likes to sleep with this type of people and not really the emotional aspect of it. And so, it's kind of uncomfortable talking to my dad about relationships and everything that comes with that.

These remarks address the relationship between Hmong fathers and daughters as well as the perception of GLBT identity. Together they provide us with important insight for understanding the experiences of Hmong GLBT youth in particular and GLBT identities more generally. As an issue that is rarely discussed in Asian American communities, (homo)sexuality may be even more difficult to talk about in some Hmong families, where the interactions between fathers and daughters do not facilitate intimacy and conversation. Additionally, Ong's comment about the association of GLBT identity exclusively with sexual intimacy reveals the need to dispel misconceptions about that identity.

Taken together, the reactions to the bisexual and gay identities of Ong,

Tougeu, and Brian included disapproval and disappointment from their families. Many of these difficulties were derived from Hmong gender expectations of Ong, Tougeu, and Brian, as the next section shows.

Navigating Gender Expectations

The process of identity negotiation for my Hmong GLBT participants was imbued with family and community pressures to conform to heteronormative ideas about femininity and masculinity. The experiences of Ong and Tougeu are especially illustrative of the expectations to look and behave in particular ways as a Hmong woman and a Hmong man. For example, as a woman who prefers to have her hair cropped short, close to her scalp, Ong was frequently mistaken for a boy. She has been especially embarrassed at large family gatherings with extended family members:

> I went to a funeral home because my sister, I believe one of her in-laws or a relative of her in-laws had passed away. I went there and one of the older ladies—I don't know how they're related, but—asked her if I was my sister's brother. And she's like, "No, this is my sister." And they would laugh a little and make comments about my appearance. I'm really just embarrassed in front of the people. And that happens even now with my own clan. There was another incident where—we call him grandpa, but he's an older relative in the clan. He was getting remarried and his older brother was there and we called him grandpa also. He has a son-in-law who has long hair. And at the time, I had really short hair. He said loudly in front of everybody, "Oh, I wondered who you were. I wondered whose son you were" and "Girls shouldn't have short hair and boys shouldn't have long hair."

For GLBT Hmong women such as Ong, choosing to not conform to gender expectations—to look and dress in particular ways—resulted in ridicule. While such condemnation occurs across racial and ethnic groups and thus is not unique to Hmong Americans, it proved salient in Ong's experience. As a member of the Hmong American community, it was important for Ong to be involved in family gatherings such as funerals and marriage celebrations. However, the response of family members to her outward appearance discouraged such community engagement.

Beyond her extended family, Ong also faced criticism from colleagues at a Hmong nonprofit agency. While her Hmong coworkers were not "in your face" with scorn, she noted that "there's this undercurrent" of disapproval. One subtle way that coworkers conveyed their criticism of Ong's androgynous appearance occurred through comments about a photo from a prom event the agency organized for local teenagers. As Ong explained,

> So we actually took a picture with the teams. You can see me with my hair all done, my makeup all done in this prom dress. There's a picture by my desk with me in this prom dress. I have a co-worker who's in the other department and every time she'd walked by, she'd say, "You look more mature in this picture. I like this picture. You look more mature in it."

This remark that Ong looked "more mature" wearing a dress and makeup is significant. At one level, the coworker implied a desire for her to conform to expectations for femininity in her clothes and appearance. At another level, the coworker seemed to suggest that Ong's GLBT identity was childish, immature behavior. At an agency with over forty employees, Ong had few supporters: "I think that I can literally count the number of GLBT supporters that work at [my agency] with one hand. There's one hand."

For Tougeu, the negotiation of his sexuality required consenting to the wishes of his parents and grandmother to "fix" him and the family reputation. Tougeu explained his attempt to appease his mother in this way:

> I don't want her to feel like I don't love her. I told my mom, "Mom, if you really want me to be straight I'll try to be straight to make you happy." And my mom said, "Can't you just please try to see if you can be straight?" Me and my mom had that conversation and I was like, "Yeah, I'll try to be straight. But I'm not going to guarantee that I'll be straight. Because you telling me to be straight is like me telling you to fall in love with a girl, a woman."

After months of tension, Tougeu agreed to "try to be straight" out of a deep love for his mother and the desire to mitigate her unhappiness.

Similar to the experiences of GLBT individuals in other communities, Tougeu went through a period where his family attempted to change him into a heterosexual man. As Tougeu's parents struggled with his gay identity, they sought on three separate occasions the assistance of Hmong shamans to perform healing ceremonies. On the one hand, attempts to "heal" Tougeu of his homosexuality presuppose that he is in some way "sick." As Tougeu explained this perception, he painfully noted, "I think to my mom and my family—my cousins, aunts and uncles and them—they think that being gay is when you're deformed." The seriousness of his family's disapproval is also illustrated in the time and expense put toward multiple ceremonies.[8]

On the other hand, it is important to also note the difficulty faced by Tougeu's parents. As we saw earlier, Tougeu's parents believed that his sexuality would have negative implications for the family's reputation and his siblings' marital potential. At one of the ceremonies, Tougeu overheard his father asking the shaman to "just keep it between us": "I remember when my dad and those shamans were talking, it seemed like my dad told me not to tell anyone. My dad is like, "This is between us. Don't tell anyone that you're here to do this for my son and just keep it between us." At the same time, family actions such as the request for secrecy about Tougeu's sexuality point to the complexity of navigating sexuality within Hmong social relations. According to Zha Blong Xiong and his colleagues, conflicts between Hmong parents and children may be explained by parents' attempts to save face or preserve the family's good reputation. This is necessary because "a family that has a problem child (e.g., a child who has problems in school and/or engages in delinquent activities) tends to become a 'headline' during social gatherings." The struggles of Tougeu and his parents cannot be simplified to explanations that underscore malicious actions. Arguably, more than a harsh attempt to make Tougeu straight, his parents' actions and attitudes may be motivated by their concern to keep kinship networks—present and future—intact.[9]

Support

While Ong, Tougeu, and Brian shared experiences of pain, harassment, and anguish in their relationships and interactions with their family and the Hmong American community, they also received support from friends and family. All three participants acknowledged that their siblings were especially supportive. They generally attributed this acceptance to the difference in attitudes between the younger and older generations of Hmong Americans. Ong explained the acceptance of her bisexuality by siblings and Hmong friends in this way: "They accept me even though I identify as GLBT. They're willing to talk when I want to. Not pressure me into talking or asking questions when I'm not ready to. Yeah, I'm grateful for that." In the same vein, Tougeu said of his siblings, "They're all cool about it. They don't even make much of a big deal about it. It's just my parents." Tougeu also developed a closer relationship with his twenty-three-year-old brother. His brother proudly told friends, "Oh I have a gay brother." They also talked more, providing Tougeu with a way to share his struggles: "I would talk to him more about how I felt. When people would put me down and my parents said this and that to me I would go, 'Okay, this is how I feel.'"

Of the three participants, Brian has perhaps experienced the most remarkable support from his family. He explained this support through a story that highlighted the transition from disapproval to acceptance. According to Brian, a few years before he came out, he was leaving a gathering for his grandmother's funeral. As he walked down the street with a cousin, they struck poses, pretending to be models. While they were doing this, friends of his aunt passed by in a car and witnessed the "modeling." Soon after, these friends asked his aunt and uncle if Brian was gay. A couple of months afterward, his aunt and uncle decided to confront Brian:

> They decided to go to Chinatown in Georgia. They called me and I really didn't want to go. I was like, "No, it's four hours. It's a four hour drive. I really don't want to go." Somehow, someway, they got me to go. So I sat in the front seat. My dad sat all the way in the back and then my mom and my aunt sat—it was a van—and they sat in the seat behind us. And then my uncle was driving. Right when we hit the road, almost hitting South Carolina, the speech begins. My uncle and my aunt basically just torture and torment me all the way. They were like, "Why are you like this? You're gay. You shouldn't be like this. There's no such thing. You have to act straight. If there's a way that you could be straight, you need to be straight." All the whole nine yards. That coming from a very

conservative Hmong family. They don't want me to be gay. They
want you to be straight. They want you to get married. They want
you to have a family.

His aunt and uncle lectured Brian until they were just outside of Atlanta.
And then, remarkably, his father—who Brian pointed out was part of "a
very conservative Hmong family"—spoke up in support of him:

And then, that's when my dad—I get teary when I say this—My
dad was in the back seat and that's when he was like, "Brian, don't
listen to nobody. You shouldn't listen to nobody. Just as long as you
go to school, have an education, have a successful life, I will accept
you no matter what or how you are."

For Brian, this experience—especially his father's support—made a last-
ing impression. He was not out at the time but was comforted that his
father did not mind his flamboyance and "girly ways."

In addition to his father, Brian's mother, aunt, and uncle are now allies.
Since he came out in 2004, they have transformed from staunch critics to
supporters. After he recounted the confrontation, he stressed this change
and noted, "What is ironic about that is that now my aunt and uncle are
so supportive of me. My mom is so supportive of me now. They gave me
an earful, but now they're so supportive of me." Indeed, the support Brian
received from his mother was extraordinary:

She's been a really big support of the whole Hmong GLBT issue.
She actually walked in the parade at Pride. She's really involved. She
came to the Hmong GLBT New Year and she made a speech, a very
emotional speech. She was a performer at the GLBT Hmong New
Year as well, so she's very, very involved with the Hmong GLBT community. She actually met a lot of the gay boys, so I'm very happy for
that. I'm very fortunate to have such an accepting mother.

This support is particularly significant given the dominant perception that
the Hmong American community is traditional and conservative. It critically illustrates that Hmong parents such as Brian's mother are capable of
shifting their stance on complex issues from positions as harsh critics to

that of staunch allies of their GLBT sons and daughters, who march in a GLBT Pride parade and make speeches at Hmong GLBT events.[10]

Discussion

This chapter provides a counterstory to the dominant narratives that depict Hmong culture and identity as rooted in static customs and practices. It specifically attests to the ways Hmong American youth and adults are changing understandings and attitudes toward gender and sexuality. As the stories of Brian, Ong, and Tougeu reveal, this process is neither simple nor painless but infused with conflict and censure. To be sure, families and relatives disapproved of their sexual orientations. Brian and Tougeu went through periods of estrangement from their parents and family. Ong's mother still hopes she will marry a man, and she cannot discuss her sexuality with her father. Yet, the experiences of these GLBT young adults cannot be defined only by alienation. Acceptance and support were also part of their lives. They found support in their siblings, and, for Brian, eventual support from parents and relatives.

My work suggests that we need to pay more attention to the value and complexity of nuclear and extended family relationships for Hmong Americans. As many scholars of Hmong studies have documented, aspects of Hmong kinship networks may be deployed for social control. For example, Jo Ann Koltyk observes that Hmong family decisions more often than not involve kinship networks: "Where a family chooses to live, when they will buy a car or a home, where they will send their children to school, how they will confront an illness, all of these issues fall under the decision-making powers of families and their extended kinship network."[11]

Significantly, kinship networks are also social, political, and economic support systems that contribute to the spiritual, emotional, and physical well-being of Hmong Americans. Koltyk notes that the Hmong "lineage and clan system are involved in helping kin find employment, training, and housing, and assist in accumulating capital to buy cars, houses, and to pay for education. The wider network of clan affiliations is mobilized in times of crisis, or when moving, visiting, and traveling." Indeed, Dwight Conquergood and Paja Thao suggest that from the perspective of many members of the Hmong community, a "sick society" is one that is highly individualistic.[12]

However, and problematically, we have a propensity to frame the experiences of immigrants within binary oppositions of traditional or modern. It would be too easy—and inaccurate—to explain the experiences
of Ong, Brian, and Tougeu within a storyline of "traditional" or "oppres-
sive" Hmong culture. The experiences of these GLBT Hmong Americans
are simultaneously unique to them as well as shared with other GLBT individuals across racial and ethnic groups. Yet, the complexity of Hmong
social relations is often understood within negative representations of
tradition and culture that highlight the actions and attitudes as particular
to a backward, immigrant culture. This obscures complexities such as the
value of kinship ties and ongoing changes in Hmong social relations. For
example, changes include shifts in the role of women and relationships
between parents and children. While homosexuality in the Hmong community was once denied as a part of social relations, there is increasing
visibility and support for GLBT Hmong Americans.[13]

Speaking about Asian American GLBT identities, Mark Ng insight-
fully describes our tendency to view the complexity of identities "in a
linear way along a bipolar spectrum—that one can only be either male or
female, gay or straight . . . Asian or queer." The experiences of GLBT young
adults in my study challenge all of these simplistic dualisms. Indeed, Ong,
Tougeu, and Brian are reenvisioning and rearticulating Hmong culture
and identity. As researchers, scholars, and community members, our task
is to do the same.[14]

NOTES

1. Nancy Donnelly, *Changing Lives of Refugee Hmong Women* (Seattle: University of Washington Press, 1994). Stacey J. Lee, "More than 'Model Minorities' or
'Delinquents': A Look at Hmong American High School Students," *Harvard Educational Review* 71.3 (2001): 505–28. Joy Lei, "(Un)necessary Toughness?: Those 'Loud
Black Girls' and Those 'Quiet Asian Boys,'" *Anthropology and Education Quarterly*
34.2 (2003): 158–81. See, for example, Bic Ngo, "Contesting 'Culture': The Perspectives of Hmong American Female Students on Early Marriage," *Anthropology and
Education Quarterly* 33.2 (2002): 163–88.

2. Pam Louwagie and Dan Browning, "Shamed into Silence," Minneapolis *Star
Tribune*, Oct. 8, 2005, www.startribune.com/local/11594631.html (accessed Nov. 15,
2011).

3. For full analysis of the special series, see Paul Jesilow and Machiline Xiong,

"Constructing a Social Problem: Suicide, Acculturation, and the Hmong," *Hmong Studies Journal* 8 (2007): 1–43. Anne D. Ellis, "Embracing the Forbidden—'Pa Nhia Xiong.' Special Report: Lost in America," *Fresno Bee,* Aug. 11, 2002, 7, www.capm. state.mn.us/pdf/HmongTeenSuicideReport.pdf (accessed Nov. 15, 2011).

4. Alice Y. Hom, "Stories from the Homefront: Perspectives of Asian American Parents with Lesbian Daughters and Gays Sons," in eds. Min Zhou and J. V. Gatewood, *Contemporary Asian America: A Multidisciplinary Reader* (New York: New York University Press, 2000), 561–71. Kevin K. Kumashiro, ed., *Restoried Selves: Autobiographies of Queer Asian/Pacific American Activists* (New York: Harrington Park Press, 2004). Russell Leong, ed., *Asian American Sexualities: Dimensions of the Gay and Lesbian Experience* (New York: Routledge, 1996). Mark Ng, "Searching for Home: Voices of Gay Asian American Youth in West Hollywood," in eds. Jennifer Lee and Min Zhou, *Asian American Youth: Culture, Identity and Ethnicity* (New York: Routledge, 2004), 269–83. Joan Varney, "Undressing the Normal: Community Efforts for Queer Asian and Asian American Youth," in ed. Kevin Kumashiro *Troubling Intersections of Race and Sexuality: Queer Students of Color and Anti-Oppressive Education* (Lanham, MD: Rowman & Littlefield, 2001), 87–105, quotation 87.

5. Katherine Charmaz, *Constructing Grounded Theory: A Practical Guide through Qualitative Analysis* (Thousand Oaks, CA: Sage Publications, 2006).

6. Norman Denzin and Yvonna Lincoln, eds., *The Handbook of Qualitative Research,* 3rd ed. (Thousand Oaks, CA: Sage Publications, 2000). Michelle Fine, "Dis-stance and Other Stances: Negotiations of Power inside Feminist Research," in ed. Andrew Gitlin, *Power and Method: Political Activism and Educational Research* (New York: Routledge, 1994), 13–35.

7. Jo Ann Koltyk, *New Pioneers in the Heartland: Hmong Life in Wisconsin* (Boston: Allyn and Bacon, 1997). Zha Blong Xiong, Arunya Tuicomepee, and Kathyrn Rettig, "Adolescents' Problem Behaviors and Parent-Adolescent Conflicts in Hmong Immigrant Families," *Hmong Studies Journal* 9 (2008): 1–21.

8. See, for example, Douglas C. Haldeman, "The Pseudo-Science of Sexual Orientation Conversion Therapy," *ANGLES: The Policy Journal of the Institute for Gay and Lesbian Strategic Studies* 4.1 (1999): 1–4.

As scholarship has documented, shamanism (*ua neeb*) is an important aspect of spirituality for many Hmong Americans. Hmong shamans play a central role in rituals such as "soul calling" and healing ceremonies. The Hmong shaman is similar to healers of numerous cultures, where spirituality and health are viewed as interlinked. See, for example, Dia Cha, *Hmong American Concepts of Health, Healing, and Conventional Medicine* (New York: Routledge Press, 2003); Dia Cha, "The Hmong 'Dab Pog Couple' Story and Its Significance in Arriving at an Understanding of Hmong Ritual," *Hmong Studies Journal* 4 (2003): 1–21; and Dwight Conquergood and Paja Thao, *I Am a Shaman: A Hmong Life Story with Ethnographic Commentary* (Minneapolis: University of Minnesota, Southeast Asian Refugee Studies, 1989).

9. Xiong, et al., "Adolescents' Problem Behaviors," 11–12. Julie Keown-Bomar, *Kinship Networks among Hmong-American Refugees* (New York: LFB Scholarly Publishing, 2004).

10. See also Alice Y. Hom, "Stories from the Homefront."

11. Donnelly, *Changing Lives;* Koltyk, *New Pioneers in the Heartland,* 38.

12. See also Julie Keown-Bomar, *Kinship Networks among Hmong-American Refugees* (New York: LFB Scholarly Publishing, 2004), and Kou Yang, "Hmong Americans: A Review of Felt Needs, Problems, and Community Development," *Hmong Studies Journal* 4 (2003): 1–23. Koltyk, *New Pioneers in the Heartland,* 42. Conquergood and Thao, *I Am a Shaman.*

13. Bic Ngo, *Unresolved Identities: Discourse, Ambivalence, and Urban Immigrant Students* (New York: State University of New York Press, 2010). Donnelly, *Changing Lives,* 1994. Christopher Thao, "Hmong Customs on Marriage, Divorce and the Rights of Married Women," in eds. Brenda Johns and David Strecker, *The Hmong World* (New Haven, CT: Yale Center for International and Area Studies, 1986), 74–98. Kathy Mouacheupao, "GLBT Hmong Coming Out Party." *Hmong Today,* Feb. 3, 2006.

14. Ng, "Searching for Home," 272.

< 8 >

The Challenges and Contributions of Hmong American Elders

A Personal and Professional Perspective

SONG LEE

Stereotypes and misunderstandings of elders in the Hmong American community have serious consequences; they can cause damage to elders' self-worth and diminish the empathetic assistance they need from their families as well as professional caregivers. Common perceptions of them as frail and senile, for example, overlook the reality that elders make important contributions to their families and society. While many communities need to improve care and perceptions of their elderly, the situation of the Hmong American community is complicated by two factors: research and literature focused on its elderly population is very limited; and Hmong culture, for thirty years, has undergone major transitions in response to immigration and subsequent resettlement in the United States. Furthermore, health and wellness of Hmong American elders go beyond caring for visible or measureable illnesses. For them, sound mental health and social satisfaction are as important as physical health. Additionally, from anecdotal data taken from my personal experience and professional practice, the Hmong American elderly population needs to feel acknowledged, respected, and understood in the context of their overall well-being.[1]

This chapter will address the situation of Hmong elders in the United States aged fifty and older. As refugees of the Vietnam War who sought political asylum during the 1970s and 1980s, most arrived in the United States when they were in their late teens or older; usually they came as part of family groups, whether immediate or extended. Even though the U.S. Census Bureau defines an elder as someone above age sixty-five, Hmong people tend to regard anyone in their fifties or older as an elder. This perception of age is influenced by two factors: a cultural expectation to take on adult roles at an earlier age than is common in the West; and

< 133 >

the deterioration of Hmong health at an earlier age due to traumatic war and refugee camp experiences. Currently, about 2.6 percent of the Hmong American population is above sixty-five years old. Hence, the elderly population aged fifty and above is higher.[2]

Most important, regardless of their number, the contributions of the elderly are immeasurable to their families, clans, communities, and American society. The roles elders play continue to ensure the vibrant health of Hmong culture as well as the financial prosperity of the Hmong American community. Today, for example, Hmong American elders are involved in organizing Hmong festivals and holiday celebrations that are a thriving part of America's rich cultural diversity in general and of Hmong American life in particular.

To increase awareness of and respect for Hmong American elders, in this essay I address their roles, contributions, and emerging needs. To supplement the limited professional literature focusing on Hmong American elders, I integrate their voices from personal interactions, surveys, interviews, and radio programs in which I was involved. In addition, I incorporate professional and personal experiences shaping my personal epistemology, that is, the "conceptions of knowledge and knowing" that derive from what I have learned through my life history. I am a counselor, therapist, educator, researcher, daughter, and daughter-in-law of elderly Hmong Americans. Consequently, my views are influenced by both Western training in counseling and lifelong experiences with Hmong customs and values.[3]

Vital Roles and Contributions of Hmong American Elders

Most of the Hmong in the United States reside in California, Minnesota, Wisconsin, Colorado, and North Carolina. In all of these communities, Hmong American elders provide childcare for working parents, which is essential to maintaining family stability and achieving economic prosperity. They also pass on knowledge of Hmong culture and language to younger Hmong generations, keeping them anchored to their heritage as they search for their place in American society. Some of the key roles that Hmong American elders fulfill in Hmong and American society include those of clan leaders; educators and supporters of spirituality; leaders in preserving Hmong culture and language; and advocates for political justice in American society.[4]

As clan leaders, the elderly provide highly significant service. A Hmong clan consists of families with the same last name and lineage. To date, only men have been allowed to assume leadership positions. The hands-on involvement of these leaders in community affairs adds quality and integrity to everyday life. By providing guidance in culture, history, and ancestral relationships, they ensure that traditions and rituals are appropriately practiced. Furthermore, clan leaders skillfully facilitate communication among family members within the same clan and between members of different clans to resolve conflicts. They also assist with marriage negotiations and funeral proceedings. Most important, clan leaders are vital for clan recognition and identity, especially for Hmong elders. For example, when Hmong elders meet each other, they often ask, "*Nej tus coj noj coj haus yog leej twg?*" or "Who is your clan leader?" This question helps to identify individuals in terms of the relationships they already may have with each other through that leadership.

Elders also provide guidance and support in the spiritual health and development of younger generations. Even though Hmong Americans have been influenced by multiple religions from Laos, Thailand, and the United States, most practice either traditional religion or Christianity. Many elderly Hmong Americans prefer to stay with the traditional beliefs of their upbringing. Yet, it is not uncommon to see Christian elders who support the decision of younger individuals to join churches or even to become pastors and leaders in churches.[5]

Hmong American elders who still adhere to traditional ways of life are active in performing rituals and educating others about how to do so. Some elders (male and female) are *txiv neeb* or shamans who provide spiritual protection and healing. In this form of Hmong spirituality, *txiv neeb* serve as mediators between the human world and the spiritual world. Through their rituals, they strive to keep the health of individuals and families in balance. Hmong elders have sought *txiv neeb* for treatment of dementia, healing of various illnesses, and prolonging of life. As a Hmong elderly woman remarked on my radio show, "Although the *txiv neeb* may not be able to cure everything, he or she is able to help us 80 percent of the time."[6]

Today, *txiv neeb* help to maintain beliefs central to the spiritual health of Hmong people in the United States. One of the most important ways of doing this is to act as mentor to novices. Once someone has been identi-fied as destined to become a shaman (after suffering and recovering from a debilitating illness), the *txiv neeb* who has healed that person will usually (but not always) agree to serve as mentor and teacher, training that per-son until he or she is ready to step into the full responsibilities of this vital cultural role. Even then, the mentor will continue to supervise some of the more complex rituals the new *txiv neeb* is asked to perform.[7]

Although not every Hmong elder is a *txiv neeb* or clan leader, most Hmong American elders play a role in passing on their knowledge of tradi-tional rites, rituals, and the Hmong language. Culture for Hmong people, like health, is traditionally tied to spiritual and ancestral worship to ensure well-being, good fortune, and linkage to ancestors and rebirth. Rituals such as *hu plig* (soul calling) for new brides and *nqee plig* (birth ceremony) for newborns as well as funeral rituals for the deceased are carried out to ensure that individuals are able to join with their ancestors in life and after death. Those who still practice traditional beliefs do not have written doc-trines to guide them but instead rely on elders to pass down knowledge of traditions and rituals orally. Moreover, Hmong American elders possess wisdom that reflects a deep understanding of Hmong identity as it has developed through hundreds of years.[8]

In modern society, Hmong American elders often encourage Hmong American youth to attend ritual ceremonies and practice sessions to learn more about their cultural heritage. When my brothers became young adults, for example, they met regularly with an elderly Hmong *qeej* master to learn how to play this traditional musical instrument. They also con-tinue to observe my father set up a *xwm kab* (family altar) and perform New Year rituals to remember the ancestors. Their responsibilities are to learn the family customs and religious practices. When my father is no longer around, they are expected to know exactly what to do. As Mr. Thao, a Hmong American elder, stated on my radio show, "Once our sons marry, we would like them to learn our *kev dab kev qhuas* [traditions]."[9]

Even though the elders serve as teachers and encourage their children to learn about Hmong culture and practices, it has been a struggle to reach many Hmong American youth. Ms. Yang, an elderly Hmong American woman, asserted on my radio show, "We are the first doctors and teach-ers of our children. We teach our children from the day they were born.

We started by cooing, *as qwg*. Then we teach them every day that they are with us. It is harder to teach children Hmong culture and traditions in the U.S. because once they know how to speak, they are being taught by their teachers [in school]."[10]

Despite such difficulties, Hmong American elders are determined to continue their instruction. Without knowledge of Hmong culture, they understand that younger people cannot develop culturally informed identities or acquire the basic skills to meet the expectations of family and community. For example, after giving birth, I did not enter other people's homes, adhering to a postpartum taboo traditionally observed by Hmong women, because I respect the belief of my mother's generation that my entrance could bring harm to myself or others. Also, as an adolescent, I detested the white or red strings that I had to wear on my wrists after a blessing ceremony. The strings embarrassed me because none of my peers had to wear them. As an adult, I now embrace them and feel protected by them. When others inquire about the strings, I have the opportunity to educate them about Hmong cultural practices. Furthermore, current Hmong American university student groups proudly showcase Hmong culture through campus activities such as multiethnic educational fairs. While the teachings of elders may not influence every youth to embrace the values and practices they share, continuity of Hmong culture is made possible through their efforts.

Lastly, Hmong American elders also advocate for political justice in the United States. Progressively, they have come to understand the need for unified participation in public policymaking and the selection of politicians who represent their values and needs. Their attempts to gain voice in the United States have led to establishing nonprofit organizations such as Lao Family and Lao Veterans of America, Inc. (LVA). Lao Family associations throughout the United States secure federal and state funding to coordinate programs to assist Hmong with employment, housing, and education. Representing Hmong and Lao veterans who served the United States during the Vietnam War, LVA lobbies legislators for veteran rights, such as keeping Supplemental Security Income (SSI) benefits and securing burial rights.[11]

In recent years, Hmong American elders also have supported politicians by joining their campaigns, voting, and encouraging others to vote. Although Hmong Americans have a high poverty rate (37.8 percent compared to the national rate of 12.6 percent), Hmong American elders nonetheless have provided financial support in small donations to politicians, such as city council member Blong Xiong in Fresno, California, and (former) state senator Mee Moua in Minnesota. In general, Hmong American elders have become more involved in mainstream politics due to the influence of Hmong American politicians and the outreach of local organizations and media. Compared to ten years ago, Hmong American elders today are more knowledgeable and proactive in the election system. Personally, I have seen a change in my elderly parents as well. Five to ten years ago, my parents would ask me to select whomever I believed would be the best candidate on their mail-in ballots. A year ago, when I was helping my mother with her ballots, I was surprised when she informed me exactly whom to vote for and for what causes. Elders have helped to elect Hmong American and other Asian American officials and have encouraged the Hmong American community to be more involved in politics and voting.[12]

Other civic engagements of Hmong elders include participating in peaceful protests against perceived mistreatment of Hmong individuals or groups. In California, they came together to save a small community farm in Fresno and to demand a fair trial for General Vang Pao when he was charged in 2007 with plotting to overthrow the Lao government. In doing so, they make Hmong American issues visible by ensuring that their voices are heard through news media and public forums. More important, their devotion encourages younger people and other ethnic groups to support Hmong American concerns.

Challenges and Concerns of Hmong American Elders

Although Hmong American elders now appear to be much more at ease with life in the United States, they face ongoing challenges. Their limited English proficiency prevents them from pursuing employment sufficient to support their families, leading to a loss of status and respect that they once wielded in Laos. Many have had to accept changes in family roles, handing the decision-making power to their spouses, sons, or daughters. In addition, as they grow older, they encounter health problems that they do not fully understand, such as depression, diabetes, hypertension, arthritis, chronic obstructive pulmonary and cardiovascular diseases, Alzheimer's disease, cancer, and Parkinson's disease. With all of these changes converging on them, many elders have acknowledged that they feel trapped as if "living in a cage" and helpless "like a child."[13]

While their children and grandchildren are acculturating rapidly into American society, Hmong American elders are concerned that culture and tradition be maintained as everyday practice. As Ms. Yang admitted, "We [elders] have not changed much. We are still the same as when we were in Laos." Elders believe their children should learn not only Hmong language but also respectful behavior. In their eyes, young people should "obey or listen to parents, help around the house, show respect to parents and elders, and stay home or do not go out." Yet younger Hmong Americans find it difficult to fulfill those expectations because they have been taught in school to be independent and assertive.[14]

Intergenerational differences have led Hmong American elders to believe that their children and grandchildren are rejecting many of the values they grew up appreciating. As one elderly Hmong woman commented, "Everyone is more knowledgeable than before. If the youth do not agree with the elders, they will not do as the elders say." Another added, "There are some problems that I have with my son and daughter-in-law. I also see these problems with other families who have daughters-in-law as well. There are some daughters-in-law who do not do things when you tell them or do anything to help around the house. I paid for my son's wife and so do others, hoping that the daughters-in-law know how to cook, clean, and help around the house." Respect for the elders includes listening to them and knowing one's role in the family. "We are their parents and they should respect us," Mr. Thao reported. Through my work, I have come to realize that youth and elders differ on what the word "respect" means. In contrast to Mr. Thao, young people have expressed the desire to develop their own values and follow their dreams by pursuing education and professional careers.[15]

Although empirical studies are still few, those that have focused on Hmong American college students have pointed to intergenerational differences as sources of family conflicts, stress, and depression. Miscommunication between Hmong American elders and younger Hmong Americans are common. Elders cannot communicate with their children in English; their children and grandchildren cannot communicate with them in Hmong. Even if younger Hmong Americans could speak Hmong, they often prefer to be direct in expressing views and opinions, creating tensions and misunderstandings. Hmong American elders are disappointed that their children do not speak to them "nicely." As one noted in our conversation, "We [elders and children] communicate differently. The children sometimes speak directly and sometimes don't watch what they say, so they end up hurting our feelings. We, the elders, speak indirectly so it is difficult for them to understand what we mean."[16]

Some elders fear that their children will forget all of the rituals that connect them to their ancestors, disregard the importance of *kwv tij* (extended clan families) and *neej tsa* (relationships formed through marriages), and abandon them in old age, a dereliction of duty that could disrupt continuities essential to the health of families. There is validity to these concerns. For example, Hmong American scholar Yer Thao has stated that "the loss of Mong [Hmong] tradition, culture and language causes the Elders [*sic*] to be harmed physically, mentally and spiritually."[17]

Lessons Learned Outside of Professional Setting

Despite my educational training, extensive research, and professional practice, some of the most meaningful insights into the lives of Hmong American elders have come from everyday interactions with family members. My elderly parents and mother-in-law have helped me to be aware of the challenges that come with aging, the wishes of Hmong elders to be heard, and the need to do more to reach out to others as a multicultural counselor. I consider my parents to be traditional because they still *coj kev cai qub* or practice traditional Hmong customs and beliefs. My mother-in-law, on the other hand, is a Christian. Despite their different religious affiliations, my parents and mother-in-law still have Hmong dreams. In their old age, they wish to be taken care of by their children. Traditionally, when Hmong parents reach old age (fifty and over), they expect their sons and daughters-in-law to help provide for them. A proverb reminds Hmong of all ages of this fact: "Raise crops anticipating a famine; raise a son to alleviate the sufferings of old age."[18]

Even though Hmong American elders are still capable and independent, they believe that children should love them enough to provide for their daily needs. According to my parents and other elders I have met, they feel that their strength has decreased with old age. Therefore, they expect the daughters-in-law to assist with domestic chores and sons to assist with yard work. A recent conversation with my mother helped to clarify for me what it means "to care for an elder":

> When you care for an elder, you respect them. You acknowledge that they no longer have the same strength as when they were young. If you see that they cannot do something, go do it for them. Do not wait for them to ask for help. Talk to them with kindness. Say good things to them. Also, offer them something to eat. If children are disgusted with caring for their elders, they should think about how their parents took care of them when they were young. In Laos, there were no diapers. When a child urinated or had a bowel movement, the secretions were all over whoever was carrying them.[19]

Even though I am aware of my role as a daughter and daughter-in-law, I guiltily admit that I am unable to fulfill many of their expectations. Part of my duty as a Hmong American woman is to take care of the family and older parents by cooking and cleaning for them. However, occupational demands leave little time for meeting those obligations. As shown by the research of Linda A. Gerdner, Xa Xavier Xiong, and Deu Yang, employment and other responsibilities prevent sons and daughters from taking care of their elders. The shift in priorities from family responsibilities to professional pursuits has not made life easy for elders. At a time when they should be enjoying quiet living, they end up caring for their grandchildren and cooking and cleaning for the family. Because of the demands imposed on them by modern society, Hmong American professionals are forced to neglect many of their responsibilities to their aging parents.[20]

Multicultural Considerations: Implications for People Serving Hmong Americans

Both personal experiences and professional trainings have contributed to my development as a health care consultant and provider, enabling me to discuss with clients their religious healing practices, their expectations in life, and how they can use counseling services in addition to other resources available to them. Working effectively with Hmong American elders requires counselors and other professionals to adopt a multicultural perspective, particularly in terms of modifying interventions "in ways that are both developmentally and culturally appropriate." Additionally, counselors are required to "possess cultural and diversity awareness and knowledge about self and others, and how this awareness and knowledge is applied effectively in practice with clients and client groups."[21]

Professionals need to be aware that the religious beliefs of Hmong elders affect their approaches to health care. In Hmong culture, health involves physical, emotional, and spiritual aspects of the person. Hmong elders in both traditional and Christian faiths still believe in spiritual healing as an important component of their well-being. Although some Hmong American elders strictly adhere to either traditional beliefs or the Christian faith, others choose to be eclectic, using whatever seems necessary to cure illnesses and to deal with difficult life situations. Regardless of their differing religious affiliations, many still seek the expert advice of traditional herbalists for assistance with physical ailments. Major health concerns should be discussed with family members, especially sons (and daughters-in-law), since they are expected to be the first line of caregivers. Careful explanation of medical procedures must be provided to the patient and family members so they understand what is being done and the risks involved. Overall, understanding the worldview of Hmong elders and their family support system will help enhance sensitivity to their needs and improve treatment compliance.[22]

According to researchers, Hmong are the least likely among Southeast Asian Americans to seek Western interventions for health care. One reason is that they do not fully understand their health problems, especially with regard to illnesses and treatments described in a manner foreign to them. Furthermore, as a minority group in this country, they may not find health services useful because interventions tend to be based on Western values and focused on client compliance rather than family involvement. Additionally, most health care providers are fluent only in English, while most Hmong elderly are fluent only in Hmong.[23]

Soliciting patients' views about what is happening could help counselors determine whether mental health education is needed before providing treatment. For example, realizing that one of my Hmong clients has a strong belief in traditional Hmong healing practices, I was careful to explain how she could use counseling services in combination with shaman rituals. I informed her that professional counseling could help her to view life from a healthier perspective and find approaches to better manage her overall symptoms, while she could turn to a shaman to give her the spiritual support she needed to confront her ailments.

I agree with researcher Stanley Sue that "changing the client to fit the services and changing the services to fit the client" is required when working with minority clients. Hence, education should include informing clients about helpful services as well as guiding providers on how to modify services to fit client needs. To that end, I have tried providing mental health education to the Hmong American community via *Suab Kaj Siab*, a Hmong radio program in Fresno, California. An encouraging recent development is that Hmong American elders have reported becoming more open to counseling services after learning about mental health issues through those broadcasts.[24]

Conclusion

In my personal and professional view, Hmong American elders have knowledge, wisdom, challenges, and contributions that should be recognized in their families, accepted by their communities, and carefully considered in the American health care system; otherwise, they cannot receive the care they deserve. Hmong American elders are doing their best to adapt to contemporary life at an advanced age, but they find it difficult to accept many of the modern shifts in family roles, responsibilities, and social values. Caregivers should respect the resiliency and strength of this elderly population. Despite obstacles, Hmong American elders take on roles that contribute to family unity, youth identity, and cultural continuity; the visibility and voice of Hmong Americans in modern society; and the passage of "important heritage, knowledge, wisdom and information about Mong [Hmong] tradition from one generation to the next generation." In sum, our recognition of Hmong American elders will contribute to their health by affirming that they are accepted and welcomed in our lives.[25]

NOTES

1. Robert Gingold, *Successful Ageing* (New York: Oxford University Press, 1999), 2.

2. Linda A. Gerdner, Xa Xavier Xiong, and Deu Yang, "Working with Hmong American Families," in eds. Gwen Yeo and Dolores Gallagher-Thompson, *Ethnicity and the Dementias* (New York: Taylor and Francis Group, 2006), 211. Terrance J.

Reeves and Claudette E. Bennett, "We the People: Asians in the United States. Census 2000 Special Reports," Dec. 2004, www.census.gov/prod/2004pubs/censr-17.pdf (accessed June 2, 2010).

3. Song Lee, "Hmong Elders' Needs Assessment" (Study in Progress, California State University, Fresno, 2010). "Role Reversal," *Suab Kaj Siab*, Central California Asian Voice (Fresno, CA: KBIF 900, July 7, 2008); "Role Reversal Part 2," *Suab Kaj Siab*, Central California Asian Voice (Fresno, CA: KBIF 900, July 14, 2008); "Learning from Hmong Elders," *Suab Kaj Siab*, Central California Asian Voice (Fresno, CA: KBIF 900, Sept. 6, 2010). Barbara K. Hofer, "Personal Epistemology as a Psychological and Educational Construct: An Introduction," in eds. Barbara K. Hofer and Paul R. Pintrich, *Personal Epistemology: The Psychology of Beliefs about Knowledge and Knowing* (Mahwah, NJ: Lawrence Erlbaum, 2002), 9.

4. Wendy Mattison, Laotou Lo, and Thomas Scarseth, *Hmong Lives: From Laos to La Crosse* (La Crosse, WI: The Pump House, 1994), xv.

5. Gerdner, Xiong, and Yang, "Working with Hmong," 212–13. Pastor W. Tra Xiong, telephone conversation with author, July 27, 2011.

6. Linda A. Gerdner, Toni Tripp-Reimer, and Deu Yang, "Perception and Care of Elders with Dementia in the Hmong American Community," *International Psychogeriatrics* 17 (2005): 125. Linda A. Gerdner, Soua V. Xiong, and Dia Cha, "Chronic Confusion and Memory Impairment in Hmong Elders: Honoring Differing Cultural Beliefs in America," *Journal of Gerontological Nursing* 32.3 (2006). Linda A. Gerdner, Dia Cha, Deu Yang, and Toni Tripp-Reimer, "The Circle of Life: End-of-Life Care and Death Rituals for Hmong-American Elders," *Journal of Gerontological Nursing* 33.5 (2007): 22. Quotation, "Learning from Hmong Elders."

7. Yer Lor, telephone conversation with author, July 10, 2010.

8. Gary Yia Lee, "Cultural Identity in Post-Modern Society: Reflections on What Is a Hmong?" *Hmong Studies Journal* 1.1 (1996): 8, hmongstudies.org/LeeCulturalIdentHSJv1n1.pdf (accessed July 7, 2010).

9. "Learning from Hmong Elders."

10. "Learning from Hmong Elders."

11. Michael Doyle, "Bill Would Allow Hmong Veterans to Be Buried in U.S. National Cemeteries," *Merced Sun-Star*, Oct. 28, 2009, www.mercedsunstar.com/2009/10/29/1139754/bill-would-allow-hmong-veterans.html/ (accessed June 29, 2010); Lao Veterans of American Inc., "Lao Veterans," www.laoveterans.com/ (accessed June 29, 2010).

12. Yang Lor, "Hmong Political Involvement in St. Paul, Minnesota and Fresno, California," *Hmong Studies Journal* 10 (2009), www.hmongstudies.org/YangLorHSJ10.pdf (accessed July 12, 2011). Poverty figures from Reeves and Bennette, "We the People," 17. Matt Leedy, "Council Run Motivates Hmong: Win or Lose, Blong Will Draw Southeast Asians into Fresno's Civic Life," *The Fresno Bee*, Oct. 25, 2006, quoted in Seng Alex Vang's Blog, www.myspace.com/gqcaliguy/blog/190193739 (accessed

July 28, 2011). Pakou Hang, "Hmong-town, USA," *Colorlines Magazine*, Dec. 22, 2002, www.thefreelibrary.com/Hmongtown,+USA%3A+This+year,+Mee+Moua+became +the+first+Hmong+American . . . -a095266753 (accessed July 28, 2011). Laura Yuen, "Hmong Leaders Consider Value of Identity Politics after Losing Seats," Minnesota Public Radio, Aug. 17, 2010, minnesota.publicradio.org/display/web/2010/08/17/ hmong-politics-legislature/ (accessed July 28, 2011).

13. Deborah Helsel, Marilyn Mochel, and Robert Bauer, "Chronic Illness and Hmong Shamans," *Journal of Transcultural Nursing* 2 (2005): 152. Yer Thao, *The Mong Oral Tradition: Cultural Memory in the Absence of Written Language* (Jefferson, NC: McFarland & Company, Inc., 2006), 105, 159.

14. Yu-Wen Ying and Meekyung Han, "The Longitudinal Effect of Inter-generational Gap in Acculturation on Conflict and Mental Health in Southeast Asian Adolescents," *American Journal of Orthopsychiatry* 77.1 (2007): 61. Miriam Potocky-Tripodi, "Refugee Economic Adaptation: Theory, Evidence, and Implications for Policy and Practice," *Journal of Social Services Research* 30.1 (2003): 75; Thao, *The Mong Oral Tradition*, 173. "Learning from Hmong Elders." Zha Blong Xiong, Patricia A. Eliason, Daniel F. Detzner, and Michael J. Cleveland, "Southeast Asian Immigrants' Perceptions of Good Adolescents and Good Parents," *The Journal of Psychology* 139.2 (2005): 166.

15. Lee, "Hmong Elders' Needs Assessment"; "Role Reversal"; "Role Reversal Part 2"; Thao, *The Mong Oral Tradition*, 65, 170. "Learning from Elders."

16. Jenny Su, Richard Lee, and Shary Vang, "Intergenerational Family Conflict and Coping among Hmong American College Students," *Journal of Counseling Psychology* 52.4 (2005). Ying and Han, "The Longitudinal Effect"; Richard M. Lee, Kyoung Rae Jung, Jenny C. Su, Alisia G. T. T Tran, and Nazneen F. Bahrassa, "The Family Life and Adjustment of Hmong American Sons and Daughters," *Sex Roles* 60.7–8 (2009): 554. Lee, "Hmong Elders' Needs Assessment."

17. Lee, "Hmong Elders' Needs Assessment,"170. Gerdner, Tripp-Reimer, and Yang, "Perception and Care," 134. Thao, *The Mong Oral Tradition*, 173.

18. Sue Murphy Mote, *Hmong American: Stories of Transition to a Strange Land* (Jefferson, NC: McFarland & Company, Inc., 2004), 271.

19. Yer Lor, interview by author, Fresno, CA, July 20, 2011.

20. Gerdner, Tripp-Reimer, and Yang, "Perception and Care," 134.

21. American Counseling Association, *ACA Code of Ethics* (Alexandria, VA: American Counseling Association, 2005), www.counseling.org/Resources/ (accessed June 16, 2010), 4, 20.

22. Gerdner, Tripp-Reimer, and Yang, "Perception and Care," 113–14. Lisa L. Capps, "Change and Continuity in the Medical Culture of the Hmong in Kansas City," *Medical Anthropology Quarterly* (New Series) 8.2 (1994): 161–77. Dia Cha, *Hmong American Concepts of Health, Healing, and Conventional Medicine* (New York: Routledge, 2003), 23.

23. Rita Chi-Ying Chung and Keh-Ming Lin, "Help-Seeking Behavior among Southeast Asian Refugees" *Journal of Community Psychology* 2 (1994): 114. Sharon Johnson, "Hmong Health Beliefs and Experiences in the Western Health Care System," *Journal of Transcultural Nursing* 2 (2002): 128; Helsel, Mochel, and Bauer, "Chronic Illness," 153. Jacqueline Wallen, "Providing Culturally Appropriate Mental Health Services for Minorities," *The Journal of Mental Health Administration* 19.3 (1992): 289.

24. Stanley Sue, "Mental Health in a Multiethnic Society: The Person-Organization Match" (paper presented at the American Psychological Association convention, Toronto, Canada, Sept. 1978), quoted in Wallen, "Providing Culturally," 290.

25. Thao, *The Mong Oral Tradition*, 171.

< 9 >

Hmong American Professional Identities

An Overview of Generational Changes since the 1970s

PAO LOR

Introduction

Since the 1980s, researchers have addressed many aspects of the Hmong American experience. These encompass a broad range of topics including history; religion and culture; education and youth; health, spirituality, and medicine; the Hmong diaspora; and Hmong identity. Against this background, I am interested in the emergence of Hmong American professional identities, a process that is influenced by generation, education, cultural competency, language proficiency, and other aspects of self-formation and socialization. A *professional* is defined as a person whose job requires a certified level of knowledge and training.[1]

Although variations certainly can be found, three broad categories of Hmong professional identity are evident in the more than thirty years since the initial resettlement of Hmong refugees in the United States:

- *Hmong Immigrant Professionals:* born and raised in Laos and educated in Laos or Thailand; fluent in Hmong, Lao, and possibly other languages such as Thai, French, or Vietnamese; possessing a high degree of cultural competency, including a keen awareness of tradition and values shaping family and community life; and holding a strong sense of what it means to be Hmong.
- *Hmong Professionals of 1.5 Generation:* born in Laos or Thailand; arrived in United States as teenagers or at a younger age; received education mainly in the United States; and completed college or technical training. Most are fluent in Hmong and are bicultural in social outlook and adaptability; most also have a strong cultural identity as a Hmong but have adapted well to their new American identity.

< 147 >

- *First-Generation Hmong American Professionals:* born in the United States; not necessarily fluent in Hmong (speaking, writing, and reading), but definitely proficient in English. Their connection to the Hmong American community may be limited and their sense of what it means to be Hmong is likely to be much more open ended, not constrained by a firm understanding of tradition.

A snapshot of these Hmong professional generations is captured in the census of 2010. However, that census does not offer a complete picture of how these categories have emerged and become distinctive since the 1970s. Here, my intention is to share key characteristics of each generation of Hmong American professionals. In broad brushstrokes, I will explore each generation's professional credentials and careers; cultural competency and language proficiency; and the duality of being Hmong and a professional, particularly in terms of responsibilities to family, clan, and community.[2]

Hmong Immigrant Professionals

Hmong immigrant professionals came to the United States as adults in the mid-1970s, 1980s, or 1990s when refugee camps were being closed across Thailand. Their formal educational credentials usually include six years or so of schooling in Laos and Thailand. Some attended postsecondary education and earned degrees or certificates. A handful even studied abroad in Canada, France, Vietnam, and Russia. Their language proficiency includes fluency in Hmong. Many also are fluent in Lao and French. However, even if they had studied English in Laos or Thailand, only a few could speak it well when they arrived in the United States. Before Laos fell to communism in 1975, some held positions as teachers, police officers, electricians, politicians, or business owners in Laos.[3]

When they arrived in the United States, many Hmong immigrant professionals who were proficient in English began their careers in the public sector as interpreters and case managers for state agencies to help assist new Hmong immigrants in navigating the welfare system, the educational system, and the complexity of urban American life. Eventually, starting from these entry-level professions, some became executive directors for nonprofit organizations that serve the Hmong American community. In addition to these public sector professions, others entered fields such as medicine, law, higher education, business management, skilled craftsmanship, and other public service.

Because few Hmong immigrant professionals held such prestigious positions, other Hmong highly respected them and looked to them to serve as role models for younger Hmong generations. Many became symbols of hope for Hmong in the United States. In their professional capacity, they provided the outlook and reassurance necessary for Hmong Americans to rebuild their community. Most important, their employment would inspire younger Hmong Americans to pursue higher education and become professionals in other disciplines. When committed to making a better life for Hmong Americans, members of this generation are a backbone of community strength.

Their Hmong language proficiency and cultural competence are advanced. Whether at professional meetings or at cultural gatherings, they readily can switch between English, Hmong, or Lao. Their English is efficient for carrying out their responsibilities, and in my view, their resolve to help Hmong refugees adapt to the United States has accelerated their language development. In terms of cultural competence, most are very familiar with traditional practices, such as *ua neeb* (shaman rituals), *kev ploj kev tuag* (funeral), *hu plig* (soul calling), and *ua tshoob ua kos* (wedding ceremonies). Those who have converted to Christianity still are likely to participate, when appropriate, in traditional and religious practices within their clan and in the community.

For the most part, their views on what it means to be Hmong include many of the qualities, characteristics, and perceptions described by Gary Yia Lee, who notes, for example, that at a fundamental level, to be Hmong, one has to speak Hmong, know and practice Hmong cultural traditions and religion, respect the elders, know his or her roles and responsibilities in the clan and community at large, contribute to his or her clan and community, and know his or her family history and background. Without these cultural identifications, a person's degree of being Hmong is diminished. This generation's efforts to maintain these characteristics have been tireless and persistent.[4]

Since 2000, there has been a slow fundamental shift. Some have come to recognize that changes to Hmong identity are inevitable. Many agree that being Hmong is a transformative process; to justify this, they point to hallmark changes in Hmong history, such as the transitions Hmong people have made from being predominantly farmers and hunters to holding key professional positions as medical doctors, university professors, attorneys, business owners, politicians, and information technology experts. Also, they cite the educational and professional advancement of their children, grandchildren, and great-grandchildren as examples of new possibilities opening up for Hmong identity development and progress in adaptation to American society.

Although much has changed since they began coming to the United States, Hmong immigrant professionals still hold a deep appreciation for agrarian ways of life extending back many generations in Laos. They are the last Hmong generation to hold firmly to an identity based on traditional values. For this group, choosing to be Hmong is not an issue to be debated; they know without a doubt that they are Hmong. They place a high priority on maintaining what it means to be Hmong and helping to preserve much of the knowledge passed down from previous generations. As they always tell me, "It's the way of our parents and before them, our grandparents and ancestors." Today, many play a critical role in adapting traditional cultural practices such as weddings, New Year celebrations, and funerals to modern life in the United States. They have a deep commitment and willingness to work with younger Hmong generations to advance the Hmong American community.

1.5 Generation of Hmong Professionals

This category includes Hmong born in Laos or Thailand who were educated in the United States after their arrival as young refugees (in their early teens or younger). All are proficient or advanced in English. Many also speak Hmong well, although they are not likely to read and write in the language. They are the first to have completed postsecondary education in the United States, representing a small but significant percentage of Hmong Americans who have earned associate, baccalaureate, or graduate degrees. Praised for this achievement, they also have been expected to serve as role models for success in modern society. Indeed, their accomplishments have been interpreted by community elders as proof that the sacrifices made by their parents and grandparents to come to the United States were not in vain.

With their college education, most have secured public or private sector positions, becoming social workers, teachers, attorneys, school counselors, academic advisors, business owners, police officers, sheriffs, school administrators, dentists, chiropractors, and medical doctors. Established in respected positions, many have chosen to advocate for social justice for Hmong American and other ethnic groups. Today, they are active in community service, volunteering their time in local Hmong and non-Hmong organizations.

As pointed out by Susan Bosher, individuals in this group possess complex bicultural identities; thus, they balance their Hmong values and ideals adroitly with their new American life. They are capable of developing a highly functional American identity without sacrificing their Hmong values. Many honor traditional practices while also incorporating Western approaches in creating a new urban lifestyle. For example, this generation easily can move between Western medical treatment and traditional spiritual healing.[5]

Their views on what it means to be Hmong resonate from the previous generation of Hmong professionals, with some important modifications. They continue to regard fluency in Hmong and knowledge of Hmong culture and history as important keys in maintaining Hmong identity. Moreover, this identity stems from shared life experiences, which include the Secret War in Laos, refugee camp life in Thailand, and resettlement in the United States. From the war, many learned that being Hmong meant being unwanted by an international community. As refugees, all experienced displacement on multiple levels: emotional, physical, cultural, and political. They grew up at a time when Hmong were persecuted in Laos and mistreated in Thailand. Furthermore, their early challenges in adjusting to a new life in the United States heightened and solidified their sense of purpose and vision, particularly the necessity of becoming educated, working hard, and elevating the status of Hmong people in America. Most have a strong commitment to give back to the Hmong community. Their appreciation and understanding of their cultural heritage have been enhanced by their attentiveness to stories of family history told by parents, grandparents, and other elders.[6]

Many would like to pass on these Hmong identity markers to their children and grandchildren, but the dynamics of life in modern society make that difficult, particularly the demanding reality of adults working and children going to school. Learning from past generations and their own experiences, they recognize that Hmong identity is neither static nor stable. Many will continue to maintain the language and culture, but they know it will be difficult for the next generation to do so.

For example, based on extensive conversations with these professionals, I have concluded that they tend to believe the following: Hmong children are too Americanized; they live in a different world and time; they do not speak or understand Hmong anymore; they are losing knowledge of Hmong traditions; and they often are detached from their families and communities. To me, because of this sudden shift in outlook, what it means to be Hmong for the 1.5 generation and their children may be contentious but also allows room for negotiation.[7]

First-Generation Hmong American Professionals

In the last decade or so, a new generation of Hmong American professionals gradually has begun to emerge. This group includes those who were born in the United States, received their entire education in the United States, and are professionally certified. Their professional credentials are similar to those of the 1.5 Hmong generation. They hold undergraduate and perhaps graduate degrees, professional training, and licenses. Currently, many hold entry-level positions or are in middle management in the private and public sectors.

Intent on advancing their careers and raising families, they may not necessarily be thinking about how they can use their professional expertise to benefit the Hmong American community. Also, due to upbringing, their community ties may not be as strong as those of the first or 1.5 generation. In fact, because they may not claim a public identity as Hmong American professionals, they are only beginning to be recognized by the community as a distinct group.

This generation of professionals will face different challenges than the previous two. One major change is they must acquire necessary skills, competence, credentials, and dispositions to work with mainstream constituents. In a positive light, this change is a measure of Hmong American integration into modern society and our increasing ability to work across ethnic and racial lines in a wide range of professions. This level of success is crucial in reassessing Hmong identity and progress in this country.

Unlike earlier generations, members of this professional generation tend to have minimal proficiency in Hmong language and culture. They grow up mainly speaking English and experiencing a world much different from that of their parents, families, and ancestors. Their comprehension of Hmong history is likely to be superficial. Most know conversational Hmong but are not proficient in writing and reading the language. Limited knowledge of traditional Hmong customs, traditions, and rituals makes it difficult for them to qualify for positions in community organizations requiring a high level of Hmong cultural and language competency. More important, they are not likely to be closely connected to the Hmong American community in their daily lives. Their perception of what it means to be Hmong will not be the same as previous generations.

As I have learned from college students and professionals, they are ambivalent about their Hmong identity. Is being Hmong a birthright, or can they choose to be Hmong or not, depending on personal circumstances? Does the inability to speak Hmong fluently mean one falls short of being Hmong? Does being fully Hmong mean knowing and practicing Hmong cultural traditions? Many do not know or practice Hmong traditions. They also are concerned that if they do not meet their parents' expectations, they might fall short. What about those who have chosen to live different lifestyles and pursue unorthodox careers, such as rapping, fashion design, film making, and fine arts? Their generation also is facing identity complications related to sexual orientation, gender roles, and the need for equality between men and women in modern society. Do these concerns, which were largely unaddressed by older generations, make young people today less Hmong?

Choosing to be Hmong is a fulcrum in the current formation of the ethnic and cultural identity of Hmong American professionals. Making sense of the many dimensions of what it means to be Hmong can be challenging and daunting; the landscape of Hmong identities described by Gary Yia Lee offers some clues into the complexity of the situation. However, increasingly clear to me is that young people today are poised to venture into new areas of achievement that older generations could only begin to imagine. For example, as new graduates compete for jobs beyond the community, they are expected to develop a repertoire of skills and abilities broad enough to serve both Hmong and non-Hmong. Through many careers, young professionals are proving to be highly capable in social integration and success.[8]

Especially during the first decade of the twenty-first century, I have seen positive developments in the identity formation of youth. Research suggests that most Hmong students begin to be aware of their ethnic identity in late elementary or middle school. Studies I conducted on Hmong American teachers and university graduates show that Hmong American students begin to notice social groups and form cliques in late elementary school and middle school. Many of the participants I interviewed, once they became aware of these social and cultural groups, wanted to learn more about their own cultural heritage and history; at the same time, many were also proud to be Hmong and did not want to lose their Hmong identity. Rather, they wanted to enhance and advance it. This process of increasing self-awareness frequently continues in high school when they find association with other Hmong students to be beneficial, giving them a sense of belonging based on shared experiences and established norms for their peer group.

However, there are exceptions to this trend. As some students move through the school system, their assimilation leads them to disengage from other Hmong students and from the Hmong American community. They perceive being Hmong as negative due to various influences: social media coverage of negative stories; current cultural practices and rituals that to them are hard to understand; and other Hmong ways of life that do not seem to fit into what they consider to be their lifestyles—modernized, civilized, and Americanized. Consequently, they immerse themselves into mainstream culture. To many of them, a good indication that they are successful is, ironically, isolation from the Hmong American community.[9]

Personal and Professional Experiences: The Duality of Being Hmong and American

Like many of my fellow Hmong American professionals of the 1.5 generation, I was born in Laos. I lived there for about six years before fleeing the Secret War with my family to Thailand. From 1978 to 1980, we stayed in Nongkhai and Loei and then moved to the United States. We stayed in Long Beach, California, for about six months before relocating to Wisconsin, where I attended elementary, junior, and high school. I completed undergraduate and graduate studies at the University of Wisconsin campuses of Green Bay, Oshkosh, and Madison. Since the mid-1990s, I have held positions as university academic advisor, middle school and high school communication arts teacher, soccer coach, school administrator, and associate professor. Before then, I had many odd jobs, such as picking cotton in Thailand, cleaning bathrooms in school facilities, washing dishes and cooking in the Rathskeller at University of Wisconsin–Green Bay, and driving a combine harvester for Stokely USA.

These personal and professional experiences have given me both a front-row seat and an active role in the Hmong American professional experience. Like many other Hmong American professionals, I feel a heavy responsibility to promote understanding between older and younger generations of Hmong. Whether I like it or not, I am part of the bridge connecting past, present, and future.

Since the 1990s, I have seen within my own family the changing landscape of Hmong American identities. Our oldest son is nineteen years old, and our youngest child is six years old. The other two are thirteen and fifteen. Already, the range in their ages greatly affects their perception of what it means to be Hmong. Our youngest is quickly losing his Hmong language. He speaks almost 100 percent English. He understands some Hmong when we speak to him, but he cannot respond in Hmong. One good sign is that he recently learned to count to twenty in Hmong. Our oldest is fluent enough in conversational Hmong; he also can read and write at a beginning level. Our two middle children are somewhere in between. They know enough about Hmong history and culture to understand there is much more to learn, as I am encouraging them to do. My own experience reflects a common trend among Hmong American families with children who were born and have grown up in the United States. I know my children will have a different Hmong American identity and different professional opportunities than I do.

Looking beyond my own family, I recognize that Hmong American high school and college students are struggling to understand the importance of cultural identity in modern life. Many find it challenging to balance academic, personal, and cultural responsibilities. Without high school teachers, guidance counselors, and university professors who are readily accessible, youth today will have a hard time finding their place in American society. With limited cultural knowledge and tenuous connections to the Hmong American community, many students lack a sense of purpose and direction. These new dynamics will certainly affect the development of Hmong American professional identity in the future.

For me, it is still surprising to hear Hmong American students speak mostly in English, not Hmong, the opposite of what was true for me in school. Also, I notice that many students are not interested in helping families at weddings, funerals, and rituals, which I and others of my generation usually would be expected to do; instead, students talk among themselves about which bars or clubs to go to on the weekends. However, amid these challenges, I find reason for optimism and hope. Many Hmong American high school and college students and first-generation Hmong American professionals still share an unspoken understanding and appreciation of what it means to be Hmong. Many speak of giving back to the Hmong American community; many aspire to achieve leadership positions in the community and larger society; and many hope one day to visit Thailand, Laos, and China to see where their parents, grandparents, and ancestors once lived. These experiences can make the culture meaningful for them in enduring ways.

Conclusion

Today, the achievements of Hmong American teachers, attorneys, medical doctors, business owners, and other trained professionals should be lauded. However, we also should recognize that the cultural foundation for Hmong professionals has been set firmly in place by highly respected individuals across generations who have fulfilled essential roles as *txiv neeb* (shaman), *mej koob* (intermediary in a wedding ceremony), *tswv zos* (village chief), *kws tshuaj* (herbalist), and *txiv qeej* (qeej player). Typically, hands-on training and cultural knowledge are required for all of these roles. In daily life, those who possess qualities Hmong refer to as *nquag* (demonstrating a good work ethic) are models for professionals today. Moreover, from past to present, the value of each person's contributions is measured in terms of how he or she fulfills the needs of family, clan, and community.[10]

Since the 1980s, three distinct categories of Hmong American professionals have emerged—Hmong immigrant professionals, Hmong professionals of the 1.5 generation, and first-generation Hmong American professionals—which provide a framework for understanding contemporary Hmong American identity development. Furthermore, these categories are useful benchmarks for measuring ongoing Hmong American community progress.

Hmong American professional identities will continue to evolve as we move into the twenty-first century. In the process, some contentious questions remain: Can Hmong American professionals who denounce their ethnicity still proclaim themselves Hmong? Will divisive politics regarding linguistic and religious differences within the Hmong American community determine who is more or less respected as a "true" professional? With the recent emphasis on global categorizations of identity and culture, are we possibly losing sight of the extensive work that still needs to be done in investigating what it means to be Hmong in particular families, neighborhoods, and communities? Through careful examination of such questions, we can gain deeper appreciation of the roots and values that not only bind us to each other in this country but also shape our unique contributions to its advancements.

Most intriguing to me are Hmong American professionals who choose to work and reside in places where they will have only minimal connections to the Hmong community. Other than their names and obligations to family members, their ties to the Hmong American community often seem tenuous. They blend into the community in which they live. Their cultural and language proficiency may no longer be crucial to their individual identity. Yet, based on my personal and professional experience, I recognize that people's decisions regarding where they live and work reflect influences far more complex than language ability (proficient or deficient) or cultural obligations (accepted or rejected). In my view, one defining characteristic of Hmong American professionals in this category is the diversity of their cultural affiliations and assimilations.

Personally, I have come to embrace the reality that being Hmong helps define who I am, but it is not all that I am. My viewpoints on Hmong identity development and formation are informed by my roles as a son, son-in-law, father, teacher, and scholar of Hmong American studies. Such diverse life experiences have taught me the importance of community service; respect for family, humanity, and nature; personal humility; and dedication to social justice. In my professional career and personal life, these are invaluable guideposts. It is essential for Hmong Americans to embrace the best of their culture even as they pursue other opportunities contributing to modern society.

NOTES

1. Please see Recommended Reading (below) for helpful sources on these topics.

2. U.S. Bureau of the Census, *Census 2010*, http://2010.census.gov/2010census/. See also Hmong National Development, Inc., *Census 2000: Data and Analysis* (Washington, DC, 2003).

3. Throughout this chapter, I draw on pertinent conversations with members of the three main groups under consideration to support my conclusions and speculations. In addition to my personal experience, primary sources for this chapter also include extensive observational notes that I have kept as a teacher and researcher over the past three decades.

4. Gary Yia Lee, "Cultural Identity in Post-Modern Society," *Hmong Studies Journal* 1 (1996): 1–4.

5. Susan Bosher, "Language and Cultural Identity: A Study of Hmong Students at the Post-Secondary Level," *TESOL Quarterly* 31 (1997): 593–603.

6. Jane Hamilton-Merritt, *The Hmong, the Americans, and the Secret Wars for Laos, 1942–1992* (Bloomington: Indiana University Press, 1999); Fungchatou Lo, *The Promised Land: Socioeconomic Reality of the Hmong People in Urban America 1976–2000* (Lima, OH: Wyndham Hall Press, 2001).

7. Hmong National Development, Inc., *Census 2000*; Christopher T. Vang, "Hmong-American Students Still Face Multiple Challenges in Public Schools," *Multicultural Education* 13.1 (2005): 27–35; Zha Blong Xiong, Daniel F. Detzner, Zoe Hendrickson Keuster, Patricia A. Eliason, and Rose Allen, "Developing Culturally Sensitive Parent Education Programs for Immigrant Families: Helping Youth Succeed Curriculum," *Hmong Studies Journal* 7 (2006): 1–29.

8. Lee, "Cultural Identity in Post-Modern Society."

9. Lee, "Cultural Identity in Post-Modern Society."

10. Pao Lor, "Hmong Teachers' Life Experiences and Their Perspectives on Teaching," *Kaleidoscope II Newsletter* (Milwaukee: University of Wisconsin System Institute on Race and Ethnicity, 2010), 2–8.

RECOMMENDED READING

Chan, Sucheng, ed. *Hmong Means Free*. Philadelphia, PA: Temple University Press, 1994.

Clarkin, Patrick E. "Hmong Resettlement in French Guiana." *Hmong Studies Journal* 6 (2005): 1–27.

Conquergood, Dwight. *I Am a Shaman: A Hmong Life Story with Ethnographic Commentary*. Minneapolis: University of Minnesota Center for Urban and Regional Affairs, 1989.

Davy, Joseph. "Por Thao's Funeral (Documentary Photo Essay)." *Hmong Studies Journal* 2.1 (1997): 1–5.

Fadiman, Anne. *The Spirit Catches You and You Fall Down.* New York: Farrar, Straus, and Giroux, 1997.

Falk, Catherine. "Upon Meeting the Ancestors: The Hmong Funeral Ritual in Asia and Australia." *Hmong Studies Journal* 1.1 (1996): 1–15.

Hamilton-Merritt, Jane. *The Hmong, the Americans, and the Secret Wars for Laos, 1942–1992.* Bloomington: Indiana University Press, 1999.

Hang, MayKao. "Growing Up Hmong American: Truancy Policy and Girls." *Hmong Studies Journal* 2.1 (1997): 1–54.

Hein, Jeremy. "From Migrant to Minority: Hmong Immigrants and the Social Construction of Identity in the United States." *Sociological Inquiry* 64 (1994): 281–306.

Hendricks, Glenn L., Bruce T. Downing, and Amos S. Deinard, eds. *The Hmong in Transition.* New York: Center for Migration Studies, 1986.

Hutchinson, Ray. "The Educational Performance of Hmong Students in Wisconsin." *Wisconsin Policy Research Institute Report* 10.8 (1997): 1–36.

Lee, Gary Yia. "Diaspora and the Predicament of Origins: Interrogating Hmong Postcolonial History and Identity." *Hmong Studies Journal* 8 (2007): 1–23.

Lee, Mai Na. "The Thousand-Year Myth: Construction and Characterization of Hmong." *Hmong Studies Journal* 2.1 (1997): 1–23.

Lor, Pao. "Hmong Teachers' Life Experiences and Their Perspectives on Teaching." *Kaleidoscope II Newsletter.* Milwaukee: University of Wisconsin System Institute on Race and Ethnicity, 2010, 2–8.

———. "Life Experiences Contributing to Hmong Student's Graduation." *Multicultural Education* 16.1 (2008): 39–47.

———. "Tale of a Minority Administrator." *American School Board Journal* 196.8 (2009): 24–6.

McGinnis, Kathleen. "Ethnic-Sensitive Work with Hmong Refugee Children." *Child Welfare* 70 (1991): 571–78.

Quincy, Keith. *Hmong: History of a People.* Cheney: Eastern Washington University Press, 1995.

Timm, Joan T. "Hmong Values and American Education." *Equity and Excellence in Education* 27.2 (1994): 36–43.

Vang, Christopher T. "Hmong-American Students Still Face Multiple Challenges in Public Schools." *Multicultural Education* 13.1 (2005): 27–35.

Watt, Hilary. "The Power of the Spoken Word in Defining Religion and Thought: A Case Study." *Hmong Studies Journal* 9 (2008): 1–25.

Wayne, Carroll, and Victoria Udalova. "Who Is Hmong? Questions and Evidence from the U.S. Census." *Hmong Studies Journal* 6 (2005): 1–20.

Yang, Dao. *Hmong at the Turning Point.* Minneapolis, MN: WorldBridge Associates, 1993.

Yang, Kou. "An Assessment of the Hmong American New Year and Its Implications for Hmong American Culture." *Hmong Studies Journal* 8 (2007): 1–32

———. "Hmong-Americans: A Review of Needs, Problems and Community Development." *Hmong Studies Journal* 4 (2003): 1–23.

———. "A Visit to the Hmong of Asia: Globalization and Ethnicity at the Dawn of the 21st Century." *Hmong Studies Journal* 9 (2008): 1–50.

< 10 >

Forging New Paths, Confronting New Challenges

Hmong Americans in the Twenty-First Century

KOU YANG

During the summer of 2010, many Hmong American families celebrated their thirty-fifth year in the United States. From a population of about five hundred at the end of 1975, the Hmong American community has grown to about three hundred thousand persons in 2010, making it the largest Hmong population living outside of Asia. Today, Hmong Americans are an ethnic group whose lives have been woven into the social, economic, and political fabric of this nation. Yet, their status as a double minority—a minority within the Asian American community and in American society—remains. Compared to that of other immigrant groups, Hmong integration into American society has been equally remarkable, undergoing rapid and progressive changes within a short time. In a 2006 plenary address at the First International Conference on Hmong Studies, I divided the Hmong American experience into three phases: The Refugee Years (1975–91); The Transitional Period (1992–99); and The Hmong American Era (2000–present). This third phase of Hmong adaptation to American society is a promising starting point to explore two crucial aspects of understanding Hmong identity formation: namely, the educational experiences of Hmong Americans and recent developments in Hmong studies as a scholarly, global field of inquiry. To encourage critical reflection on the complex lives of Hmong Americans in the twenty-first century, I begin this chapter with a discussion of how Hmong people have been represented in the media and scholarly publications.[1]

< 161 >

Questioning Stereotypes and Looking for New Stories

As a social worker in California from 1980 to 1996, I was astounded at the way academic and popular literature represented Hmong Americans. In *Asian Americans,* for instance, Harry Kitano and Roger Daniels depicted Hmong culture in the 1990s by citing the *Los Angeles Times:* "Every winter in the Central Valley of California, Hmong men search for brides, often as young as 12 and 13 years of age." Kitano and Daniels readily accepted the newspaper's claim that a Hmong man in the area had married a twelve-year-old girl. However, because of my work in the community at the time, I knew that she was at least five years older than the birth date on her immigration document indicated. Until recently, Hmong children born in Laos and Thailand customarily were not given birth certificates. Furthermore, Hmong refugees sometimes lowered their children's ages on official documents with hopes of qualifying them for public schooling in the United States. Consequently, the popular media made many misjudgments about how Hmong families were finding their way in American society.[2]

Enduring to the present day is another popular stereotype found in *The Contemporary Asian American Experience,* where Timothy Fong labeled Hmong soldiers "mercenaries." All too common in the 1980s and 1990s were images of Hmong in Laos as fierce mountain fighters eager to enlist in the U.S. cause. Unfortunately, missing in most accounts of the war were more accurate depictions of Hmong as people with their own deeply held reasons for risking everything in the name of defending their families, way of life, and territory. Widespread in academic literature and mass media are many more misrepresentations of Hmong and Hmong Americans.[3]

Scholars researching Hmong and Hmong Americans in the early 1980s had to work with a very limited pool of literature. For example, in 1979, a friend and mentor of mine took me to the library of the University of Southern California, where we could find only three books on Hmong: all were authored by Christian missionary workers in China in the early twentieth century.

In all of these early accounts, Hmong people were seen through a Western lens, as a group living in remote places isolated from the rest of the modern world. My perspective as a professor of Asian American studies, a former social worker, and a member of the Hmong American community offers an alternative approach to telling the stories of Hmong and Hmong Americans.

Hmong History Retold through Personal Experience

My interest in Hmong history, culture, and contemporary experience is both personal and intellectual. I was born into a large extended Hmong family in the highlands of northwestern Laos. As the first son of the oldest son of my grandparents, I was in line to lead the family and, possibly, the community. However, I disappointed my elders when they discovered that I was not as skilled as other boys. I could not shoot arrows straight with a bow, play *qeej,* weave *kawm,* or help elders make tools essential to daily village life. More important, I was not adept in verbal skills necessary for performing religious rites and leadership duties.

Moreover, I asked many questions that no other boy in our family had asked before. For example, I vividly remember that during the ritual offering of the first harvest to our ancestors, my grandmother gently told me, "Don't run around; be quiet. Your grandfather is calling the ancestors to take part in our feasting, so you must be a good boy." When I stopped running and turned my eyes to the table surrounded by empty chairs, I saw no one except my grandfather, sitting alone and calling the names of our ancestors one by one to join us for the first meal of the new harvest. Puzzled, I turned to my grandmother and said, "I see no one there except grandfather." My grandmother then patiently explained that our ancestors are always present in our hearts and on the family altar. Even though they have passed on, they remain a part of our family lineage, extending many generations back to China.

At eight years of age, I was sent with other Hmong children to a school in Ban Namone, a Lao village in Sayaboury Province. Ranging in age from eight to sixteen, we were taught in a one-room schoolhouse by a single teacher who valued curiosity and hunger for learning. Traits my family considered to be shortcomings thus became my strengths in school.

Most of my classmates, including my youngest uncle, eventually left school to join the Royal Lao Army in the mid-1960s. Five years into his service, my uncle was killed in action. A year after his death, my father and another uncle, who were well liked by everyone, were killed while traveling for our family business. We and our fellow villagers suspected their assassinations were linked to the divisive politics of the war.

As the situation in Laos deteriorated, most Hmong students left school, returning to their villages to help their families. However, I continued in school as my uncles and father would have wanted. A Buddhist temple and later a Christian youth hostel provided me with food and shelter while I contemplated what was happening in my family and the country. Buddhist teaching helped me tremendously through its emphasis on peace and love, compassion, self-sacrifice, and the non-permanence of this world. Gradually coming to accept what happened to my father and uncles, I found my way out of misery to a new life. In 1974, I passed the entrance examination to Lycee de Luang Prabang, the only high school in northern Laos. Because my family did not have any money, I attended Lycee only for a short time and then transferred to a teacher-training school on a scholarship. Like other successful students in those days, I dreamed of studying abroad in France and returning to serve the country in peacetime as a teacher or civil servant.

In 1975, my dream shattered when the war in Laos ended and the country went into turmoil. Most of the right-wing politicians and military leaders left Laos. Thousands of Hmong and other people who had sided with the former Royal Lao Government became refugees abroad. Pressured by family and friends, I soon left for Thailand.

The first month in the refugee camp was full of self-doubt and depression. Camp leaders distrusted me because I had been part of the student movement in Laos, which had supported the end of war. To make the best out of this difficult situation, I began to collect oral histories as a way to document refugee life and to better understand Hmong culture and tradition. In addition to gathering proverbs and personal narratives, I composed poems about various aspects of Hmong society, including camp life, gender inequality, and the effects of the war on families.

My American journey began in 1976 when my family arrived in New Orleans, Louisiana. Because I spoke a little French, our sponsor, a staff member of Catholic Charities, found me a dishwashing job in a French restaurant at the International Trade Building. At the same time, by memorizing the meaning of one word per day, I managed to increase my vocabulary by 365 words in a year. Soon I was able to understand and speak English; through two years of practice, I found that my new language made my new life much more meaningful.

In 1978, I moved to Long Beach, California, where I worked as a cultural orientation teacher at the Asian Pacific Family Outreach and later as a community worker with a private Asian American mental health center.

In 1980, I was hired by the Los Angeles Department of Public Social Services and worked there until 1984, when I moved to Fresno, California, to become the first social worker of Southeast Asian ancestry in Fresno County. My education progressed slowly but steadily during the nearly twenty years of my advancement from ESL classes to completing master of social work and doctor of education degrees.

Since the 1980s, I have researched what it means to be Hmong and American. To better understand how Hmong Americans have adapted to life in this country, I have visited many Hmong American communities across the United States. In addition, the need to know how Hmong people live in different parts of the world has taken me to China, France, Germany, Australia, Thailand, Laos, and Vietnam. Since 1986, I have been to China eight times; these have included leading a Fulbright-Hays Group Study in 2004 and an international scholars trip in 2009 focusing on Hmong/Miao studies in Guizhou. What I have discovered on these research trips is that we have much more to do before we can begin to understand the complicated history of Hmong people. Like many other Hmong Americans, I am deeply interested in finding the connections between the Hmong past and present.

Hmong Americans in Higher Education: Making Connections through Hmong Studies

In 2010, institutions of higher education in the United States employed twenty-one tenured and tenure-track professors of Hmong ancestry on their faculty. Of these twenty-one, three were full professors, eight were associate professors, and the rest were assistant professors. Five of the twenty-one were women. Nearly one-half of the professors were working in the California State University and the University of California systems; the others were employed in Minnesota, Wisconsin, Oregon, and Georgia. Most of them were teaching outside the discipline of Hmong studies. On the one hand, I hope to see these professionals stay connected to their communities in carrying out innovative research and developing new courses. On the other hand, they have an invaluable opportunity to expand understanding of what it means to be Hmong beyond traditional views held by people in our community. When I started teaching Asian American studies, there was no demand for courses on Hmong or Hmong

Americans. Even in courses on the Vietnam War and Southeast Asia, mention of the Hmong was superficial at best. As I did in the 1980s and the 1990s, Hmong American faculty members now need to collaborate with colleagues across academic fields to include more substantial representation of Hmong and Hmong Americans in the university curricula.

Four aspects of development seem particularly important in contemporary Hmong and Hmong American studies. First, scholars must build the discipline of Hmong studies from the ground up with very little foundation in place. In the process, we need to explore how Hmong studies can be defined. Scholars have taken steps in that direction at the first, second, and third International Conferences on Hmong Studies sponsored by the Center for Hmong Studies at Concordia University in St. Paul, Minnesota. Second, Hmong studies should be offered as an undergraduate major in colleges and universities. At present, only two Hmong studies certificate programs are in place. Third, we need to establish a professional association to provide direction for the future, to ensure academic integrity and quality by establishing research standards and publishing guidelines, and to promote the dissemination of knowledge through annual meetings. Built into the vision of Hmong studies should be community support here in the United States and abroad. Finally, it is important for scholars of Hmong studies to acquire multilingual and multicultural skills, such as fluency in Chinese and the languages of Miao subgroups. This will enable us to build academic bridges with scholars of Hmong studies in other countries, mainly in China, Vietnam, Thailand, and Laos.

Some important efforts have already been made in both the United States and China. For example, in 2009 the Guizhou Miao Studies Association organized a two-day Hmong and Miao panel with more than forty multinational scholars at the sixteenth World Congress of the International Union of Anthropological and Ethnological Sciences in Kunming, China. In the United States, the Center for Hmong Studies at Concordia University offers a Hmong studies minor and hosts a biannual international conference on Hmong studies; along with the Hmong diaspora studies certificate at the University of Wisconsin–Milwaukee, these are important stepping stones in the advancement of research. A final example is the peer-reviewed *Hmong Studies Journal,* which since 1996 has contributed much to our understanding of Hmong history, culture, and lives across the globe.

Fulfilling American Dreams

Although it is not yet the norm, Hmong Americans have made headlines in their local newspapers regarding their educational achievements. In Spring 2009, the graduation of the daughters of the Xiong family of Merced, California, provided a clear example of Hmong American educational success: the oldest daughter earned a doctor of medicine degree from Georgetown University Medical School; the second graduated from Lake Erie College of Osteopathic Medicine in Pennsylvania; the third earned a pharmacy doctorate from Creighton University; the fourth completed a bachelor of science in microbiology from the University of California at Davis; and the fifth received her special education diploma from Merced High School. These young women have become role models for all young Americans.[4]

Equally noteworthy are the numbers of Hmong Americans who have become teachers and administrators. Prior to the early 1990s, Sacramento City School District had no teacher of Hmong ancestry. As of 2010, approximately eighty teachers and bilingual specialists worked in that district, as did many school administrators. Among these are Lee Yang, the director of the Multilingual Literacy Department; Mao J. Vang, the director of Assessment, Research, and Evaluation; Yee Yang, principal of Hollywood Park Elementary; Annabel Lee, principal of Noralto Elementary; Bao Moua, principal of Clayton B. Wire Elementary; and several vice principals, such as Shane Yang at Grant Joint Union High School.

Prior to their resettlement in the United States, very few Hmong had basic literacy skills. The formal educational level of the Hmong of Laos was low; in some remote mountainous areas, according to Yang Dao, very few knew how to read and write. Despite these challenges, the Hmong American community did have its first doctorate in 1982, its first lawyer in 1987, its first physician in 1988, and its first university professor in 1991. Since the late 1970s, many young Hmong have successfully navigated the educational system; since the late 1980s, they have entered many professions.[5]

According to Mark Pfeifer, the number of Hmong Americans who have completed bachelor degrees increased from three percent in 1990 to 10.4 percent in 2006. My own tracking indicates that the number of Hmong people who have completed a doctoral or professional degree increased from one in 1982 to about three hundred in 2008. Data from the 2009 American Community Survey shows improvement in educational attainments, although Hmong still lag behind the general U.S. population. The number of Hmong twenty-five years and older (93,936 out of 236,434) who have completed graduate or professional degrees increased from 1.5 percent in 2000 to 3.5 percent in 2009. More significant are those who hold college degrees, up from three percent in 1990 to 11.1 percent in 2009. As suggested by these statistics, at least three hundred to five hundred Hmong Americans completed graduate or professional degrees as of 2010. Given the fact that the first doctorate awarded to a Hmong American did not occur until 1982, this development is encouraging, even if this group still lags behind the national average of 10.3 percent for people holding graduate or professional degrees.[6]

Educational advancement definitely affects the economic opportunities of Hmong American families. Mark Pfeifer notes that the median Hmong family income in 2006 was $42,875 compared to $58,526 for the U.S. population, up from $32,384 in 2000. Despite the economic recession from 2006 to 2009, median family income continues to increase. The 2009 American Community Survey reveals that Hmong family median income was $45,611, a small increase from 2006. Moreover, a majority of Hmong American family households are two-parent households: about 70 percent of Hmong American families in 2000 compared with 24 percent of the U.S. population. On an even more optimistic note, the poverty rate of Hmong Americans was 26.4 percent, down from 40 percent in 2000. However, this number was still much higher than the 9.8 percent for the general U.S. population.[7]

On the one hand, more and more Hmong Americans are entering a range of professions, such as information technology, journalism, engineering, teaching, the military, and medicine. On the other, if the Hmong American community is to develop the full educational potential of its young people, then schools and families have to solve the problem of low test scores and high dropout rates. For example, a 2005 study indicated that language barriers and limited parental education are two leading challenges for many Hmong families in the Twin Cities of Minnesota. In the Sacramento City School District, 80 percent of Hmong students scored below the fortieth percentile in math and reading on the 2001 SAT9. The California State Office of the Secretary for Education reports that Hmong K-12 students are California's third most common English Language Learners, a situation that complicates their educational needs as they advance through the public school system. Because the majority of the Hmong American population is under the age of eighteen, the most realistic approach to preparing this group for the twenty-first century is education, so its members can become productive citizens of this country and build a vibrant Hmong American community.[8]

Gender issues in the Hmong American community also need more attention. First, the 2006 American Community Survey (ACS) indicates the Hmong population to be 50.1 percent male compared to 49.9 percent female. Second, in our analysis of the 2000 Census, Mark Pfeifer and I found that "56.8% of enumerated Hmong women across the United States reported having completed no schooling, compared to 33.5% of Hmong men." Overall, the 2000 Census revealed that more than twice the number of Hmong men (compared to women) reported earning associate and bachelor degrees, with a 2:1 ratio for graduate degrees. However, a new trend of increasing Hmong female participation in higher education is emerging. According to the 2009 ACS survey, for example, 13.9 percent of Hmong females at age twenty-five or older, compared to 15.4 percent of Hmong males, had associate, bachelor, or higher degrees, an impressive increase from 2000.[9]

Yet, what these statistics do not show are social or cultural explanations for this trend. Is the educational achievement of Hmong American women the result of self-determination alone? Or could the upbringing of daughters in Hmong American families have given them the life-shaping discipline and other self-strengthening qualities necessary to persevere and succeed in school? Moreover, do young women view educational advancement as a way not only to overcome gender discrimination but also to bring credit to their families and communities? Exploring such questions will be an important part of understanding how the Hmong American community may be changing.

Doing More to Promote Education

The educational attainment of Hmong Americans still lags behind that of the general U.S. population. Fully understanding both the progress and the problems in the Hmong American community today requires that more research be undertaken to investigate problems facing Hmong American students in higher education. In general, students I have worked with tend to be the first in their families to attend college; consequently, they often lack realistic educational and career goals, going along with the advice of friends and family without carefully assessing their strengths, shortcomings, and future job prospects. Additionally, they tend to have limited access to information about educational and financial resources essential to college success. Although supportive of sons and daughters pursuing higher education, many Hmong American parents are not certain how to guide them through school.

In my view, Hmong American youth need educational advocates and educational leadership. Local and national Hmong American organizations, such as mutual assistance associations and Hmong National Development, can include these services in their long-range vision. For example, parents and youth would benefit from workshops on how to apply to college and how to succeed in higher education. Further, I encourage Hmong American student clubs to take even more active roles in providing orientation to new students, guiding them to resources available on campus and introducing them to faculty who understand their needs and could serve as mentors. Hmong media, including radio stations, newspapers, and magazines, should address topics related to higher education, particularly stories featuring outstanding students and their strategies for success. Last, I want to commend Hmong parents for organizing community-wide events to celebrate the graduation of their children from high schools, colleges, and universities. These events clearly demonstrate the value that Hmong American parents place on education.

Building International Bridges, Overcoming Internal Divisions

Prior to 1985, Hmong American visits to China were rare, mostly because Hmong refugees were focusing on adapting to life in the United States. In the past decade, many young Hmong Americans have developed a yearning to explore the paths of their ancestors; consequently, they are interested in building bridges with Hmong of other countries, such as those from Australia, Argentina, Canada, China, Germany, France, Laos, Myanmar, Thailand, and Vietnam. Most important of all is the reconnection between Hmong in the United States and in Asia. As a college professor, I have found that when Hmong American students have the opportunity to learn about transnational influences that Hmong have on each another, they are eager to know more. For example, they are intrigued by my discovery (during a 2008 visit to Vietnam and Laos) that young Hmong in North Vietnam can adeptly text message in the (Hmong) Romanized Phonetic Alphabet (RPA) language and know the names of more Hmong American pop singers than I do. Moreover, many Hmong in Laos can recite the telephone area codes of the metropolitan areas of Fresno and the Twin Cities. At the same time, I have seen that young Hmong Americans proudly wear to their annual Hmong New Year gatherings the contemporary costumes of their cousins in Laos, Vietnam, and China. These developments are partly the result of young people's education, access to the Internet, and involvement in popular global culture.[10]

In the twenty-first century, people of Hmong descent will become more diverse in their cultural outlook, economic status, educational achievement, political affiliation, and religious beliefs. At the same time, the longer they are in the United States, the more likely they are to resemble other ethnic groups in this country. In my view, Hmong Americans are shifting from a group orientation toward individualism. The clan, which has long served as a foundation of Hmong society, will take on new significance in the twenty-first century. My hope is that differences between White Hmong and Green Hmong will eventually phase out; as the majority of Hmong Americans become more educated and visionary, they will be less inclined to accept division.

Conclusion

In this chapter, my observations of the Hmong American community have emphasized transcentennial change, including new opportunities for individual achievement, family success, and collective advancements. Hmong in the United States are different in many aspects from their cousins in Europe, the other Americas, and Asia. As scholars analyze the ongoing journey of becoming American, more attention should be given to stories of success as well as ongoing challenges in achieving full citizenship. The relevance of Hmong American accomplishments in modern society will depend on more fully utilizing their resourcefulness and adaptability as proud members of a multicultural country. Their contributions can include helping to close ethnic and racial divides. As Hmong and American cultures interact, this productive process will ensure a secure place for Hmong Americans in American society.

From a humble beginning, I have made the leap from an elementary student in Ban Namone, Laos, to a university professor in Stanislaus, California. My life in higher education may not be representative of many other Hmong lives in the United States, but my path there reflects Hmong struggles and determination that stem from our shared longing for peace and security. Hmong are flexible. They can adapt to any country, whether rural or urban, Asian or Western. Despite life-changing experiences, the identity of Hmong people remains intact and perhaps is becoming even stronger in the process.

NOTES

1. This number is estimated based on the inclusion of offspring of Hmong Americans born between 2000 and 2010, the entry of fifteen thousand Hmong refugees from Thailand to the United States since 2004, and documented and undocumented Hmong immigrants and those who overstayed their visas. It should be noted here that data from the 2010 U.S. Census counted the Hmong American population as only about 260,076.

Kou Yang, "The Experience of Hmong Americans: Three Decades in Retrospective Review," in ed. Gary Yia Lee, *The Impact of Globalization and Trans-Nationalism on the Hmong* (St. Paul, MN: Center for Hmong Studies, 2009), 79, 84.

2. Harry H. L. Kitano and Roger Daniels, *Asian Americans: Emerging Minorities,* 2nd ed. (Upper Saddle River, NJ: Prentice Hall, 1995), 144.

3. Timothy P. Fong, *The Contemporary Asian American Experience,* 2nd ed. (Upper Saddle River, NJ: Prentice Hall, 2002), 34. For discussions related to this topic, see Mai Na Lee, "The Thousand-Year Myth: Construction and Characterization of Hmong," *Hmong Studies Journal* 2.2 (1998): 1–23; and Keith Quincy, *Harvesting Pa Chay's Wheat: The Hmong and America's Secret War in Laos* (Spokane: Eastern Washington University Press, 2000).

4. Mike Tharp, "Five Graduates, 3 Doctors: A Tale of Laotian Refugee Triumph," *Modesto Bee,* June 5, 2009, www.modbee.com/2009/06/05/732638/five-graduates-3-doctors-a-tale.html (accessed Nov. 15, 2011).

5. Yang Dao, *Hmong at the Turning Point* (Minneapolis, MN: WorldBridge Associates, 1993), 83–84.

6. Mark Pfeifer, "Census Profile of Hmong Americans," *Asian American Press,* Oct. 26, 2007.

7. U.S Bureau of the Census, "Selected Population Profile in the United States, Population Group: Hmong Alone or in Any Combination," Data Set: 2009 American Community Survey 1-Year Estimates, hmongstudies.org/HmongACS2009.pdf.

8. Bob San, "Hmong Kids Lack Early Learning Help," Asian Week.com, Dec. 2, 2005. For a discussion on this issue, see Suanna Gilman-Ponce, Sacramento City Unified School District Multilingual Education Department (2001), a manuscript circulated by the department.

9. Kou Yang and Mark Pfeifer, "Profile of Hmong Educational Attainment," 21, 22, and Mark Pfeifer and Serge Lee, "Hmong Population, Demographic, Socio-economic, and Educational Trends in the 2000 Census," 4, 11, both in *Hmong 2000 Census Publication: Data and Analysis* (Washington, DC: Hmong National Development, Inc., and the Hmong Cultural and Resource Center, 2004), www.hmongstudies.org/2000HmongCensusPublication.pdf (accessed Nov. 15, 2011).

10. Kou Yang, "A Visit to the Hmong of Asia: Globalization and Ethnicity at the Dawn of the 21st Century," *Hmong Studies Journal* 9 (2008): 1–50, hmongstudies.org/KouYang2008.pdf.

PART III

Cultural Integration through Education and the Arts

< 11 >

Pieces of the Puzzle

A Hmong American Teacher's Multifaceted Identity

MAY VANG

I sat in my graduate educational statistics course anxiously awaiting the results of the latest quiz. I had looked forward to taking a course related to mathematics. When I scanned my answer sheet for errors, my eyes fixed upon a response marked as incorrect. I wanted to ask for clarification, but because I did not want to prolong the gathering any further for my classmates, I decided to wait until after class. As the last of my classmates left the room, I quickly approached one of the two instructors. I asked her to explain what she had expected the answer to be. However, even before I could finish, she interrupted me with her response. She looked at me and without any hesitation stated that I would not understand the concept because I was an ESL (English as a Second Language) student similar to those she had previously taught in her *remedial* computer class. Therefore, there would be no point in explaining anything to me. I simply was not going to ever get it.

Needless to say, I was blindsided by her simplification of me as "just another" ESL student and her belief that such a label actually corresponded to my abilities. In that brief moment, my identity as an educated American was called into question. The presumptions of this instructor left no room for the multiplicity of my identity, which included being a graduate student, an experienced teacher who had provided teacher in-service workshops, and an individual who had grown up in the United States. The last time I had been labeled as ESL was in third grade.

As a Hmong American student, I had long rejected the pervasive belief that coming from a different ethnic background was somehow an indicator of deficiency and defect. However, this incident served as a reminder that who I am would always be defined by more than my personal experiences or accomplishments. As I examine how my identity has been shaped

< 177 >

by interactions with my family, Hmong people, and the world around me, I am motivated to make a positive difference in the lives of students and other Hmong Americans. More specifically, as an educator, I hope to expand opportunities for Hmong American students to explore identity formation as a combination of self-reflection and social critique. In this chapter, my intention is to suggest the complexities of this process by focusing on what I have learned through my own experiences of schooling and socialization. In particular, I continue to ask my students and myself: what can we do to ensure that our bicultural identities incorporate Hmong language as a vital component?

Influence of Family Experiences

A foundational part of my identity has always been my understanding of family and childhood. Early in life, the transmission of my family's history became woven into my understanding of the world around me and my identity within that world. Orphaned at a young age, my father spent his childhood earning his keep with a relative. He was never afforded an education because that was usually reserved for only the most beloved male son of the family. My mother shared a similar background because her father died when she was a little girl. After my maternal grandmother remarried, my mother lived under the roof of her stepfather. Although he was a good father to her, he did not allow her to pursue the education she desired. From my parents' personal stories, I understood their regrets and the childhood circumstances that made it impossible for them to go to school.

Early on, I also heard many stories of our family's journey to the Thailand refugee camps. As my father detailed the harrowing journey by foot through the jungles with my sister strapped to his back, I could not help but feel the fear that lingered with every step—the dread of being discovered, ambushed, or killed. Today I understand that my place in America did not come without great sacrifice. My family's struggle for survival became intertwined with my own sense of obligation and determination to succeed.

My mother told a tale of the destitution that awaited us as our family was forced to spend the last of our monetary assets to ensure safe passage through the varied dangerous points of transition. With nothing left but diminishing hope and only the few immediate possessions that could be carried, my mother had no choice but to seek out the local Buddhist temple to ask for food to feed her children. She was met with compassion and kindness and the essence of humanity was shown to her as she was given enough to feed her children that day. Her story of kindness, at a time when there was nothing left, instilled in me a strong sense of compassion toward others.

Somehow my parents made it to the refugee camps in Thailand with all my siblings still alive. Everyone who started the journey with them had made it. However, our family's journey to the United States was temporarily put on hold, and they remained in those refugee camps for many years. During that period of transition, I was born. Shortly thereafter, the family boarded an airplane headed for the United States. Like thousands of other refugees, they could not have anticipated all of the challenges ahead.

Once in America, my parents were met with seemingly unyielding compassion by some and immense contempt from many others. The earliest memory I have of our new life in America seems like a dream from a long forgotten past. I am seated in a chair which seems to go on forever (a toddler high chair), and there is a new sensation, an overly salty, almost bitter taste, which lingers as I taste the new exotic foods. Overwhelming fear wells up inside, and all I can do is cry. I keep crying, and no matter how much my older sisters try to calm me, it does no good. Our sponsor's patience remains steadfast, and without much fuss I am returned to the comfort of my mother's arms. Over a brief period of time, sponsors helped to guide our family's adjustment to the new country and provided me with early experiences of life in America. Through them, I learned that there are sincere individuals whose kindness is extended to everyone, including those who may have had exceptionally different experiences and perspectives.

However, not everyone my parents encountered was willing to accept people who were different. My father told of a woman who must have been our family's caseworker. My parents routinely met with her to report their earnings at an assembly line factory. Every time my father made his weekly trip to her office, he was met with resentment and contempt, exemplified by a piercing, hate-filled stare. Although my father could not fully understand what the woman was saying, she always seemed to have a smugly crooked smile and suspecting eyes, which told him all he needed to know.

He never forgot those eyes, and as he recounts the story to me, I learn about the deep, long-lasting effect of hatred and contempt.

At that time there was no public knowledge that my father, along with many other Hmong, had been members of the Special Guerrilla Unit (SGU) secured by the United States to rescue downed soldiers during the Vietnam War and provide tactical support. Like many other refugee groups who have immigrated to America, Hmong people upon arrival were concerned with how to survive in a new country; they needed time to fully participate in America's educational system. Because their involvement in the Vietnam War was not widely recognized and because their skills as rice farmers were not readily transferrable, they were perceived as yet another minority group who came to America to live off of hardworking citizens. Moreover, we were met with hate signs spray-painted on the walls of the houses in our neighborhood. A new understanding of my place in this world then developed as those symbols could only mean that my family and Hmong people were not welcomed.

Those early experiences of racism, hatred, and discrimination supported my nascent sense of unity with Hmong people because I understood that at the very least we shared a language and the cultural experience of readjustment to a new life in America, filled with both exciting opportunities and daunting challenges.

Unity of a People

During my childhood, Hmong were closely clustered together in ethnic neighborhoods. My immediate family originally arrived in Illinois but subsequently relocated to Arkansas and finally to Wisconsin in search of our extended family. We moved to both Arkansas and Wisconsin precisely because we knew our relatives also had settled there. The Midwest was a far cry from my life back in Southeast Asia. Yet, it was in these clusters that I enjoyed endless days interacting with cousins, aunts, uncles, and grandparents. Out of these experiences, I came to understand the meaning of family and the richness of culture and heritage. My step-grandmother would tell stories of the old days, and I would listen to her folktales about how the world was created or how the Hmong people became the way they are. My language flourished as I interacted with elders. I revered my step-grandfather, father, and oldest brother. I secretly wondered if there could ever be anyone who would measure up to my father and oldest brother. To me, they were the two tallest people in the world. This belief manifested a vivid impression that the physical stature of my father and brother made on me. Through the dignity of their self-presentation, I also gained a deep reverence for Hmong people of worth in the world.

As I saw how my family remained tied to the people from the old country through letters and tapes, my beliefs about the importance and stature of my father were reinforced. Those letters and audiotapes allowed families to stay connected no matter where they lived. Moreover, the reality of fragmented traditional families and dispersed villages—consequences of the Hmong diaspora following the Vietnam War—reminded me that I was a member of a larger community. This knowledge and connection was a significant part of who I was, whether or not I knew it as a child. Early on, I developed this foundational identity strongly tied to the language of a people and its culture of hard work, family obligation, and responsibility. Unfortunately, this unity that I understood so long ago would become a faded and forgotten backdrop as my identity began to evolve through the personal experiences with the world outside of my family and outside of the Hmong community.

Personal Experiences

Today I am a Hmong American nearing the end of my doctoral studies in urban education. Humbly, I know this achievement exceeds what my parents had dreamed would be possible as we boarded that plane to America long ago. I have successfully completed a master's degree in reading and language arts despite prevailing assumptions that students of disadvantaged backgrounds are at higher risks for academic failure. When this assumption remains unchallenged, schools lower their expectations at all levels, as exemplified by curricula for at-risk students. As a Hmong American who values education as a path to the American dream, I am compelled to reflect on my struggles in the public school system; the experiences of fifth graders whom I interacted with; and the ability of schools to give all students access and opportunity to achieve.

Entering school as a young child, I was identified by teachers and school administrators as needing ESL services. Not only was I a student with "limited English proficiency" (based on particular criteria that schools were expected to follow at that time); I was also labeled as coming from a low socioeconomic background. Therefore, I was twice as likely to not succeed because I was doubly "disadvantaged" and twice "at risk." Advancing through the school system, I began to identify more and more with the ideals and values of mainstream society because I was acutely aware of these perceptions of my disadvantages. In addition, I understood the underlying assumption that I needed to fix myself so that I could be accepted as normal. Part of being accepted would be to improve my limited English proficiency. As researcher Lily Wong Fillmore points out, to be accepted in school and society, I needed English for everyday functioning—a reality every refugee and immigrant group must internalize as a fact. In the process, my native language gradually was displaced along with ethnic and cultural identity. Subconsciously, I not only aimed to reach that English proficiency but also subscribed to the dominant ideology of individualism and competition as innately good for everyone. I needed to become what was considered to be a good citizen—patriotic and loyal only to American values. I did not want to be different and was continually reminded by teachers to speak in English only; every day of school reinforced the idea that if I did not speak Hmong, then I would become even more American.[1]

In fact, the schools recognized my Hmong identity only when I had to attend ESL classes, usually located in the basement or a secluded corner of the building, and when I was asked to bring in egg rolls for multicultural events. These recurring incidents served to reaffirm my acceptance of the need to assimilate. Within educational structures reinforcing the inequality of ESL and non-ESL learners, I yearned to become what the dominant society wanted me to become. I grew up believing that if I did not do well in school, it was because I was not a hardworking individual. Would it be possible to shed my Hmong identity and blend in completely with my white American peers? I did not realize that as I was working so hard to become American, my language was being displaced, as was my connection with being Hmong.

It was not until I was well within the reach of a high school diploma that I started to long for a clearer understanding of who I had become. In fact, I had done a great job of learning what the educational system deemed essential. I knew all about U.S. historical figures. I learned how to speak and write well in English. My hard work paid off; I was accepted into the advanced placement track in high school. I read literary classics and was in all the right classes. I even surpassed many other American students in achievement. School staff supported me, and every one of my teachers thought only the best of me. In that situation, I met the only acceptable Asian identity for me, that of a model minority, despite my early at-risk beginnings. At that point, I was feeling accepted and as American as any of my peers; I had found a niche.

Then one day, a friend whom I had known since third grade asked me what language I dreamed in. The immediate answer was English, but then I began to question why it was not Hmong. At what point in my life was my first language displaced? My friend's curiosity made me realize how troubling the relationship between language and identity was for me. This incident marked the beginning of a long search for an integrated identity. Perhaps I was not simply American, but had been Hmong American all along.

Growing up, I did not realize that as my English language skills and American identity flourished, my sense of being Hmong, including the many memories of storytelling that I had been fond of as a child, had slowly slipped away. At home, my siblings and I spoke English only, which meant we did not communicate much with my parents and grandparents. We enjoyed doing things that many American kids do. Whenever the Hmong New Year or soccer tournaments rolled around, I felt awkward putting on Hmong clothes or being in large Hmong gatherings. In my own ways, I rebelled against Hmong traditions by accepting only mainstream American values. Gradually I had lost the language skills needed to effectively communicate with my parents, and they did not know enough English to ensure that I understood our history, traditions, and heritage.

My father had often said, "Your hair will still be black and your eyes will still be brown." I never understood the depth of his statement until I began searching for an identity existing beyond the American model minority, who is able to prevail above a so-called disadvantaged background. Being Hmong, I always had a wealth of advantages. As I identified myself more and more as a member of this group, I made conscious efforts to learn the language and culture. Only when I embraced a fuller understanding of my complete identity did I begin to realize the urgency for capturing and regaining a language and culture in danger of being lost. Without ever rejecting my identity as an American, I have realized that my identity as Hmong is ever present. Being Hmong did not mean that I was somehow abnormal. Being Hmong and having those early connections to the identity of my family and Hmong people had been the underlying source of my determination and motivation for success all along.

It was never my naïve belief that if only I could reject my ethnic identity, then somehow I was going to turn into someone who would be acceptable to the dominant society. I realized I had been wholly misguided because, up until college, my American education did not include courses on Hmong history, culture, or contemporary issues. While in school, I gave no credence to having built a strong foundation for resiliency and success from my early childhood identification with being Hmong and my connections to my family. Realizing that students in many ethnic groups share similar experiences of exclusion and misguidance, I chose to become a teacher because, at the very least, my presence would attest to the multiple identities possible in America.

As a teacher, I have worked with ethnically and linguistically diverse students who reflect the multicultural character of this country. I have witnessed the disparities between schools, even though they are all, in theory, designed to serve students of all socioeconomic backgrounds. This situation reflects a social paradigm in which those who have the most maintain a system to ensure continued success, while those with the least must make do with what is availed to them. Educational institutions continually operate according to such spoken or unspoken policies and pedagogy serving the interests of majority social groups. Teachers can be in a position to promote educational equity if they are willing to confront the many challenges involved.

More specifically, I am acutely aware of being a minority teacher in a predominantly white, middle-class, female profession. Complicating my situation is that even among Hmong American teachers there is tension regarding the educational standards to which all students should aspire. For example, although teachers may be from the same population of marginalized people, who have often been labeled as adhering to what educators refer to as a "deficit paradigm," this group membership does not necessarily provide inoculation against a pervasive system of inequality. Without the willingness to examine the structures allowing some to succeed and gain upward mobility while suppressing others, one cannot begin to understand the effects of such socially constructed paradigms. Simply because one has also been victimized by the larger dominant structure does not automatically mean that one is willing to work against it.

Knowing this, I am still continually disheartened when I hear some of my Hmong American colleagues insist that Hmong American students should speak only English. I am reminded of my own education, stripped of any substantive representation of perspectives and languages divergent from those of the dominant society. In my view, speaking students' home language with them at school would at the least validate their identity outside of the school setting. My colleagues insist, however, that doing so would result only in more confusion, believing that those students would not be able to learn either language well enough to succeed, even though much research has indicated that a strong foundation in students' first language will help them to acquire the target language.[2]

I am dismayed at how fellow Hmong American colleagues push for remedial teaching practices as a means to correct perceived deficiencies without so much as a cursory examination of the tools that have been used to measure these supposed deficiencies, given that the consequences of such a label can have far-reaching, long-term effects. Once again, the deficit educational paradigm is applied to groups of learners who have been deemed as outside the dominant group. The true outcomes for these students categorized as deficient or at risk are far worse than just receiving remedial instruction. The effects are much more damaging because *at risk* is a label that is not as easily removed and may always position these students as underachieving, marginal, and abnormal. Investing in the dominant belief that the failures of Hmong students are due in total to their own inadequacies (to learn English, to have "active and supportive" parents, to work hard) and the subsequent need for remediation continues to allow a cycle of inequality to prevail over not only Hmong children but also minority students in general and the society as a whole.[3]

As a fifth-grade teacher, I have tried to open up spaces welcoming all language varieties and all identities. I remember how discouraging it was to hear some of my Hmong American male students talking about how one of their classmates did not speak English correctly (without an accent). Although this school had a large number of Hmong students and various groups put up multiple ethnic displays in the hallways during ethnic celebrations, the deeper meaning of what it means to be successful remained decisively mainstreamed. Most of my students acted in accord with a prevailing belief in American individualism; many outright refused to acknowledge their Hmong heritage or to participate in the Hmong New Year program.

Reflecting on my own education, I remember rejecting my own ethnicity during those stereotypical school celebrations. However, a significant difference is that I am a first-generation Hmong American, whereas current Hmong American students in public schools are mostly second or third generation. I believe that although my education was also devoid of any substantive representation of Hmong identity, I had already developed a strong foundational identity with my family and Hmong culture, which was ultimately the underlying force that contributed to my motivation and success.

I fear many of my students do not have the opportunity to develop an understanding of their ethnic identity. Consequently, they struggle, as I did growing up, to find an acceptable and well-situated identity in the dominant society. Outside of the acceptable model minority identity, are alternatives accessible to students? With that concern in mind, I am motivated to work within current educational structures to expand opportunities for young Hmong Americans to develop identities surpassing society's expectation of them. Through educational reform, students can reconnect with their history and culture. Stepping outside my role as the classroom teacher, I have been able to witness the possibilities and the openings for such changes.

A Shift in Identity

While attending a science fair as a guest at a different school, I was happily surprised to hear many students speaking in Hmong. Several young men were animatedly discussing the energy required to carry out different kinds of work. They insisted that it was hard work to carry water back and forth and to cut down and carry wood, as if they knew firsthand about carrying water and wood on their backs. They chuckled and stated that they knew all about it because that is what Hmong people do. Although this incident was simply a friendly exchange about a shared cultural experience, it revealed not only how these young men constructed their identity as Hmong through collective history but also how this social group respected homeland experiences shared by many Hmong. Group identification as Hmong created an opening for the development of the language, similar to what Stacey Lee has posited in her research with Hmong American high school students. This membership meant not only the possibility of a mainstream American identity but also a Hmong identity connected to the language and shared cultural experiences of a people.[4]

Reflecting on this encounter, I realize that intergenerational transmission of cultural knowledge helps to create fuller comprehension of the world around us. As we listen to and absorb the experiences of others, we expand our understanding of who we are and what our identity potentially encompasses. Our ability to maintain a cultural identity is tied to the ongoing intergenerational transmission of the history and cultural practices of Hmong people. Through the rich oral tradition of our elders, we can remember and develop the part of our identity that is intimately tied to a unique identity as both Hmong and American.

Although we are a part of America's history, our contributions to this country have yet to be fully recognized. Educational reform must include acknowledgment of Hmong involvement in the Vietnam War. My father and many other Hmong soldiers sacrificed life and limb, yet they are still waiting for the day when their courage and convictions are honored. Their stories should be incorporated into public school curricula. As a teacher, I would like to hear more Hmong American voices in public debates on these and other issues related to educational reform, so that we can begin to reshape what is being taught to our children.

Instead, we see that the current educational debate on the use of first languages (other than English) is a barometer of America's tolerance for diversity. The successful passage of propositions to make bilingual education illegal in both California and Arizona reflects the wider disdain toward not only language diversity but also racial diversity. In essence, these propositions make English the only language that can be legally used with children in both California and Arizona public schools. Yet, research across many disciplines has recognized the integral connection that language has with identity. Knowing that language and identity cannot be separated, I am convinced that restricting the use of minority languages in public education systems is part of the larger sociopolitical discourse to make the United States linguistically and ethnically homogenous. A people's language represents identity, worldview, and creativity. Although the minority language most obviously targeted in both propositions is Spanish, Hmong Americans must understand that our language too is threatened. In this multicultural society, Hmong lives are tied inevitably to those of other ethnic groups.[5]

As an educator, I must ask: is Hmong language in danger of dying as the last of its linguistic reservoir evaporates with the final waves of Hmong immigrants? Hmong speakers pass on without having been able to fully transmit the language to younger users. At the same time, as its written language is still in its infancy, the language is in real danger of also fading away and becoming a forgotten language. With the loss of our language comes the distinct possibility of losing an ethnic identity and an understanding of what it means to be both Hmong and American. This reality is quickly approaching Hmong Americans as we are now fully integrating into mainstream America at an ever-quicker rate.

In my personal and professional view, Hmong Americans must make a conscious decision to be active advocates for the rights of ethnic minority groups to maintain their native languages for themselves and future generations. Although the Hmong American population is low compared to that of other ethnic groups across the nation, our growing presence and active citizenship in California, Minnesota, and Wisconsin give us the opportunity to help reform public education. We have been silenced too long. We must demonstrate civic responsibility, which has been idealized as part of the American democratic identity. The call to preserve the Hmong language is urgent. Ultimately, as Collin Baker posits, through our language we will identify who we are as a people, and when we use our language, we will be able to express who we truly are. We cannot allow for policies and institutions to remove our language because, by doing so, we would lose a large part of what identifies us as Hmong Americans.[6]

Choosing to be Hmong American

Hmong Americans are at a pivotal moment as the responsibilities for maintaining our language and culture are passed down from our elders. The successes Hmong Americans have attained since the late 1970s must be considered in the context of their connections with community, family, and cultural values. Hmong American youth need the support of their ethnic communities to succeed. However, without meaningful connections to the language and culture, youth are likely to resist Hmong values and ideals as essential to their own identity, a situation often pushing them to the margins of society. Indeed, all of us must critically examine the societal influences on our individual and collective self-concepts, including the potential for English to displace Hmong and other minority languages. If we are not careful in maintaining the essence of what makes us Hmong—which to me resides in language and culture—we may forever lose our unique identities. As more and more Hmong Americans make carefully calculated decisions to secure economic and educational advantages, they may find themselves reassessing the essence of what it means to be Hmong. If we lose our ties to family and community, I fear we will become not only more individualistic but also more isolated from each other.[7]

My identity as a Hmong American encompasses the experiences of many others. Who I am today is not who I was as a child or even who I was just a few years ago. With a clearer understanding of my own experiences and those of Hmong within an ever-changing multicultural society, I come away with a deeper sense of belonging and a truer sense of myself. I do not exist as two different people, one Hmong and the other American, but as an individual with an identity encompassing the multiplicity of my lived experiences as a mother, wife, daughter, professional, educator, and citizen of a hopeful nation and a proud people. Within the last thirty years, I have seen how Hmong American identities have continually evolved. Our very ability to adapt while maintaining an ethnic identity is a testament to the strength of a people and provides the means by which we remain interconnected to one another. Moreover, this flexibility is a cultural strength as we build new lives in the United States. Ultimately, as a Hmong American, I have discovered that just as my personal history continues to influence the development of my identity, so too do the histories of my family, people, and country show me who I am.

NOTES

1. Lily Wong Fillmore, "When Learning a Second Language Means Losing the First," *Early Childhood Research Quarterly* 6 (1991): 323–46.

2. Collin Baker, *Foundations of Bilingual Education and Bilingualism*, 4th ed. (New York: Multilingual Matters Ltd., 2006); J. David Ramirez, "Executive Summary," *Bilingual Research Journal* 16.1–2 (1992): 1–60.

3. Elaine M. Garan, *In Defense of Our Children: When Politics, Profit, and Education Collide* (Portsmouth, NH: Heinemann, 2004); Eugene E. Garcia, *Teaching and*

Learning in Two Languages: Bilingualism and Schooling in the United States (New York: Teachers College Press, 2005); and Elana Shohamy, *The Power of Tests: A Critical Perspective on the Uses of Language Tests* (London: Pearson Education Limited, 2001).

4. Stacey J. Lee, *Up Against Whiteness: Race, School, and Immigrant Youth* (New York: Teachers College Press, 2005).

5. Baker, *Foundations of Bilingual Education;* Garcia, *Teaching and Learning in Two Languages.* Hye-young Jo, "Negotiating Ethnic Identity in the College Korean Language Classes," *Identities: Global Studies in Culture and Power* 9 (2002): 87–115; and Rosina Lippi-Green, *English with an Accent: Language, Ideology, and Discrimination in the United States* (New York: Routledge, 1997).

6. Baker, *Foundations of Bilingual Education.*

7. Lee, *Up Against Whiteness;* Stacey J. Lee, "More Than 'Model Minorities' or 'Delinquents': A Look at Hmong American High School Students," *Harvard Educational Review* 71.3 (2001): 505–28.

< 12 >

Transforming the World and Oneself

The Arts and Hmong American Identity

DON HONES, SHERVUN XIONG, MA LEE XIONG, CHAN VANG,
HUE VANG, AND AMY DEBROUX

I have a mind, and I have hands.
This is enough for me to make dreams into reality.

Hue Vang

When one thinks of centers of culture and the arts, Oshkosh, Wisconsin, may not come immediately to mind. True, Oshkosh has gained fame as host to a large gathering of aviation enthusiasts each July, and it's a great place to spear a sturgeon in February. Yet, the casual visitor to the city might be forgiven for finding the cultural landscape as flat as the surrounding terrain. However, despite the cold of an April evening, things begin to heat up inside Albee Hall on the University of Wisconsin–Oshkosh campus. Inside, at this kickoff event for Asian Heritage Month, tables ring the floor and groups of students representing China, Japan, Pakistan, Sri Lanka, and other nations share images, arts, and delicacies with the audience. Onstage in the front of the room, dancers whirl and spin in a variety of styles including traditional, hip-hop, and Bollywood. Performers sing romantic ballads to the accompaniment of a guitar. A pan-Asian fashion show ignites the crowd. All of Asia is celebrated in this evening of culture and the arts. An observer might be surprised that most of the performers are Hmong Americans.

The arts appear to have a high profile in the Hmong American community, especially at celebrations such as New Year, which typically feature dozens of dance groups, singers, and musicians. Some scholars have suggested that New Year highlights the adaptability and flexibility of Hmong culture. In larger cities, such as St. Paul, Minnesota, centers devoted to the encouragement of Hmong artistic talent are prominent (for example, the Center for Hmong Arts and Talent and the Hmong

< 191 >

American Institute for Learning). Hmong artistic talent contributed to the success of Clint Eastwood's *Gran Torino*. Even in smaller cities such as Oshkosh, young Hmong Americans often stand out in the quality of their visual and performing arts. Yet, some fear that changes in how young people approach the arts, such as the playing of the bamboo flute, *qeej*, jeopardize traditional Hmong customs.[1]

The role of the arts within ethnic identity formation has been documented widely, including the role of music, theater, and community change; murals and photography within urban spaces; and ways in which the arts are connected specifically to culture within schools. Certainly the arts have played a tremendous role in the lives of Hmong people. Mai Neng Moua writes of Laos, "We Hmong lived our art ... It was such an integral part of our everyday lives that there was no separation between what was art and what was culture." Traditional Hmong arts still practiced in the United States include sewing *paj ntaub*, playing instruments such as *qeej*, singing and dancing, and storytelling. *Paj ntaub* traditionally contains intricate geometric patterns; since the 1970s, it also represents folktales and real history, such as the flight of Hmong refugees from Laos. Traditional instruments played by Hmong people range from the blowing of leaves, to flutes, to *qeej*, an instrument that has a particular importance at Hmong funerals. At a New Year celebration, one might hear the poignant sounds of a traditional Hmong song or view the stylized, intricate patterns of hand and foot movements associated with a traditional dance. Storytelling is an art that allows Hmong people—and, in fact, all cultures—to pass on important information, ideas, and beliefs to younger generations.[2]

This chapter focuses on the role of arts in the identity of four young Hmong Americans. For these young people, painting, animation, hip-hop, and drama may provide different tools not available in the traditional arts, yet the influence of tradition is present in their lives. In weaving together disparate cultural styles with elements of traditional arts, these four Hmong Americans are transforming their own identities as well as the community around them.

Portraits of the Artists as Hmong Americans

The concept of identity has come to have many different meanings. In discussing the influence of the arts on the identity formation of Hmong

Americans, this chapter acknowledges that an individual is continually involved in rewriting his or her self-concept over time. Moreover, the concept of "protean identity," wherein the postmodern self can adapt to a variety of shapes and forms, seems particularly relevant to the bicultural experiences of young Hmong Americans. This chapter also affirms that the performing and visual arts can play a powerful role in reshaping ethnic boundaries and identities.[3]

This chapter presents portraits of four university students whose artistic pursuits have helped to shape their identities as Hmong Americans: Chan Vang, a painter whose work depicts the war, the refugee crisis, and the struggle to adapt to life in the United States; Ma Lee Xiong, a dancer and singer whose stylistic influences range from Southeast Asia and India to China and the urban United States; Shervun Xiong, who experiments with song, drama, and creative writing; and Hue Vang, who uses animation and theater to retell Hmong folktales and history. Although each of their stories is unique, they are also representative of dozens of Hmong American students on the University of Wisconsin–Oshkosh campus who participate actively in artistic endeavors. Ma Lee Xiong, Shervun Xiong, Hue Vang, and Don Hones met through classes and conferences at the university. Indeed, Don Hones teaches with Txawjthoj Vang, who is the father of Chan Vang, and the families have known each other for more than ten years. Amy Debroux, a graduate student and writer interested in Hmong culture, assisted in completing this project.

Reflecting on Hmong American identity formation as mediated by the arts, the coauthors engage in a process of narrative research and analysis. Intending to choose narrative forms that engage readers aesthetically as well as critically, we occasionally represent the young artists' spoken word as poetry. We use grounded theory to examine important themes that emerge from the portraits of the coauthors.[4]

Chan Vang

Chan's wife opens the door to the Vang home, welcoming us inside. Kia, his mother, gives us a big smile and warm "Nyob zoo!" A visiting Hmong couple sits on the couch. Groups of smiling people—and some not smiling—dressed variously in traditional Hmong or "American" attire, look down from photos lining the wall. Chan leads us past them

*to the basement. It could be any basement, except for the oil paintings
of war and refugee camps that rest against the cinderblock wall. The
final painting in the series shows an elder, seated, telling stories to a
group of children; in the background, the stories take shadowy shapes
of village huts, mountains, and helicopters. When interviewed about
his growth as an artist, Chan will say, "I think many of our artistic
skills come through these stories, which our imagination paints so well,
we only need to transfer it to our hands and a brush." The washing
machine whirs and Hmong voices hum upstairs as Chan explains his
artistic journey.*

Many Hmong students growing up think: How can I help my culture? How can I preserve something? There is much in our history that people, including my younger brother and sister, do not know about. They know about the Vietnam War, but they do not know the stories behind it. We grew up hearing the stories that my mom and dad told us, but my younger brother and sister never heard those stories. So painting is my way of preserving the stories for the next generation, a generation that is more visual, that does not have much time to sit down and listen to a story. Through these paintings, I can preserve the stories they told me.

The first painting I did was based on a dream. I always remember my dad saying that he still has nightmares about being back in Laos during the war. So I started with a watercolor of my dad sleeping and his nightmare. My professor saw that and said, "You should hold onto this theme." The professor involved me in a collaborative grant project with funding to purchase materials and develop a theme. Last summer, I went out and talked to elders, interviewing them about the stories they remember and then interpreting the stories through my own eyes. I am not seeing through their eyes; I am just getting the stories and interpreting in my own way. I wanted to do a storyline with a beginning, middle, and end. This is the first time in my life where I could find a theme and go with it.

A painting of a man on a motorcycle, pulling a long chain tied to a cloud of people and events, is one I call "Chained to Your Past." Growing up, I really wanted to be American. When I was in kindergarten, I did not know English, and the first thing I did was to look around to see if there was anyone with black hair like me. I did not know how to communicate, so I had to find someone who could help me. Luckily, I had a friend who got here before I did. He knew English, so I stuck with him. Later, others would stick with me, too. We had a little group that could communicate together.

Growing up we wanted to be
American
instead of being Hmong.
Being Hmong was so old-fashioned,
like your mom.
Everyone wanted to be Americanized.
You try to run from the past,
being Hmong,
the war,
history.
In my painting,
I accept the past.
This is my past.
I have to either cherish it,
to help other people realize it
and learn from it,
or ignore it,
like many people do.

Another series of paintings entitled "Evolution" shows that there are certain defining moments in our lives. The first one I did was of a Hmong lady at the garden. The second one was a soldier going to war. After the war, Hmong were put into refugee camps, fleeing the genocide in Laos, crossing over to Thailand. Then the first generation had to get used to life in America. The painting I did for that was of a little girl staring across the street at a park. She wants to be at the park but is separated. The idea and the feeling I wanted to get across was that we always wanted to be American, but other people were judging us for the way we dressed and the way we lived. The child is wondering if she can go there or not. With the Main Street Bridge in Oshkosh as a backdrop, the last painting is of a father in a suit, with his child, taking a picture near the lake. As Hmong Americans, we do not know where history is going to take us.

I want to go back to Laos and Thailand, especially where the refugee camp used to be. I want to be in the presence of the place where I was born.

I want to paint the landscape, the people in the villages, the real life, and the beauty of the land. I also plan to go to graduate school for a degree in art. Because teenagers are losing the language and culture, I want to show how they feel confused. Hmong are being separated from each other even within their culture. We deal with problems that other Americans deal with, but the battles are different. I want to reach into Hmong culture and my own history.

Ma Lee Xiong

I got to know Ma Lee Xiong as a bright, cheerful, and hardworking student assistant at the office down the hall. Last spring, at the kickoff to Asian Heritage Month, I saw her dance for the first time. She and her three partners were dressed in white T-shirts and white pants, their music was hip-hop, and they had some great moves. She has danced to Bollywood tunes and the music of Thailand, but she likes to go back to the traditional dances of the Hmong in Laos, too. Much of her connection to music and song comes through the Christian and Missionary Alliance church.

Throughout my childhood, I was involved in some form of arts. I was active in choir until high school, when I decided to pursue fashion design and interior design. I loved the classes, but I was also afraid of the competition, so I moved on to elementary education, something with opportunities closer to home.

My family did not encourage me. I had my interests, so I motivated myself, but when I got scared, I did not pursue them. Except for when I learned how to play the violin. My mom thought that if I learned a musical instrument, it would help me with my studies, and that was definitely true! I was the oldest child in my family, so my siblings got stuck with me in practices, so that influenced them. When I see how much they have grown musically, I wonder how I would have turned out if I had been given more encouragement. Yet I am content, knowing that it is never too late for me to pick up something new.

Most of the music I sing is Christian, and I do much of it through our church, the Christian and Missionary Alliance. We sing in both Hmong and English. We are trying to make the programs more contemporary, but it is kind of hard because the older generation is still used to the Hmong hymns. Our pastor is very dedicated to the music. He also started the theater ministry, and my sister is involved in that. They have done a play about the Columbine shooting.

In dance, I like the more contemporary
hip hop.
But I like our traditional styles, too.
I think it is nice to do something traditional.
You do not see as much of that anymore.
What you do see are Indian songs.
Growing up we saw a lot of
Indian movies
dubbed in Hmong,
so someone would find some song they liked
put on the saris,
and dance to it.

The arts do not really make me feel Hmong. I feel more American. I suppose it is because Hmong girls are not encouraged to pursue these roles as much as boys since there are few Hmong instruments meant for girls to play. I was not encouraged to play the traditional music growing up.

I used to sew growing up because my mom did it. My grandma also taught me how to do some. She often made Hmong clothes for us. It is meaningful because it is the only real Hmong art that I was encouraged to do. I was too young to actually remember if my mom or grandma told me what the patterns symbolized, but I know that each pattern has a meaning. It is only a memory for me because I do not do it anymore, and I do not see my grandma as much anymore.

My identity is shaped by Christian music. Listening to it, I remember what I am supposed to be doing. That plays a role in who I am. Open to new ideas, I never had a problem with identifying myself as Hmong and American.

When I was growing up, our parents wanted us to study, to be lawyers and doctors. They still want us to get those high-paying jobs, but many realize that it is important for us to be happy.

Shervun Xiong

She sings Hmong love songs. She directs and acts in a full-length play about life in Laos in the 1950s. She is a voice in an animated film. She is writing a book, in Hmong and English, for children. Despite these and other endeavors, Shervun Xiong denies having any special artistic gifts. What is apparent about this tranquil young woman is her strong inter-personal connectivity and her willingness to collaborate in many artistic genres with other Hmong Americans of her generation.

When I was a child and we were naughty, we were forced to learn how to do cross-stitching and to make the different parts of the Hmong clothing. Learning it was special, but as we grew older, we had less time for it, and now I notice that we are starting to forget how to do it. Also, we do not wear Hmong clothing much anymore, not even at New Year celebrations. I try to encourage my friends to wear Hmong clothing, but they always say no. In the past, it was popular. Traditional sewing is a dying art, which is sad because it is something very special in Hmong culture. That is one reason why I want to do a children's book about Hmong New Year, explaining what happens each day, with some photographs on each page.

The Asian Heritage Month kickoff last year was my first time singing in public. But I wanted to participate, and I asked a friend if she wanted to sing in Hmong, so we picked out a song about a girl in a relationship and how she has to let go. Last year also was my first time acting in a play. Doing a play was an activity I had pushed for us to try. We had attended a Hmong conference where they acted a play out. We talked about it when we came back and decided we should do it.

As a group on campus, we have gotten to know each other as friends, engaging in various social activities, such as eating together, having a snowball fight, or ice-skating. Because we have become close, when we pass on the word about projects like the play, many people are excited to take part. When Kao and Malee wrote the most recent play, Hue added his ideas about traditional Hmong life, making the story more realistic. He has been a big part of all of the plays. Nancy and I directed, but Hue helped us. In the fall, we made the story, and in the spring we practiced and performed.

The 1950s and 1960s were an important time for Hmong people. In the play, we show young people talking through the wall at night, going to the New Year, and ball tossing. Everything is changing now, so we try to relate back. Many of our actors and actresses do not know much Hmong language and history, so as they go through the play, they are learning more about their heritage. They learn what you do in a traditional kitchen, what a kitchen looked like, and how the work was done. They are learning about history by acting.

Theater is a form that will interest children growing up today. They do not just have to look at history by reading a book. Instead, children can see history come to life on the stage. Then, what they read in school and on their own will be more meaningful.

I think the elders are sad, and I, too, am sad, because we are losing the traditional arts. I miss the songs, and I do not even know what they are saying anymore. But we are developing new arts. At the conference, we heard an artist talk about "the new *paj ntaub.*" He painted over a *paj ntaub.* Some of the elders were very angry with him for doing that, but he explained that our culture is changing. In his view, we need a *paj ntaub,* but a different kind of *paj ntaub.* You can still see the *paj ntaub* behind his work.

Art is what we relate to.
When I think about Hmong,
I always think about
paj ntaub
and the mountains.
We always relate to *paj ntaub,*
and to the countryside
Laos and Thailand.
We relate to the New Year.
That is who we are.

Hue Vang

In the fall of 2008, several Hmong students in the Hmong Language, Culture, and Learning class developed a two-hour presentation for the campus community entitled "Being Hmong and Being American." A highlight was a thirty-minute animated film (Hmong with English subtitles) entitled Txoj Dab Neeg Kawb[kawg] *(Myth of End). It was a tale combining the story of the flood with the story of Shee Yee, the first shaman. There were scary demons, heroic rescues, and final scenes depicting the plight of Hmong refugee people, including those who continue to die in the jungle. Behind these scenes we hear the voice of the boy saved from the flood:*

"Now I know why the clouds cried tears of never ending rain that day and flooded the world . . . But I am not the sky, nor am I the clouds. I am a man . . . a person with a dream. I have a mind. I also have hands, and so this is enough for me to make dreams into reality."[5]

Hue Vang, the soft-spoken young author of this work, has been a leader in the artistic endeavors of Hmong Americans at University of Wisconsin–Oshkosh, as they strive to define who they are and to make a difference for their community.

I make art because it can express ideas and feelings that words cannot. I respect the power of words, but personally I am intrigued that a couple of ebony strokes can open up a person's conscience.

Growing up, I loved doing art so much that it would get me in trouble. In elementary school, my teacher sent a letter to my parents reporting that I was drawing a Ninja Turtle during my reading hour. While it was true that I should have been reading, I had promised a friend I would draw him a picture. My friends, then and now, have always encouraged me to keep on making art. People admire my drawings, and that has inspired me to keep going. So, in ways, I make art for them also, for believing in me.

In high school many Hmong students spoke highly about Hmong culture, and yet they criticized the New Year celebrations or complained that the traditional clothing was silly looking. That behavior is contradictory. I did not mock my culture, nor at the time was I interested in it. When I came to the University of Wisconsin–Oshkosh as a freshman, I barely had any Hmong friends because I was shy. Semesters later, I met so many Hmong students who wanted to do things for their culture. Coming to college, joining the Hmong Student Union (HSU), and seeing how united the members were made me realize how important culture is. I knew that people liked my art, so I thought, *why not use my art to support my culture, a culture that is disappearing?*

I loved directing and handling the annual plays for HSU, which brought Hmong American students closer. The plays were about Hmong lives, and we were amazed to realize how little we knew about our own culture. We would have questions and discussions about why Hmong people did certain things, then go and ask our friends and families for answers. We would regroup and share what we found out. Doing so became a great learning experience. The play attracted many Hmong American students that I had never met before on campus; some of them were very talented. If it had not been for the plays, I doubt I would ever have met them.

Animation to me was fascinating, but I never had the opportunity to use the technology. In high school I took a class that taught animation using Photoshop. In college, for the HSU Conference, I had the opportunity to make a visual presentation of the Hmong folktale "The Orphan Boy and His Wife." The feedback was overwhelming. I was also glad that non-Hmong found my work interesting, so I focused on folktales as a central theme in my art.[6]

I created *Myth of End* for the University of Wisconsin–Stevens Point Hmong Student Conference. I have always wanted to do the flood story (about the origin of the eighteen clans) because every culture has a flood story. But I did not follow the traditional story. A character named Shee Yee was placed into the story, which would be like putting Paul Bunyan in the tale of Pecos Bill. They are two completely different stories. Before I presented, I made sure to tell the audience that this was not a traditional depiction of the story. In my version, Shee Yee took the role of the main character because he was the first shaman. Shamanism is so important to our culture, and I wanted Shee Yee to be the hero. These two stories fit so well together for me: Shee Yee would help the boy and the girl to ward off the demons, escape the flood, and in doing so, the couple would go on to re-create the world anew, without evil and hate.

The main point of *Myth of End* is the final ten minutes. Pictures of Hmong people from the 1960s to now show the audience that we have a choice to make a difference with our opportunities, so our culture will not be a myth that is ending. Many viewers have told me afterward that the final moments of the animation were what they remembered most because it had an emotional impact on them. As an artist, that was my sign of successful work: for them to be intrigued enough to watch with their hearts but also to see this deeper meaning.

In *Myth of End,*
the man who has survived the flood says,

"I am not the sky,
nor the clouds.
I am just a man,
a person with a dream.
I have a mind,
and I have hands.
This is enough
for me to make dreams into reality."
We don't have to be godly
to have special powers.
A brain and hands is enough.
We have the tools already.
We can create anything.

I would like to make something original that means more than just car-toons. With the world as the curious child and my animation as the elder storyteller, I want to use art and the folklore of Hmong people to express my culture.

Portrait of a Teacher Scholar

He gardens, but he has never planted rice. He has made many journeys of choice and can never really comprehend what it was like to flee for one's life out of Laos. He loves music but cannot blow a leaf to save his soul. As the ninth of eleven children, he finds common ground with Hmong Americans with large families. As a language learner, he can only marvel at his friend Txawjthoj Vang, who speaks Hmong (White and Green), Laotian, Thai, Chinese, French, English, and a few phrases of Spanish. Through his work with Txawjthoj at the university and his engagement with Hmong friends in the community and in the garden, Don Hones has embarked on a journey of discovery that has influenced his scholarship, his teaching, and most importantly, his personal life.

I first encountered Hmong refugees in San Francisco, California, back in the 1980s. Little children used to come through the sidewalk cafes sell-ing garlic that had been gleaned from the fields in area farms. I remember seeing an elderly Hmong woman walking down the street, a long pole balanced on her shoulders, with two full bags of crushed aluminum cans at either end of the pole.

In Minneapolis, I had many refugees from Laos in my adult ESL classes. I will always remember what they taught me about human strength in desperate situations. One day, we were working with an "easy reader" with a story about a very small woman who picked up the front of her car so that her son could crawl out from under the wheel. "Isn't that amazing?" I asked my students. "Have any of you ever done anything amazing like that?" There was a pause before one of the students raised his hand and said, "I swam across the Mekong River in thirty minutes!" Then all the people in the room started talking excitedly about how they had escaped from Laos. In the next few days and weeks these refugee students from Laos, working with basic expressions in English, opened up a new world for me.

I believe my work with the Hmong American community definitely has shaped my career as a scholar and a teacher. My dissertation concerned the story of Shou Cha, a Hmong refugee in Lansing, Michigan, whom I had read about in the newspaper: he was shot and seriously wounded when exiting a grocery store a few blocks from his house. Shou's story combined family tradition (his great-grandfather had called down lightning to thwart the attacking Chinese); real history of Laos before and after 1975; spiritual beliefs ranging from shamanism to fundamentalist Christianity; family concerns; and the importance of education. As a bilingual liaison at a school of choice, Shou played an integral part in connecting the school to the community. This dissertation and subsequent book and articles were largely responsible for my invitation to work at the University of Wisconsin–Oshkosh.

Since coming to Wisconsin, I have been blessed with many wonderful teachers of Hmong culture. However, Txawjthoj Vang stands out as my greatest teacher for Hmong language and cultural practices. We met shortly after my arrival in Oshkosh in 1997. Like Shou Cha, Txawjthoj plays the integral role of bilingual assistant and liaison between the public schools and the Hmong community. Furthermore, since 2000, he also has been my partner in teaching a university course: Hmong Language, Culture, and Learning. Originally, this course was intended for teachers adding licenses in ESL or bilingual education, with the goal of building cultural knowledge about Hmong people as well as empathy and support for native speakers of Hmong who are learning English. Txawjthoj has taught basic Hmong language to hundreds of our teacher candidates. He also provides an understanding of history and cultural practices that brings much authenticity to the course. When we are not teaching together, my favorite times with Txawjthoj and his family are out on the farm, where we share some garden space. I admit most humbly that I will never be able to garden as well as the Vangs, nor be able to butcher a chicken with the ease and skill that Kia (Txawjthoj's wife) possesses. Yet, it is a pleasure to learn from the Vangs and spend some time tending the field together.

The Hmong Language, Culture, and Learning course recently has attracted dozens of Hmong American university students, most of whom are not education majors. Most are seeking a course that in some way will inform them about—and honor—their heritage. These young people have transformed the course by their presence and the many perspectives about culture and cultural change they bring. Moreover, in the area of the arts, already addressed by Txawjthoj in the realm of traditional music, Hmong American students have made a huge contribution: through song, theater, storytelling, and animation, they have informed our class about Hmong American culture in transition. Acknowledging the impact of the arts on his own son, Txawjthoj has encouraged other Hmong youth who are in the process of exploration and identity development through the arts. I look forward to further evolution of the artistic strand in our course and continued flowering of the arts among Hmong Americans at our university and in our community.

Themes in the Portraits

Despite important differences among the four young Hmong Americans, several common themes emerge from their portraits. First, they all address the role of their families in shaping their artistic choices. They also highlight the deep support they have from a community of friends. They all mention how a strong oral storytelling tradition has influenced their art. Each feels compelled to use the arts to honor traditions as well as give something back to the community. Finally, they all address through their art a dialogue between the old and the new, between traditional Hmong culture and Hmong American identity.

Family plays a huge role in the lives and the artistic endeavors of the Hmong Americans in this study. All of the young Hmong Americans who share their views in this chapter speak about the career goals their parents have for them. Most parents in the Hmong American community have endured many hardships and therefore wish their children to be economically successful. For this reason, it is not surprising that Hue Vang has been channeled toward a medical career, or that Chan Vang, Shervun Xiong, and Ma Lee Xiong all have pursued careers in teaching, at least initially. The arts may be overlooked due to this focus on economic betterment. Hue was encouraged to study his math and science and not to draw so much. Shervun was discouraged from dancing, and Ma Lee was encouraged to take up the violin largely in the belief that it would help her academically. Both Shervun and Ma Lee participated in the art of *paj ntaub*, although over the years they have not continued with sewing. Chan gained the encouragement of his family once he had shown his success by selling a piece of sculpture and by his efforts to include elders in his project to depict the history of Hmong refugees through painting. Hmong parents do often tacitly support their children's artistic pursuits. Many attend cultural events on campus such as Asian Heritage Month kickoff and the Hmong Student Union Conference.

Leaving their families for the university, these four Hmong Americans continue the process of rewriting their "selves." The role of friends in this process of identity transformation and in supporting artistic pursuits seems paramount. Hue refers to the Hmong students who put together plays and other activities as "a happy family." Indeed, it is clear that from an early age Hue enjoyed enthusiastic support for his artwork from friends. Similarly, the public performances of people like Shervun, Ma Lee, and others testify to the solidarity these young people feel with each other. Ma Lee referred to a group of "friends here who really encourage each other, and we help each other out with artistic projects." The performance stage becomes a platform for experimentation—for testing one's own limits—with the knowledge that friends in the audience are there not only to applaud but also to collaborate.[7]

Hmong storytelling tradition is behind the paintings of Chan, the animation of Hue, and the works of theater in which Shervun and Ma Lee have taken part. Stories passed down by elders clearly have left an indelible mark on the imaginations of young Hmong Americans. The rich folklore and mythology of Hmong people inspire Hue's animation. Stories of life in Laos and America are dramatized in original plays each year at the HSU conference. Chan, who chronicles the events of the Hmong refugee experience in his paintings, commented, "In my painting, I accept the past. This is my past." Clearly, each of these young Hmong Americans cares deeply about Hmong history and culture, and each seeks ways to pass on this culture to the next generation.

Art may be individual, but it is often a contribution to a community. Chan, Ma Lee, Shervun, and Hue all worry about the fate of Hmong culture in the United States. Each seeks, through the arts, ways to share the stories and traditions of Hmong people with a new generation of Hmong American children as well as with Americans of all backgrounds. Shervun speaks of this as a learning experience for all involved, especially in the plays produced on campus: "Many of our actors and actresses do not know much Hmong language and history, so as they go through the play, they are learning more about their heritage." Hue said, "I want to use art and our folklore to tell the world about our culture." With older forms such as *paj ntaub,* traditional dance, and song as well as newer forms such as animation, these young people seek to share the world of their culture with others. They voice a strong need to give something back to the community; for them, keeping stories alive honors the elders who made the dangerous journey to the United States.

Hmong American identity for the young people in this study is forged through old traditions and new hopes for the future. It is a protean identity in its adaptability to new circumstances and new tools, yet it also features a return to traditional sources for renewal and inspiration. Ever present in the four portraits is a concern for the loss of Hmong traditions coupled with a commitment to retell old stories in new ways. Chan's paintings, especially the "Evolution" series, reflect a refugee past as well as the challenges and successes of life in the United States. In the *Myth of End,* Hue combines two Hmong stories into a new creation. The Hmong language lives on in the music of contemporary ballads sung by Shervun and Christian hymns sung by Ma Lee. The same dancers spin to hip-hop, whirl to the songs of Bollywood movies, and still strive to master the subtle movements of hands and feet that their parents brought over the mountains from Laos.[8]

Culture is in motion, like a dance. Young Hmong Americans such as Chan, Ma Lee, Shervun, and Hue are part of that dance. They know the steps, and the music may change. But they have a creative force, a tradition, and community support, and this keeps them reaching for new heights. In the words of Hue Vang: "We have the tools already. We can create anything."

NOTES

1. Kou Yang, "An Assessment of the Hmong American New Year and Its Implications for Hmong American Culture," *Hmong Studies Journal* 8 (2007): 1–32. Kristin Tillotson, "Minnesota Hmong Are Proud of Their Central Role Clint Eastwood's New Film 'Gran Torino,'" Minneapolis *Star Tribune,* Jan. 9, 2009. Yer J. Thao, "Culture and Knowledge of the Sacred Instrument *Qeej* in the Mong-American Community," *Asian Folklore Studies* 65.2 (2006): 249–67.

2. Grace Wang, "Interloper in the Realm of High Culture: 'Music Moms' and the Performance of Asian and Asian American Identities," *American Quarterly* 61.4 (2009): 881–903; and Kimberly Powell, "Drumming against the Quiet," *Qualitative Inquiry* 14.6 (2008): 901–25. David G. Garcia, "Culture Clash Invades Miami," *Qualitative Inquiry* 14.6 (2008): 865–95. Kristin Lee Moss, "Cultural Representation in Philadelphia Murals: Images of Resistance and Sites of Identity Negotiation," *Western Journal of Communication* 74.4 (2010): 372–95; and Celeste-Marie Bernier, "'You Can't Photograph Everything': The Acts and Arts of Bearing Witness in Joseph Rodriguez's Still Here: Stories after Katrina," *Journal of American Studies* 44.3 (2010): 535–52. Lisa K. Neuman, "Painting Culture: Art and Ethnography at a School for Native Americans," *Ethnology* 45.3 (2006): 173–92. Mai Neng Moua, ed., *Bamboo Among the Oaks: Contemporary Writing by Hmong Americans* (St. Paul: Minnesota Historical Society Press, 2002), 5.

3. Philip Gleason, "Identifying Identity: A Semantic History," *The Journal of American History* 69.4 (1983): 910–31; Erik Erikson, *Childhood and Society* (New York: W. W. Norton, 1950); Lev Vygotsky, *Mind in Society: Development of Higher Psychological Processes* (Cambridge, MA: Harvard University Press, 1978); and George Spindler and Louise Spindler, "What Is Cultural Therapy?" in eds. George Spindler and Louise Spindler, *Pathways to Cultural Awareness: Cultural Therapy with Teachers and Students,* (Thousand Oaks, CA: Corwin Press, 1994): 1–33. Mark Freeman, *Rewriting the Self: History, Memory, Narrative* (New York: Routledge, 1993). Robert Lifton, *The Protean Self: Human Resilience in an Age of Fragmentation* (New York: Basic Books, 1993). Kimberly Powell, "Drumming against the Quiet"; and Ephrat Huss, "Houses, Swimming Pools, and Thin Blonde Women: Arts-Based Research through a Critical Lens with Impoverished Bedouin Women," *Qualitative Inquiry* 13.7 (2007): 960–89.

4. D. Jean Clandinin, Annie Davies, Karen Keats Whelan, Janice Huber, and Chuck Rose, "Telling and Retelling Our Stories on the Professional Knowledge Landscape," *Theory and Practice* 7.2 (2001): 143–56; Donald Hones, "Known in

Part: The Story, the Teller, and the Narrative Researcher," *Qualitative Inquiry* 4.2 (1998): 225–48; and Donald Polkinghorne, "Narrative Configuration in Qualitative Analysis," in eds. J. Amos Hatch and Richard Wisniewski, *Life History and Narrative* (Bristol, PA: Falmer, 1995): 5–23. David Brunner, *Inquiry and Reflection: Framing Narrative Practice in Education* (Albany: State University of New York Press, 1994). Dwight Conquergood and Paja Thao, *I Am a Shaman: A Hmong Life Story with Ethnographic Commentary* (Occasional Paper No. 8; Minneapolis: University of Minnesota, Southeast Asian Refugee Studies Project, 1989); Donald Hones and Shou Cha, *Educating New Americans: Immigrant Lives and Learning* (Mahwah, NJ: Lawrence Erlbaum, 1999); Lauren Richardson, "The Consequences of Poetic Representation: Writing the Other, Rewriting the Self," in eds. Carolyn Sue Ellis and Michael G. Flaherty, *Investigating Subjectivity: Research on Lived Experience* (Newbury Park, CA: Sage, 1992), 125–40; and Donald Tedlock, *The Spoken Word and the Work of Interpretation* (Philadelphia: University of Pennsylvania Press, 1983). Barney Glaser and Anselm Strauss, *The Discovery of Grounded Theory: Strategies for Qualitative Research* (New York: Aldine de Gruyter, 1967); and Anselm Strauss and Juliet Corbin, "Grounded Theory Methodology: An Overview," in eds. Norman Denzin and Yvonne Lincoln, *Handbook of Qualitative Research* (Thousand Oaks, CA: Sage, 1994): 273–85.

5. Hue Vang, *Txoj Dab Neeg Kawb*/Myth of End. (2006), www.youtube.com/user/schenman (accessed Nov. 15, 2011).

6. Hue Vang, *The Orphan Boy and His Wife* (2006), www.youtube.com/user/schenman (accessed Nov. 15, 2011).

7. Mark Freeman, *Rewriting the Self: History, Memory, Narrative* (New York: Routledge, 1993). Kimberly Powell, "Drumming against the Quiet"; and Ephrat Huss, "Houses, Swimming Pools."

8. Lifton, *The Protean Self.*

< 13 >

Making the Invisible Visible

Confronting the Complexities of Identity, Family, and Culture through Art

KOU VANG

Art and History

We are surrounded by art in all the things we see, touch, hear, feel, and experience. The book you are holding in your hands was created and designed by artists. Artists also selected the colors, created the patterns, chose the fabric, and designed the style of clothing you are wearing. Art enriches our lives and adds texture to everything we come in contact with from the minute we awake. Since grade school, art has been an outlet for me to explore my innermost thoughts. Art is a form of expression that also brings about reconciliation: to make sense of situations and interpret the world and people around me. My art expresses from the heart what sometimes cannot be said. It is this inner force that has given me strength and courage to step outside of my comfort zone to examine the intersection of culture, environment, and identity.

As I reflect on my childhood in the refugee camps, my memory wanders back to a young girl with hair caked in light brown dirt. She is dressed in a dusty cotton T-shirt to keep cool during the hot, humid Thai summers. She is wearing an almond-shaped amulet, wrapped with *paj ntaub*, around her neck. Mother says it's to keep sickness away. As I start to compose and paint this vision of myself as a child, I feel bursts of energy surging through my hands as the oil paint melds with the canvas. I apply gentle brushstrokes with transparent tan colors. As I add more paint, the figure begins to emerge from the background. *Where have all the children who were there at the camp gone to? Are they alive?* I wonder as I paint dark brown, heavy lines to outline the figure. My heart longs for the worry-free mind and pure heart of the child I once was. I do not stop until I complete the image I envision. In front of me is my creation, a painting of a young girl holding a board with numbers on it, like a mug shot. This image of myself

< 209 >

also represents many with similar stories, immigrants who were persecuted and tried to escape their conflicted situation. As I look thoroughly
at the finished work, I see a young girl without a home, a country, a place
to belong. She has three things left to bring with her on her journey as a
refugee: her hope, dreams, and memory.

I appreciate and understand the sacrifices made for the survival
of Hmong people. Many from my parents' generation have died without
leaving so much as a trace that they ever existed, without anyone knowing the hardships they bore in their hearts, without ever sharing the tales
that connect the United States to Laos. Many came to America and lived
as if they had already died. Some died feeling as if they had nothing to
live for. Others tried to forget where they came from and what they had
experienced but were haunted. Overall, most feel fortunate to be alive and
to have been given a second chance, if not for themselves, then at least for
their children.

Out of tens of thousands of Hmong who died in the Vietnam War, a
small but significant percentage was spared to bear witness to the evils of
humanity. Those who have seen these evils with their own eyes help to
connect us in a more immediate way to our shared history by telling us
their stories.

We were surrounded and trapped by an army of thirty soldiers.
They were going to execute all of us. They lined us up at the edge
of a small riverbank and began to slash the throats of the people
in our group. There were only three people left before it was my
brother's turn to be killed. My father was not a Christian, but
he began to chant up to the sky asking for *tswv ntuj* (lord of the
heavens) to bring mercy and justice on us. He shouted for everyone to call. We all chanted, repeating it as the soldiers made us
kneel and placed our faces to the ground.

I remember it was ten o'clock in the morning, but the sky suddenly turned pitch black. Hail the size of eggs began to fall from
the sky. Lightning began flashing all around. Large gusts of wind
blew through. We thought that we would surely die this time, if not
by the hand of these soldiers then by the storm. I could feel charges
of lightning around my feet and legs. My father told us to begin

feeling our way out. He shouted for everyone to go to the right. I could hear frightening cries and yells all around.

There was so much confusion, but the clarity is that the storm was a miracle. This moment has always been an unforgettable memory for me. It is also an experience that determined for me that there was a greater power in the world (Chao Her).[1]

History speaks for itself; too often it repeats itself. What is not said is not and cannot be recorded into history. During my educational years in the early 1990s at Green Bay West High School and the University of Wisconsin–Green Bay, Hmong history, let alone Hmong art, was not mentioned in class or in history books. Where was Hmong history, and why was it not in the history books as part of the Vietnam War?

In the search for identity, I listened and heard the voices of others telling our stories, imposing their "educated" views on us Hmong. What I did was turn to my community and people to hear their own accounts. I found hidden stories, oral tales, spiritual and divine encounters, and collective experiences that define and bind us as a community. This newfound knowledge called out to me to be organized and translated in the only possible form I knew: through art.

For me, art exposes hidden passages through which the stories of Hmong people unfold, particularly those of women. The passion to create is driven from the heavens, explodes from within, and involves my memory, emotion, body, heart, and soul. It is in this process that I conceptualize and create art that captivates, enlivens, and is made without fear.

A Family Story

In 1979, my family and I left Laos, a war-torn country, alongside thirty-five thousand other Hmong refugees. We were a small fraction of the more than two hundred thousand Hmong who became refugees throughout the world as a result of persecution by the communist Pathet Lao regime that took over Laos at the end of the Vietnam War. We spent four years waiting in Ban Vinai refugee camp in Thailand, virtually incarcerated in cramped, noisy, impoverished conditions. We were considered nonhuman. We had no rights or privileges. We were ready to start a new lease on life.

Our destination was the United States of America. Through the compassion and generosity of a church in Rochelle, Illinois, my family was given a fresh start in a new world. From 1976 until the mid-1980s, one hundred sixty thousand Hmong resettled in the United States and other countries including Australia, Canada, and France. Many Hmong stayed behind in Thailand refugee camps, afraid to leave, waiting for peace to return. Some went into hiding in Laos, hoping for the atrocities to stop. Although the Vietnam War had ended, Hmong in Laos were still being persecuted.

My new, structured American life started with attending kindergarten, playing "Ring around the Rosie" with Caucasian children, taking naps on blue mats, and stopping by the candy shop on the way home from school for one-penny Tootsie Rolls. Though I went to school with my Caucasian counterparts, my home life was a typical Hmong life, full of responsibilities. I was the oldest daughter of ten siblings and often played the role of a parent. Having this responsibility thrust upon me at an early age forced me to think about Hmong culture in a different way: What was normal? What was cultural? What was traditional?

Here I was, in America, learning a new culture, yet I was supposed to maintain my parents' Hmong culture. This added "thinking critically about who we were as a family" to my everyday responsibilities. When non-Hmong girls were playing with dolls and just being kids, I was taking care of my siblings, washing dishes, cooking, and cleaning. My responsibilities were simply understood as a necessary part of my life. Though it made me grow up quickly, this understanding also helped me become more adaptable. I became adept at integrating my culture with my new life in America, until our family unity was threatened in a way I had not expected.

Family love is unconditional, it is sacred, and with that love comes trust and honesty, one of life's lessons that I was brought up to believe. During the summer after I finished sixth grade, my father brought home a pregnant eighteen-year-old Hmong woman to be my second mother, his second wife. He was my father, so how could I doubt his actions? I knew this could happen, but I never imagined it would happen to me. I was stunned and shocked at the betrayal, not just for my mother's sake but for the entire family.

Did my mother agree to this? How could my father betray us? Would I accept it if my future husband did this to me? All my life, my father had

searched for love and had control over his own destiny. It led him to take
another wife despite the impact it would have on our family. I have seen
the destruction of a marriage, the disintegration of a family, and the love
in my mother's eyes slowly dying. I have seen the abuse she endured at the
hands of a husband who had vowed to love and protect her.

> Domestic violence is a man's way of punishing women and putting
> them in their place. It's not right at all. That's why so many women
> in the Hmong community are emotionally and mentally disturbed.
> The abuse stays in our hearts forever. Most people never know about
> it. When it comes to committing suicide, let's not even dwell on
> that. I can't even think about that. It hurts too much. During an
> argument one time, my husband put a loaded gun up to my head
> and cocked it. I thought I was going to die at that moment. Visions
> of my children flashed before my eyes. He didn't go through with
> it, but I still hear the clicking of the bullet moving into the barrel.
> That incident vividly plays in my head like it was just yesterday.
> Even today, I'm still haunted by those memories.
>   I don't believe in love anymore. My experiences preoccupy my
> heart and soul and have given me enough suffering to last many
> lifetimes (Ying Yang, my mother).[2]

As a Hmong American woman, I cling to these poignant moments
that not only define who I am but also influence how my daughters and
their daughters will become women. Within these moments, I hear the
authentic voices that mold me—the voices of Hmong women who have
struggled to be heard, understood, respected, and loved for who they are.
I hear what I was once told—that I would have been so much more useful
to my family and clan if I had been born a male. I hear my mother wanting
to be loved as the only wife. I hear my ancestors' cries as they watched their
children being slaughtered, their siblings drowned, and their friends killed
for the sake of Hmong people gaining freedom. I hear their earthbound
spirits wandering the misty mountains of Laos.

These voices energize me to create art. As a child, I could not help my
mother when my father raised his hands to her. I did not know abuse was
wrong. I could not do anything when my father brought home another wife.
This was accepted and familiar at the time. As a newly married woman, I

did not know how to help the fifteen-year-old Hmong girl who pounded on my screen door, yelling *"Pab kuv, thov pab kuv os!"* ("Help me, please help me!") in her sarong as her husband chased after her with a stick to "discipline" her for coming home late from school. As a nineteen-year-old, I also did not know how to help the eighteen-year-old Hmong girl I translated for as she told the social worker she had been raped and had given birth to her attacker's child, or, more recently, a thirty-two-year-old Hmong woman with three children who was abandoned by her husband for a younger woman in Laos.

The Emergence of a Hmong American Artist

As math started in Mr. Amann's class, the subject and the warmth of the room easily swept my mind away from our course of study. Two hours until the school day was over, seven years of school left, four years of college to go . . . I could see myself in a suit, traveling around the world, becoming someone successful, making important decisions, finally proving that I was no different than any of my classmates. I had my goals set on what I wanted to do in life.

As a freshman at St. Norbert College in De Pere, Wisconsin, I declared pre-med as my major, thinking I would be a wealthy doctor who would heal and care for people. However, I quickly realized that biology and chemistry bored me to tears and I would be miserable in the medical field. Instead I followed my heart in pursuing a subject that might not be considered professional or looked upon highly, might not guarantee employment or a high salary, but would satisfy my soul and be something I could not live without.

Later I transferred to the University of Wisconsin–Green Bay to finish my undergraduate degree in art. I drew, painted, and sculpted, but making photos was where I felt alive and connected to the world. The artwork of Dorothea Lange, famous for her photograph "Migrant Mother," and Walker Evans under the supervision of Roy Stryker, enticed me because their work chronicled history—particularly life during the Great Depression—and their photography was art in its purest form. "One should use the camera as though tomorrow you'd be stricken blind. To live a visual life is an enormous undertaking, practically unattainable. I have only touched it, just touched it," remarked Lange. Their body of work was a catalyst to deepen my exploration of humanity, to make photos, not for the sake of making photos, but for others to carry that moment in time, whatever it was, with them.[3]

Being an artist has its ups and downs, its visionary and hesitant moments. Sometimes I am overwhelmed by the balancing act of being a mother, wife, career woman, photographer, community member, and artist, but sacrifices will always have to be made when opportunity arises or when art calls to be created. I am fortunate to have a career in the education field that allows me to be creative, serve others, and produce informational art, something that does not require as much soul but is nevertheless good practice for the trade.

Beside a strong woman stands a strong man who is defying traditional gender roles. My husband, Thai, cooks most of our family meals, helps me clean, does laundry, takes care of our daughters, and takes them wherever he goes. In our marriage, we support each other as husband and wife, true companions in life, but most important, we give each other the freedom and space to grow as individuals within our marriage, to strengthen our relationship and calling in life. My husband keeps me grounded; sometimes he pulls me back to earth, as he would say, and reminds me of the little things that need to be done. It took many years for us to fully accept one another for our quirks, faults, and individuality, but we are who we are because of each other.

Another Hmong woman, Dr. Chia Youyee Vang, a history professor at the University of Wisconsin–Milwaukee, has support from her husband and is an example of success in her profession and marriage. Although single during her undergraduate studies, she began raising a family during graduate school. In a recent interview with me, she observed, "I'm very fortunate in many ways. Everyone around me was willing to lend a helping hand while I was pursuing my doctoral degree. Grandma, my mother, and in-laws helped to watch my children. My brothers and brothers-in-law picked up my children when I had class and my husband was working. My husband took care of household chores and the children's activities. My hard work and sacrifices enabled me to achieve academically, but my husband and other family members made significant contributions."[4]

Today, she no longer lives among extended family members due to her move to the Milwaukee area from the Twin Cities. With no relatives nearby, she and her husband, Tong Yang, rely on each other. Work responsibilities, children's homework and extracurricular activities, and community involvement leave little room for error during the day. Clear communication and patience are required. The nature of her work entails frequent trips out of town, sometimes even out of the country, to conferences and symposiums. In her absence, her husband approaches the tasks with enthusiasm: "When I met my wife in college, I knew how goal-oriented she was. She studied hard but was also involved in so many other activities. She was so driven to succeed. I see our marriage as a partnership, but it is a partnership without defined roles. This means that we both do everything that's necessary for our family. When she's away, it is very difficult to get everything done. But it is also an opportunity for me to challenge myself."[5]

Paj Muas has many responsibilities as an advisor at an urban university, an adjunct instructor at a community college, an educational motivational speaker, and an advocate for human rights who speaks out against domestic abuse. She and her husband, Bon Xiong, are also redefining gender roles and what it means to be successful in a marriage: "When my husband and I married, we knew we were on our own. We understood that success meant compromising, reshaping our cultural roles for 'our' marriage to work. Without question, we both understood our positions as husband/ wife, partner, and parent. Whether he was to care for our children, cook and clean the house, or comfort the children while I was on business trips, my husband welcomes and accepts each challenge. I give thanks that he is a godly man who through his faith is appreciative and understands that when one of us succeeds, it is because we have support from the other."[6]

Art as a Perspective on Life

Listening to and learning from other women led me to conceive and create *Portraits of Hmong Women*, a combined photography and oral history collection that gives voice to Hmong American women across generations. This project exemplifies a larger theme within my work: to explore what it means to be Hmong American. *Portraits* frames specific issues, such as living with polygamy, losing cultural identity, breaking the mold of the traditional passive woman role, growing up bicultural, and coping with mental, emotional, and physical abuse. These are stories of ordinary Hmong women enduring extraordinary circumstances and surviving to share the lessons they learned. Experiences such as those of Paj Muas as a divorced Hmong woman are deeply moving:

A few months after my divorce, I began to hear rumors spread
about me. My Hmong community saw me as a threat and strongly
expressed how they felt about divorcées. People questioned why
and how I was divorced. Since I was born into a culture dominated
by men where women were blamed for "failed marriages," I was the
cause of my broken marriage. Everywhere I went people looked at
me out of the corners of their eyes and whispered behind my back.
They would tell their daughters to stay away from me and then
criticize my broken marriage. I was considered nothing more than a
slut, a whore, a bitch, a witch, and every degrading word that existed
in the Hmong language. Parents looked down on me, not knowing
my side of the story, and instead judged me as a *poj nrauj* [a deroga-
tory name given to divorced women]. Their words bit and stung me
deep in my heart and pushed unwanted tears out of my eyes. I was
regarded as someone who would corrupt their daughters' minds
and teach them to rebel against their future husbands (Paj Muas).[7]

In the process of photographing and writing, I imagined myself reliving
each woman's life, which enriched and added to my experience as a Hmong
American woman. Their contributions may seem small, but their experiences and the challenges they have overcome deserve tribute because of the
insight they offer into the untold lives of countless other Hmong women.

At the 2005 Hmong Women's National Conference, Dr. Dia Cha, a
leading authority on Hmong cultural traditions, observed, "The Hmong
woman has been told she is inferior. If one tells a peacock often enough
it is a penguin, don't be surprised if it jumps into rough waters. Likewise,
we Hmong women have for so long been told we possess only an inferior
grade of intelligence that we have come to believe it . . . we Hmong women
have been told so often—and for such a long time—that we are unintel-
ligent, that we have 'internalized' this inferiority and grown to accept it as
fact. We are peacocks in rough waters, left to wonder how we got there."[8]

For me, *Portraits* offers evidence that Hmong women are intelligent,
successful, adaptable, resilient, hardworking, compassionate, and dedicated. Hmong women are not afraid to seek justice or resolution, to try
to make sense of the situation they are in. They are not going to accept
the way things have always been done; instead, they act by doing what
is right. Their stories are a process of healing, of recognizing fear, anger,

and frustration and moving beyond these barriers to peace, love, harmony, and freedom. My motivation as an artist stems from looking at our future Hmong—my children—and knowing they will never really feel what it means to be Hmong today, right now! I want to, within my powers, document what is left. Not only sharing the stories and history of my people but also seeking justice for my mother's generation is the purpose and passion for creating art.

I have shared this body of work at dozens of universities, conferences, and presentations. The project has drawn attention in the media and surprising word of mouth interest in the Hmong American community. Many Hmong are supportive of what I am trying to highlight with this body of work, which is simply saying: hear us out, listen to our voices, feel what our hearts have been through. However, others consider me a threat to existing Hmong gender roles. I have been told that other Hmong or American women's situations are no business of mine. How dare I even question what a Hmong man does outside of the home since it does not involve me directly? At the Hmong American Women's Association, Inc. (HAWA) in Milwaukee, part of the *Portraits* collection is on permanent exhibition. In a recent incident, family members have threatened to take down some of the photographs, stating that such a display is "indecent" in a "whorehouse" and that any woman who goes there will eventually get a divorce. These family members asserted that they would not allow their relatives' respect to be blemished by any association with HAWA. How are we to change as a community when women's voices do not have weight or significance? How do we work together when self-interest and pride are stressed more than forgiveness, equality, and social justice?

Yet, I have had a surprisingly positive response from a group of elder Hmong men, who thanked me and said, "I'm so glad you came back to the Hmong American community to share your work with us. We are nobody and have lost hope in the new generation because after they've gotten their degrees, they forget about the ones who their parents called over for their high school and college graduations, who blessed them countless times with huge feasts and are proud of them for their successes. But soon they move away because they are afraid we won't be able to afford their hourly rate for their advice and expertise. They are afraid we are going to ask for help. You haven't forgotten us."

How can I forget? Born of both worlds, I will continue on my path in celebrating the Hmong journey in my creative artwork. Both of my projects now under way, *Heroes and Heroines* and *Generations,* celebrate Hmong American lives. Even in the darkest depth of human tragedy, hope is renewed.

Not long ago, I sat at the bedside holding my dying father's hand; his words of forgiveness and humility still resonate in my mind. My father said he was proud to have us as his children. He apologized for being born a poor, illiterate, uneducated person who was not able to give us the life we deserved. As he lay unable to speak or open his eyes, all that mattered at that moment was all that he did right in our lives to make us strong, successful human beings. Vitally important for me were these questions: Did I love him enough? Was I selfless in my love for him? Did I carry out my duty as his daughter to take care of and provide for him?

Progress and Resistance

Today, an increasing number of young Hmong American women are pursuing their dreams through education with the support of their family. Many Hmong American parents realize the benefits of having educated daughters. That was not always the case a decade ago. For example, May Herning Vang-Kue, a pharmacist in Green Bay, Wisconsin, found resistance in the mid-1990s from members of her family when she attempted to further her education: "Instead of support and encouragement [for going to pharmacy school], certain female members started rumors that I was having an affair [when I was married], going out, and not really studying . . . What would they gain from starting the rumors? Did they think I was going to stop what I was doing for their satisfaction?"[9]

Others have experienced similar friction within their social network. Resistance against and resentment toward women manifest themselves in many ways, and they are often worst when directed at those perceived to have defied the men in their lives to achieve their personal goals. In addition, women who hold traditional views tend to criticize those who break away from traditional roles. Often, the women who succeed in breaking away become educated and have successful careers. Many are strong-willed women who speak out against gender inequalities and live successful lives in the larger society. Unfortunately, some become targets of gossip and at times are belittled.

Although they may have successful careers in the larger community, they are not immune to such criticisms. Because they do not fit neatly into the category of what is perceived as a good Hmong woman, they are ostracized. Those in authoritative positions (e.g., parents and clan leaders) fear losing control of women who no longer have to depend on them to succeed. Maintaining control appears to be more important to some than treating the women's success as contributing to the advancement of the Hmong American community. It is, however, difficult to attribute such behavior solely to culture. On the contrary, criticism may likely be due to selfishness or envy. Some family and community members are very competitive. Rather than lending support to a successful woman, they prefer to put her down and minimize her accomplishments. Many Hmong women have used such negative treatments as motivation to achieve even more.

Individual Creativity and Cultural Expression

Today, Hmong American artists have begun to build a strong foundation in expressing who they are as writers, visual artists, musicians, poets, film producers, and fashion designers. We have taken a medium—be it writing, painting, singing, dancing, or film—to escape the noise around us, to connect and understand one another. Art brings us closer to safety or sometimes takes us to the brink of uncertainty, exposing us to new worlds that we could not know otherwise. Art is a medium to record and express authentically what is in our hearts.

Minnesota's Twin Cities are cultivating the talents of artists who have fearless energy and unstoppable momentum. Organizations such as Hmong Arts Connection (HarC) provide a place for writers, artists, and the community to experience Hmong literary and visual art in action. HarC supports emerging Hmong artists and serves as a resource center on Hmong arts and culture. It is also the home of *Paj Ntaub Voice*, the premier Hmong literary and arts journal in the United States. The Center for Hmong Arts and Talents (CHAT) is an organization that nurtures and develops Hmong artists who enhance the community; it creates a place for the arts in daily Hmong life by offering instruction, supporting creative works, and providing space for presentations. With the efforts of organizations like these, the potential for creativity is boundless.

Visual artists Seexeng Lee and Cy Thao, film artists Kang Vang and

Va-Megn Thao, and hip-hop/spoken word artist Tou Saiko Lee are among the many artists from the Twin Cities who have contributed greatly to the Hmong American community in their works. Many creative writers, such as Mai Neng Moua, Bryan Thao-Worra, Ka Vang, and Kao Kalia Yang, have garnered national and international attention. Hmong American artists have come a long way in taking risks, setting their own standards, and laying the groundwork for future generations. As Kao Kalia Yang reflected in a recent interview, "There's a real sense of urgency to the work we do: a very relevant and pervasive activism. Whether they articulate it as such or not—it is a movement of a people to the pages and the places that we feel we belong."[10]

A commonality present in the art movement shared by the artists and writers above is the lived experience of being embedded in Hmong and non-Hmong environments, neither rejecting nor accepting but being soaked in and embraced by that reality, including growing up in or surrounded by family who lived in survival mode. We are close to the trauma of great loss, when one human life mattered over another, when survival was prime and humans were put into unspeakable situations. These influences stay with us, seep into our skin, touch our hearts, and remain in our blood. Ka Vang made this clear in a recent interview:

> We, Hmong artists, are connected in our determination to express ourselves and our culture through the arts. We are individual pieces of a Hmong *paj ntaub* that will tell a story of the Hmong people . . . Some Hmong artists create art because we desire to capture our history while others create art for art's sake, . . . but regardless, we all have pride as Hmong artists. We know that we are exploring uncharted territories and what we discover and create will impact both Hmong and American cultures. Our voices will not be silenced because our talents cannot be contained. The world is just beginning to see the power of Hmong art.[11]

When the opportunity arose to escape the compounds of oppression, we sought it with a valiant heart and blazing passion. One hundred years from now, I hope my work is still alive. As I have said many times, the artwork I produce is not for me but a calling from a divine source for a devout purpose. The full intention of that purpose may or may not unfold in my lifetime but will make an impact. As Seexeng Lee told me, "Our voices, which were once shallow and weak, now have breadth and depth, because we lived it. As an artist, it is not my intention to interpret history but instead share my experiences, person to person, individual to community. This is what makes my voice authentic and everlasting."[12]

At Home as a Hmong American Artist

Being Hmong American today is profoundly humbling for me and for my generation. I cannot speak for everyone, but my observation is that our generation is the bridge between the old generation born and raised in Laos or Thailand and the new generation that was born or grew up in the United States. We have the capacity to travel back and forth between the generations—adapting, fostering, repairing, and modifying the structure within which we are placed and collecting the fragments of our invisible lives. In attempting to blend into Hmong and American cultures, we also stand at the margins of both, needing to know what came before us in order to construct what we can become. Proclaiming all the parts, positive and negative, that make up our identity can only help us become transformed in searching for the truth of our existence.

It is profound to be so aware of my culture and heritage in a time when so many people cannot distinguish who they are or where they came from. Hmong history is still tangible and living. America is home to my children and, eventually, to theirs. Though my children are of Hmong descent, they are Americans first. This makes me proud and yet fearful, for I observe so many young Hmong are unmindful of their past, wondering if life has anything else to offer them. Have they so easily forgotten or denied the odyssey that granted them existence? Without knowledge of the past, how can we build the future?

As a thirty-four-year-old Hmong woman, if I had stayed in Laos, I would hope to live to age fifty, have maybe ten children, perhaps be a first wife, possess a sixth grade education if I was lucky, be farming the land from dawn to dusk, and live simply, never knowing the awesome beauty, cultures, landscapes, and people that exist beyond the rice fields. I might be unaware of the powerful influence each of us has on the other as people of the world. To have known all the people that have crossed my path on this journey, people from all backgrounds and ethnicities, is to know that I have come home. America is my homeland, a place where my people and the community around us will flourish without being pushed to the mountaintops. It is a blessing and true privilege to be living at a time when we have the opportunity to shape and transform our Hmong American culture to prosper and have permanence.

A new chronicle of Hmong history is being written now. My story is part of that history. This is a new chapter in our long search for identity and acceptance, from China to Thailand or Vietnam or Laos to the United States. Changing and adapting to the environment around us, our identity and culture will continually transform for the good of our people. For so long, others have tried to conquer and erase Hmong people from history, but we continue to persevere. To keep our legacy alive and to have a successful future, we must revive our sense of responsibility to our people and the societies we live in as we act on our instinct for social justice. We also need to reach beyond our own communities to assist others who face injustices around the world. All humans are interconnected: the experiences of people in one corner of the world will inevitably affect all of us. As Nobel Peace Prize winner and author Elie Wiesel has explained, "Sometimes we must interfere. When human lives are endangered, when human dignity is in jeopardy, national borders and sensitivities become irrelevant. Wherever men and women are persecuted because of their race, religion, or political views, that place must—at that moment—become the center of the universe."[13]

So much has happened over the last thirty years. Still, in some ways, I feel as if life is just beginning. I once lost my homeland, my people, my belongings, and my identity. I went about searching, assembling the broken pieces of me, remembering who and what I was, dreaming of what I could be. I continue to nurture the person I have become, never losing sight of the will of my people and the power of hope. It took me many years to understand how it happened, but losing all of me was the one thing that set me free. Now, I have a home. Now, I know who and what I am: I am a Hmong American.

For more information or to be a part of the *Heroes and Heroines* and *Generations* photo documentary projects, contact Kou Vang (hmongartist@ yahoo.com).

NOTES

1. Chao Her, interview conducted by the author for *Portraits of Hmong Women,* an oral history and photography exhibition put together by Kou Vang and Christa Xiong, 2006, Milwaukee, WI (displayed at other cities from 2006–present).

2. Ying Yang, interview conducted by the author for *Portraits of Hmong Women.*

3. This quotation and additional information on the work of Lange can be found at "Dorothea Lange," www.oldstatehouse.com/exhibits/virtual/hard_times. aspx (accessed Nov. 15, 2011).

4. Dr. Chia Youyee Vang, interview with the author, Sept. 10, 2009.

5. Tong Yang, interview with the author, Sept. 10, 2009.

6. Paj Muas, interview with the author, Sept. 15, 2009.

7. Paj Muas interview.

8. Dia Cha, Hmong Women's National Conference, Minneapolis, Minnesota, Sept. 16, 2005.

9. May Herning Vang-Kue, interview with the author, Sept. 15, 2009.

10. Kao Kalia Yang, interview with the author, Sept. 15, 2009.

11. Ka Vang, interview with the author, Sept. 14, 2009.

12. Seexeng Lee, interview with the author, Sept. 10, 2009.

13. This quotation is taken from a lecture by Elie Wiesel on "Hope, Despair and Memory," which can be found at nobelprize.org/nobel_prizes/peace/laureates/ 1986/wiesel-lecture.html (accessed Nov. 15, 2011).

< 14 >

To See a Bigger World

The Home and Heart of a Hmong American Writer

KAO KALIA YANG

The chapter is an exploration of a Hmong American writer's journey into being. It is a lyric reflection of why and where a memoirist documents the internal and external landscape of belonging to a people, a place, and a dream. It is an intimate window into the heart and the mind of a young writer and an emergent teacher. This is an exploration of the intersections of the histories and realities that have fueled her abilities and aspirations to document in literature the human experience of being Hmong in America, being Hmong to the world.

"A story is like the stop sign on the road of life. It is supposed to make you stop, look both ways, check the trajectory of the horizon before you continue," said Uncle Eng. He added, "You will not find this in a book."

Uncle Eng was right. I could not find his words in any of the hundreds of books I have read over the years. This is the reason I put them into this one—so they could be found and credited to the man who gave me my first alternative reading of a story and its impact.

As a child, I wanted to be what so many other young Hmong children were encouraged to become: a doctor or a lawyer. We believed then, as did generations of immigrants and refugees before us (and as perhaps will those who come after), that we needed lawyers to protect the rights we never fully possessed and doctors to heal what was so broken in our bodies. For most of my life, I have been a Hmong girl in the United States. My family immigrated when I was six years and six months old. Like so many daughters who have crossed oceans to begin a life for a family, I was the product of what history and war had taught my people to be: creatures driven by needs, not wants.

I remember being a sophomore at Carleton College in Northfield,

< 225 >

Minnesota. We had been in the United States for nearly fifteen years, and the seasons were shifting around me. It was a lovely autumn evening. The sun was burnishing the late afternoon sky in layers of musky orange and soft pink. I was walking from downtown Northfield up the small rise to Carleton. A maroon car stopped by the side of the road in front of me. I thought the men were lost—people got lost looking for students in the small divide between Carleton and St. Olaf. I approached the car thinking I could help. When the passenger side window rolled down, I did not run. When the objects started flying out of the car window, I could not run. I stood still in the wash of soda and the cold of the ice cubes coming at me, the smell of ketchup, the refuse of McDonald's dripping down over me. Two white men were in the car, and they were calling me names I had never been. Their words again and again were "Go home!"

All of my life in America, when people ask, "What are you?"—my immediate answer is never "I am an American." It is always "I am Hmong." During my years of growing up in America, Hmong was all I had ever been and knew to be. It never crossed my mind that I was growing up Hmong American, that I fully belonged here. But in the safety of Carleton's brick buildings, its structures of learning and ideas, under the guise of education, on my way to becoming someone that few in my family had ever been—an educated person—I had forgotten momentarily that I was elsewhere than "home."

Home was a story of the tall mountains of Laos. It was a reminder of the refugee camps in Thailand, sites of dust and dirt, of children without pants sitting on pebbly ground. In Minnesota, it was a man walking from a white truck stenciled with the words "Meals on Wheels," carrying a foil tray with slices of turkey, biscuits, and gravy for our Thanksgiving dinner. Our Christmas gifts came late in the afternoon after Mom and the aunties waited in long lines for coloring books and stuffed animals at the Toys for Tots charity. Home was the annual New Year celebration at the River Centre in St. Paul and the Metrodome in Minneapolis.

It was HmongLand rising: the metaphorical space where belonging and home happens within me and, I suspect, many of my Hmong brethren. It is the community we comprise at events such as the Hmong New Year or the soccer tournaments, a site at which Hmong is celebrated and practiced, observed and examined.

It was McMurray Field at Como Park, a rented fence and high sports lights, the annual Independence Day Soccer Tournament. It was the smell of Tiger Balm on my grandma and the deep scent of the incense she burned to honor a grandpa I had never met. It was the boom of General Vang Pao's voice welcoming a people, yet one more time, yet out of time, into modernization and progress, into education and public life. Home had always been only a place from which we grew up. It was a site of departure, not a destination in the unknown.

In Northfield, Minnesota, the United States of America, the two men in the car told me to go home. I had entered into a battle that my parents had been working to keep at bay; the struggle was to achieve a belonging that they could not give because they had never owned it themselves.

The sky darkened and the wind picked up in the silence that followed the maroon car speeding away. The words they threw bounced up against me, tried to find points of entry. Across the street, a woman I had not noticed in the heat of the encounter pulled her toddler into herself and turned away. Her movement felt sudden. It, like the words, hit up against me. I fell silently inside myself. A stillness grew in the (w)hole of my being, and I felt for the first time the coldness of the wintry winds coming through. I did not know what to say. I had learned about institutional racism. I had seen men and women walk away from the stuttering accents of my mother and father. I had watched Hmong people fall and rise and get up to remember the speed of bullets flying through the jungle leaves, all because they had no place to belong to. In the stories that revolved around and inside of my home, I had learned about the fog of misunderstanding that causes so many to distrust my place in the world.

Suddenly, I yearned for the maroon car that had sped away to have left before the men could say those words to me. In that moment, the questions I had battled through experientially grew inside of me. What does it mean to be Hmong in America? To be Hmong American without the space or place allocated?

The next semester, I went to Thailand for a class entitled "Global Development and Rural Poor." In my heart, I was packing up to go home, to the refugee camps of Thailand, to the high mountains and low-lying clouds of early morning in Laos. The scent of the wild blooms, the white blossoms of my mother's girlhood called to me in ways that the lilacs of St. Paul had once done. The curling arms of the sycamore trees could not reach as high as the tall bamboos of the faraway jungles. I wanted the shortest distance between two distant points. I wanted to draw a direct line, from where I stood to where I would stand: Hmong American. And yet, I could not wrestle free from the wisdom of my grandma. Her words, "There are no shortcuts out of emotions, out of life, *Me Naib,*" breathed life into the clouds outside my plane window as I made my journey into Hmongness.

When I got to Thailand, no one knew me. They asked what I was, and I answered that I was Hmong. They shook their heads and said that I did not look like Hmong from the hills of Thailand. They said that I looked Japanese, but that I did not walk like one. They said I could be Chinese, but I did not eat like one. They suggested that I was an American. I had no room to run because the landscape was so different to me, the dirt roads with lined shops so different from the University Avenue stores of my Minnesota. My America? Me, an American? Questions were rising, unrelenting as the hot Thai sun.

In the place where I was born, Ban Vinai refugee camp, the land had grown wild. The camp had closed in 1995. It was 2001. The bushes were taller than I was. Where were the fruit-bearing trees that had once stood so tall in the compound where I had played and peed as a child, the trees that had sheltered the place where I had lived for the first six years of my life? Where were the trees that my father had climbed, with me in his arms, to see a bigger world, a better world, a world where families had enough to eat for more than three days out of a week? I looked at the hillsides. Where was the river of my youth? The open sewage canals had dried up. The rains had fallen in the wake of the monsoons, the wind had unleashed gales, the sun had channeled its scorching gaze, nature had taken over, and I could not recognize the place that had given birth to me. In order to understand, I started looking consciously for stories.

Each place I went held stories. In Thailand, it was not enough that I was Hmong. How does a Hmong person come to look, speak, and eat like me? There were stories to be told and stories to be heard. The realization happened simultaneously: in order to tell my story, I had to understand the place of stories in an individual's life. By myself, in my room, with the hungry, howling dogs prowling through the dark streets out my window, I started writing down bits and pieces of the stories around me. I started out at the outer edges of who I was, who I am, who I will be. The old Thai Isaan woman with the deep cracks in her feet, homeless now because a dam was going up that would flood the fields that had fed her family for centuries, began to look like my own grandma. The other minority groups in Thailand began to look like the Hmong. I saw myself in the little girls with brightly colored, dirty flip-flops clutching babies on the hillsides. Each story I encountered made me feel closer to the people involved, to my own people.

I came back to the United States wanting to become a writer. When I was a child, I thought that one day an asteroid would hit the earth; then from the crater of whatever would come after, I would rise up and find my place among all who had survived. While no asteroid (that I knew of) hit the earth as I stood upon its surface, two men in a maroon car sent me careening into space. My return to America was the landing of a new life direction, an affirmation of a burning motivation, an awareness of a life-giving wellspring of courage to do something I had not known that we Hmong people needed to do: speak and write our individual stories in search of a greater, fuller understanding of our shared experience. I had learned that each human being finds his or her home through telling life stories; that anyone who tries to take away a story trespasses in our heart's territory; that everyone who invites the telling of a tale thereby offers a welcome to home.

I came back to the United States to become a writer, not just a writer from the Hmong community, but an American writer telling a human story—how so many of us come from somewhere else to call this place home, how not so many generations ago we built our English on the foundations of accents not so different from my parents'. I understood that if I were any good at all, I would become, in the end, a writer contributing to world literature—putting the Hmong story into the American, adding the global context. I wanted to tell the older generations that the lives they had lived were worth learning from today.

I hope I have done that. My book *The Latehomecomer: A Hmong Family Memoir* was published in April of 2008. It took me four years to write the book. It took one year for the book to go through the publishing process. At the launch of the book at Concordia University–St. Paul, in a room containing more than three hundred people, my father took me aside. He said, "If Hmong tears can reincarnate, it would rain the world in our sorrow. Because they cannot, they can only green the mountains of Phou Bia. But through your words, if the winds of humanity blow in the right direction, then our lives were not lost."

I looked at my father with his rough hands. He is a machinist. When you use flesh to cut into metal, the flesh suffers. I looked at my father, whose supervisor at work told him, "Bee, you are here to talk to machines, not to me." I saw the man who had climbed the tall trees so I could see beyond the four hundred acres that comprised Ban Vinai refugee camp. The man who had said so many years ago, "One day your little feet will walk on horizons your father has never seen. You are not a child of war, of poverty, of despair. You are hope being born. You are the captain to a more beautiful future."

I had no idea then how that cold, stormy spring night would set my sails for a journey into an ocean of belonging. I had no idea then of the power of a community when it chooses to align, stand beside, and challenge the presumptions of itself. I knew I had written a memoir of a people. I believed that the memoir, more than any other literary form, seeks understanding. I did not know then that my writing would, or could, find it beyond myself.

Since the book's publication, I have learned many lessons about writing stories, about the responsibilities of a writer and what storytelling means to a community. Grandma was right: "Life is nothing more than moments strung on the thread of time. If we give ourselves fully and completely to one moment, it opens up the possibility for the next." When we are old and gray and sitting by a window somewhere, it will be to those moments, those memories that we speak. The people who loved us, the foods we enjoyed, and the places where we have been will become the friends we have made along the way.

The accumulation of these memories is the formation of identity. The makings of Hmong and non-Hmong identity are more similar than different. The intelligence of a world arises when relationships are built between seemingly different, unconnected elements. For example, that there is a vase and that it holds water and can sustain the life fabric of a flower out of the ground was a relationship some man or woman devised in time, and thus we as a human community have benefitted.

In the beginning, I was invited to speak as a part of the Hmong story. When people came and heard and learned my Hmong story, they discovered a young writer who thought seriously and felt passionately about writing, the chase after meaning, the process of inspiration. People began saying, "Yes, Kalia is very proud to be Hmong and live in the experience of what is Hmong in America, but beyond that, she carries a genuine love of language. She is not only a teller of the Hmong story but also a writer who feels the call and the calm of stories." Consequently, I have started to explore other relationships, such as how the Hmong story is connected to the Somali diaspora and the ramifications of the political machinations that create populations such as the Yezeti of Iraq—displaced and killed for helping the Americans in the failure of war. These days, I speak because I am Hmong, because I am a writer; equally pertinent to my identity is how I feel. Within my heart I feel tremendous compulsion to face the forces that push us together and pull us apart in the world we share. Even more important, I feel confident in the ability of the story to speak to what is good in the human heart, universal in the human consciousness.

While the Hmong are an important part of the core and the center of who I am and the history that gives rise to my life and work, I am discovering the power in my father's words, "If you dream in the right direction, you never wake up, and the dream never dies."

My dream is my identity. My identity is a bond that breaks me from the hold of simple being. It is the platform that allows my feet to bounce when my reach extends higher than I stand. My Hmong identity must be unafraid of changing. When I combine words to get at meaning, inspiration, to break out of sequence, to glue the broken edges, I have to feed my store of faith in what is Hmong so I can grow more fearless as a writer. I have to understand that when one Hmong heart is less scared, the Hmong as a people grow stronger.

I tell myself: the sun rises so we can do better at what we tried to do the day before. There is no real picture of perfection in doing productive work. Each project, each assignment, each page, each word we write or speak is always only a portrait of us in time in relation to another or many others. Because the sun rises, we receive one more chance to fight to be more effective in the world. The Hmong have words to offer in writing that will stand the test of time, creatively and productively crossing gender, cultural, and linguistic lines of belonging.

I repeat to myself: we can always be only the best of ourselves. If we try and fail, we still live in the same world that created Martin Luther King, Jr., and Rosa Parks, Ronald Takaki and Youa Lee: we try and we fail among those whose lives validate and confirm the power of trying. When we try, the world becomes the best of what we can be as a people.

I understand that life provides no guarantee. One day I will realize the folly of my convictions, but that day is not today. This is the risk of living, the thrill and excitement of being, and the promise of belonging.

The seed of who I am as one within a people was planted long before I was born; through me, the fruits of those before blossom into the world. In my case, the flower is made of paper and ink, it blooms and it wavers in the hands of strangers and friends alike, flipping through the pages. I am a writer for a community that needs many of us to be writers: an accented voice, communicating the internal and external forces that guide a young life into being, an identity emerging through the page and beyond it.

I know that the sun is only in the sky for a time. This is the long lesson many Hmong people have learned in our trek through the mountains of war and the valleys of waiting, into the rush of traffic as people travel with reason or without. Inevitably, the sun must make its descent from the center of our sky to the next.

The Hmong heart will return to its home, the place from where it opened itself to the winds of life in a world teeming with possibilities. The surprise in life is not what happens eventually. One day we will return to the earth that allowed us time on its surface. The air, the water, and the sun coax the grass out of the ground, allow the spring flowers to unfurl and reveal the bright reds and yellows of petals, turn the leaves green in summer, turn the leaves yellow come autumn, and then bury them brown beneath the fallen snow. Life issues its immortal challenge. The open sky full of splendor competes with the rich hues of a field of tulips in glorious, bright bloom. All pulls at the fluttering, the human heart.

> The pyramids of Edzná rise in the morning sun,
> To stand at its center, clap, clap, clap,
> Echoes resound, repeat, resend . . .
> The message is not lost:
> A people builds, so
> The human story grows.

This Hmong heart knows that with the emergence of each and every Hmong American writer, world literature becomes richer and we become a fabric of what is wealthy in the world of words: a story with more understanding on our side, a people getting at life, not just living through it. We become not only a part of what is written, but the authors of things written.

"A story is like the stop sign on the road of life. It is supposed to make you stop, look both ways, check the trajectory of the horizon before you continue," says Uncle Eng. He adds, *"You will not find this in a book."*

< 15 >

Stitching the Fabric of Hmong Lives

The Value of Studying Paj Ntaub *and Story Cloth*
in Multicultural Education

MARY LOUISE BULEY-MEISSNER

Introduction

The artistry of Hmong women across generations is evident in two major chapters of cultural creativity inseparable from Hmong history and heritage: first, traditional sewing in Laos to reinforce the identity and values of family and clan; and second, story cloth production in refugee camps to bring Hmong lives to the attention of the outside world. Many studies of Hmong culture have concluded that traditional forms of cultural creativity are being lost because they are unappreciated by younger generations. However, this chapter proposes that studying *paj ntaub* and story cloth potentially can become a transformative educational experience for Hmong American college students, opening their eyes, minds, and hearts to the continuing significance of their cultural heritage.

Affirming clan membership and ethnic identity, traditional *paj ntaub* designs symbolize the value of home, family, and strength gained from unity. Requiring many years of practice to refine, the patterns are as intricate as any to be found in sewing around the world. The creation of story cloths after the Vietnam War signals a major change in the purpose of sewing. Each unsigned cloth can be read as a narrative of Hmong history, often extending from Chinese origins through village life and war in Laos to resettlement in the United States. Tragic in theme yet beautiful in execution, story cloths gain even more significance as part of a worldwide indigenous movement to tell the truth of history through art.

Carefully considering the historical, social, and cultural context of how women have learned to sew, students come to recognize that the creativity of women across generations demonstrates their remarkable achievement in affirming bonds of family and clan; marking rites of passage from

< 233 >

childhood to adulthood; witnessing to the world what Hmong people have suffered; and testifying to their endurance. Moreover, *paj ntaub* and story cloth can be read as forms of narrative art emerging from both individual and collective identity.

How Hmong Language Was Lost and Saved

Many stories are told about how the original Hmong written language was lost. Some say that more than three thousand years ago, Hmong had a language so powerful that their Chinese rulers felt threatened by what it might accomplish. Suppose it were to strengthen Hmong in their relentless fight for freedom? Fearing this, the Chinese outlawed it and made its use punishable by death. Others say that the written language was lost only one thousand years ago, not when the Chinese enslaved Hmong but when the Hmong broke their chains and banded together to cross Asia in search of a land to call their own. Walking hundreds of miles, they had little to sustain them: barely enough rice to give everyone a cup a day. Alas, one night along the way, their starving horses ate the single book that contained all of the Hmong words ever written. Or starving people may have eaten this book, not realizing its worth.

Accomplished *qeej* players also say that the beginning notes of some songs—"*tuag num qeeg . . . tuag num qeeg*"—remind listeners of how Hmong writing was lost: the musical notes translated into spoken words sound similar to "*tsuag noj taag . . . tsuag noj tag*" (the mouse has eaten it all . . . the mouse has eaten it all). Past to present, older Hmong mourn the loss of this legendary book, which would have let future generations—and all the world—know how far back in time, how far back in suffering and sacrifice, Hmong have been forging their own path and identity.[1]

The tale of how the original Hmong written language was lost has another twist. Some say that the language was saved—preserved for future generations by women who cleverly sewed the script into their own clothing. How did they do it? Possibly they stitched the words into the unique *paj ntaub* of their culture: the richly symbolic "flower cloth" that Hmong women have been creating for their families and clans from ancient times until now. For example, folklore tells us that women invented geometric, highly stylized designs to represent the sounds of words—and then embroidered these designs into the folds of the elaborately, vividly colored skirts worn by mothers and daughters of the group called Blue Mong or Green Hmong.

How Hmong People Came as Refugees to the United States

By the mid-nineteenth century, half a million Hmong had migrated to Southeast Asia, taking their place in a global diaspora of Indochinese people seeking lives free of poverty, political oppression, and war. Settling in mountainous regions of Laos, Thailand, and Vietnam as farmers and hunters, they had their own spoken language, clan system, and self-sufficient villages. By the time the Vietnam War began, five generations of Hmong had lived independently in the highlands of Laos for over one hundred years. During the war, however, when Hmong were recruited to fight for the United States in the CIA's Secret War, their villages were destroyed and more than sixty-five thousand people were killed (including an estimated fifty thousand civilians). In 1975, when the United States withdrew from Laos, more than one hundred thousand Hmong tried to escape into Thailand. Nearly half died during that treacherous journey across the mountains, jungles, and "River of Death": the Mekong. In the Thai refugee camps, Hmong families waited—sometimes for years and under inhumane conditions—to secure foreign sponsorship and safe passage to another country. From 1975 to 1995, approximately one hundred thousand Hmong resettled in the United States, holding little more in their hands and hearts than their haunting, centuries-old dream that somewhere they could belong and be free.[2]

Identity and Culture

At a Midwest public university, I teach a freshman seminar called Hmong American Life Stories, which enrolls students from diverse ethnic and cultural backgrounds. Usually fifteen out of twenty students in this seminar are of Hmong descent. Our aim is to broaden and deepen our understanding of the interrelationship of history, heritage, and contemporary social issues. In exploring the textile arts of traditional Hmong life, particularly the highland village life of Laos, students across ethnic groups are fascinated to learn how individual and collective identities can be expressed through cultural creativity. Especially for female students who are constructing modern identities out of traditional backgrounds, it is intriguing to discover what we can learn from older generations about the process of cultural continuity and change; the modern significance of traditional values; and sources of creativity that can sustain self-fulfillment as well as family and community bonds. One student, Kathy Xiong, recently told me, "My identity as Hmong is forever changed by the pride I now find in that identity. Before this class, I knew very little about being Hmong and sometimes felt that not being Hmong would be better. The past seemed irrelevant, empty of meaning for modern youth. Now I want to know about the past and future, and I would not want to be anyone else."[3]

What Is It to Be Hmong?

According to Lue Vang and Judy Lewis in *Grandmother's Path, Grandfather's Way*, there is not only a preferred way but a right and readily recognized way to speak, act, and think of yourself if you are a real Hmong, if you are true to your roots and genuinely proud to be who you are. As a member of the first generation of Hmong immigrants in the United States, Vang straightforwardly observes,

> To be Hmong means that you speak the language, observe the customs and roles, live in patrilineal groups, and identify yourself as Hmong. If you were born in a different ethnic group, and adopted by a Hmong family, *you would be Hmong if you speak Hmong, act like a Hmong, and call yourself Hmong.*[4]

This passage provides a useful starting point for students to consider how attitudes about being Hmong may change from generation to generation. To a certain extent, students in my classes do believe that identity can be essentialized. They initially say it is in the bloodline; it is who they are from birth; and so it is largely predetermined. Yet, they recognize that identity also is complicated because it is inseparable from all of the people who give meaning to their lives; therefore, it inevitably involves how to fulfill (or resist) expectations, obligations, and responsibilities connecting them to others. Moreover, as we often have discussed, who you are is crucially shaped by what you choose to remember—or what you (willfully or wantonly) forget. Thus, as students learn more about their history and heritage, the realization that "it is not enough to be born Hmong" becomes a motivator for seriously considering how the meaning of "Hmongness," past, present, and future, continually evolves. As student Meng Yang told our class, "We have to take responsibility for knowing who we are as Hmong people. We have to open our eyes to what we have been missing in only thinking about ourselves one by one." One productive way to engage in this learning process is to look carefully at the artistry of *paj ntaub.*

Paj Ntaub Artistry

Many of my students' mothers and grandmothers have spent many hours making *paj ntaub,* the "flower cloth" unique to Hmong culture. Traditionally, girls in Laos as young as age three learn how to sew with their mothers, side by side and knee to knee. Hundreds of patterns have to be mastered over the years. Older women with this expertise sometimes describe sewing as an intricate "language" or "vocabulary" of stitches, including dozens of cross stitches, chain, satin, and running stitches. Appliqué, reverse appliqué, and batik also are incorporated into designs. With disciplined practice, women have no need for paper patterns, written instructions, or measurement tools. With hand and eye, they can follow a pattern perfectly. Even today, everything in a design ideally should be so carefully completed that the back will look as finished as the front. Also required for true expertise are very close stitching (with one-inch needles), perfectly straight lines, and appealing combinations of colors, threads, and fabrics. Hand-dyed, handmade cloth traditionally is blue; since the early nineteenth century, women also have enjoyed experimenting with colors such as lime green, hot pink, deep purple, blood red, earth brown, and sun yellow.[5]

For village women in Laos, excellence in sewing traditionally demonstrates home training, patience, industry, diligence, and creativity—all of which enhance marriage prospects and help to secure a prosperous future. A fortunate young woman's dowry includes an array of clothing made by and with her mother in the precious time they can find together away from daily housework and fieldwork. Requiring hundreds of finely stitched pleats, a single skirt (*dlaim tab Moob*) can take a year to complete. Feminine sleeves (*npaab tsho*) and collars (*ntsej tsho*) with delightfully intricate designs; sashes (*hlaab*) and aprons (*sev*) with eye-catching colors; even a hat (*mom suav ceeb*) to harmoniously frame a hopeful young face—every detail conveys the love between mother and daughter as well as the shared cultural values of their community.[6]

Paj Ntaub Symbolism

Because of its incomparable artistry, *paj ntaub* in the twenty-first century is becoming an object of international scholarly attention, acclaimed for the intricacy and infinite variety of its designs by textile researchers such as Gina Corrigan and Tomoko Torimaru. At schools such as the Milwaukee Institute of Art and Design, college students also are learning to take *paj ntaub* seriously as a form of highly advanced cultural expression. Yet, as Gary Yia Lee and Nicholas Tapp observe, "Traditionally, Hmong art . . . is not a separate sphere as it is in Western societies"; instead, "functional art forms help to embellish the ordinary, and to elevate common things to a plane that inspires admiration and wonder." Similarly, art historian Abby Remer emphasizes,

> In truth, there has rarely been . . . a clear-cut separation between sacred works and everyday utilitarian objects in indigenous societies. Women's ornamentation on tools, clothing, or the walls of their village homes transforms what the West considers "ordinary" items into art that carries profound meaning.[7]

Physically and spiritually, sewing can be a way to reinforce the value of home, family, and closeness to nature; protection from outside, malevolent forces; the interconnection of physical and spiritual worlds; and the strength to be gained from staying inside (the home, the clan, the community) and staying together. Most important, no matter where they have lived, Hmong people always have worn distinct clothing as a sign of ethnic identity and clan membership. Traditionally, women invest clothing with a keen awareness of both its cultural significance and its creative beauty. Designs go back many centuries. Indeed, older women say that in ancient times, *paj ntaub* symbolized the knowledge needed for safe passage from this life to the next.

Much as we read and interpret a book, what we see in *paj ntaub* patterns seems to reflect what we are prepared to see by our own cultural

Vincent Her and family in traditional Hmong clothing (Green Bay, Wisconsin, 2003). Photo courtesy of Her family.

backgrounds, including our possible relationships to those doing the sewing. Anthropologist Robert Cooper asserts that women in Laos and Thailand show "no spontaneity or originality" in their sewing and that any possible symbolic meanings in their work have been "lost through time." Similarly, ethnographer Nancy Donnelly finds little if any evidence of "shared cultural symbols" in the *paj ntaub* of refugee women in Washington state; while Jane Mallinson, Nancy Donnelly, and Ly Hang conclude in their textile research that Hmong women customarily copy patterns of sewing so exactly that "changing one motif in one corner of [a] square" is a remarkable instance of acceptable alteration. In striking contrast, anthropologist Patricia Symonds offers this observation of Hmong women with whom she made a village home in the 1980s:

> [E]very Hmong girl is expected to use her own talent and creativity to improve upon traditional patterns or create new ones . . . If she is creative in her patterns and stitches, then she will be creative in the way she cares for and manages her family . . . I was struck by the interest the women showed in every new pattern they saw . . . Although some women in Flower Village said they chose patterns and colors for their beauty, several said that specific patterns were symbolic as well.[8]

In my view, these conclusions are directly influenced by Symonds's day-to-day interactions with the women (including taking sewing lessons from them). She enjoys their company; answers many questions from them (especially about why she is living alone); and tries her best to see their world (materially poor but socially vibrant) with their eyes, including its joys as well as its hardships. To understand why women sew, my students and I try to cultivate a similar attitude of empathetic, open-minded inquiry. Impressive to us is that ever since their arrival in the United States, Hmong women have continued to experiment with new designs to beautify *paj ntaub* and to expand their repertoire of sewing skills. "Precise patterning, straight borders, and smooth surfaces" long have been criteria for achieving expertise, but so have "striking color combinations (and) innovative design motifs," according to Joanne Cubbs. As evidenced by the seventy-three biographies in "Hmong Traditional Artists," women long have taken pride in both innovation and tradition.[9]

Researching *paj ntaub* symbolism, I have found that Hmong women's designs across generations reflect the interrelationship of identity and place in everyday life. Cubbs, for example, notes that Hmong women draw extensively upon "a vocabulary of color and form rich with allusion to the natural surroundings and to Hmong myth and ritual belief." Equally important, conversations with Hmong women at organizations such as the Hmong American Women's Association, Inc. (HAWA) and the Milwaukee Christian Center have helped me to see *paj ntaub* as expressive of a highly developed sensitivity to the interrelationship of inner and outer realities.

Interviewing their own mothers and grandmothers about *paj ntaub*, students confirm that symbols hold protective, talismanic properties when sewn into daily or ritual items of clothing for enhancement of physical and spiritual health. Interpretations vary among women needleworkers, including my students' relatives, but the following meanings seem to be common:

chicken eye, foot, tail: family prosperity, respect and honor toward ancestors

cross or x-shape: spiritual health, protection against evil

diamond inside square: altar kept inside home, imprint of good and powerful spirit

dog's foot: loyalty to family

dragon's tail: longevity, power, protection

eight-sided star (also referred to as a left star): good fortune

elephant's foot: family power, status and wealth

eye of the peacock: natural beauty

fish scales: protection from outsiders, barrier against bad luck, fence to hold in good luck

goat's head: family status

heart: protection and affection

interlocking perpendicular lines ("family design"): kinship ties, linked generations

maze: many variations, including rambling of woman's soul during sleep ("dream maze"), journey of married couple through life ("love design"), road out of Laos ("crooked road"), spirit world (interlocked fingers in "hand print of a ghost")

moj zeej ("shadow self"): surrogate form (cut from red cloth) drawing attention of evil spirits away from vulnerable person

mountains: strength, protection against outsiders

rooster's comb: protection, influence over others

seeds: fertility, good fortune

snail shell: family growth (with generations spiraling out from ancestors at center), shaman's chanting and spinning

snail shell doubled: two families linked in marriage

steps: future prosperity

vegetable blossom: fertility, health, good fortune[10]

Early researchers often were confounded when different Hmong women would provide different interpretations of sewing symbols; intent on finding consistent explanations, the researchers could not see evidence of shared cultural consciousness. However, this judgment overlooks the multiple meanings that any symbol carries, depending on when, where, how, and why it is being used. How we read *paj ntaub* reflects what we are ready to read. Looking at a seed design, I think of Anthony Doerr's question: "What is a seed if not the purest kind of memory, a link to every generation that has gone before it?" Yet, a snail shell also could hold memory of Hmong origins, perhaps suggesting that rather than always being mountain dwellers, Hmong people may have resided generations ago along lowland rivers and streams. Indeed, scholars at the Third International Conference on Hmong Studies recently have raised the possibility that *paj ntaub* designs could be used by scholars to reinterpret the past, including the history of Hmong migration in Asia.[11]

The significance of well-made clothing in Hmong culture is interesting to students, whose own wardrobes are ready made and off the rack—except for the Hmong New Year outfits, which many of the young women (but few of the young men) wear at their parents' insistence. (Originally a harvest celebration, Hmong New Year is now a social gathering that attracts hundreds of people in cities such as Milwaukee, Wisconsin, and St. Paul, Minnesota.) Most eye-opening to them are ways in which *paj ntaub* traditionally has marked passages of life important to young and old. As student Jerry Yang remarked, "Hmong clothing is worth a second look! I thought it was too old-fashioned to be interesting, but now I like thinking it's part of who I am, different than what anybody else has to wear."

Traditionally, for example, pride and prosperity are displayed by newly married couples wearing outfits with *paj ntaub* designs appropriate to their clans and subclans, signifying their region of origin. For the bride in particular, this also shows her lifelong connection to her natal home, even though after marriage she resides with her husband's family. Thus, a woman's place in Hmong society may change, but her identity as a person belonging to a specific cultural group will always be affirmed through the way she dresses. For Hmong Americans from the Muang Phong (Moospheeb) region of Laos, a married daughter and her husband customarily offer *paj ntaub* squares, called *noob ncoos,* to her grandparents, parents, brothers, uncles, and aunts. This is a way for the daughter to acknowledge their continuing

Traditional paj ntaub *baby carrier (unfinished, 22.5 inches wide and 24.5 inches long, circa 1986). From author's personal collection. Photo courtesy of Daniel Meissner.*

presence in her life and a way for her husband to reinforce lifelong commitments to the family. Baby carriers (*hlaab nyas*) and hats (*mom ib* and *mom ntxhuav*) are designed to safeguard young, vulnerable souls and to protect those souls from wandering. The specific motifs used to protect the young are the maze designs, meant to keep babies close to their mothers, and the bright blossoms of color on hats, which make babies look like flowers themselves. When a parent dies, the daughters and daughters-in-law should have ready for him or her a complete set of funeral clothing known as *khaub ndluag laug* (old age clothes). This tradition shows honor for elders; allows the deceased to be recognized by ancestors in the next life; and signifies continuing prosperity in that life.

As Hmong needleworkers have known for centuries, the transition from one life to the next can leave a person very vulnerable to physical and spiritual harm. For my students and me, one of the most intriguing *paj ntaub* designs is the *moj zeej* used in *ua neeb* (shamanic ceremonies) to promote physical and spiritual healing. The *moj zeej* (shadow of a person) is a white cloth figure, edged in black and sewn onto red cloth, to be worn on the back of a shirt or jacket of a person whose soul is lost or wandering. By drawing the attention of harmful spirits to this substitute figure, a *txiv neeb* (shaman) can divert attention away from the suffering person, who then can recover balance and well-being. In the refugee camps of Thailand, *moj zeej* on the backs of children as well as adults were emblematic of their very uncertain future.

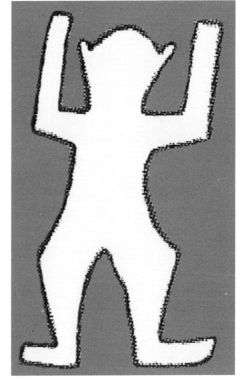

As a defense against dangerous spirits in a threatening world, *moj zeej* always are cut from cloth that is red, the color of life-giving blood—a detail that usually sparks intense student discussion about bloodlines as cultural lifelines. As May Seng insisted, "*Moj zeej* is for everybody, Hmong people, not-Hmong people, because that's the world we live in now."

Drawing of traditional moj zeej figure. Courtesy of Daniel Meissner.

Continuing Significance of Sewing

The cultural background of nearly all my Hmong American students includes growing up with mother and grandmothers spending many hours sewing *paj ntaub* for Hmong New Year, marriage celebrations, and other milestones. The women adroitly use fabric, thread, buttons, embellishments, and sometimes new patterns from local stores, their own sewing collectives, and world markets. Yet, rarely do students themselves know how to sew; home, school, and work activities keep them on the go around the clock. Noticing that "few even know how to thread a needle," Lee and Tapp conclude that among young women today, *paj ntaub* largely "has become a lost art." However, I have found that when students learn about *paj ntaub* in the context of family history and cultural heritage, they become keenly interested in needlework as an expression of identity and creativity relevant to modern life. As student Joy Moua explained in a class research presentation, "I am an art major, and I realize now that women in my family [who sew] are great teachers as I find my way to be an artist who is Hmong." Her presentation included *paj ntaub* borders and corners that she had sewn for original paintings of scenes from modern urban life, such as a multiethnic group of children playing together and flowers growing through the concrete on a city street.[12]

Studying *paj ntaub*, students say, also helps them to feel closer to their mothers and grandmothers through a new appreciation of the integrity essential to needlework creation. As Meredith McGuire points out, "memory resides in the whole body." When women sew, they not only produce handiwork; they also do the cross-culturally invaluable work of unifying the beautiful, the practical, and the spiritual in each design and every pattern. What they always remember is that the body and the spirit are inseparable; indeed, in the worldview of Hmong people for many generations, one is by nature a form of the other.[13]

Overall, careful study of *paj ntaub* reveals its significance as an ever-evolving fabric collection of fascinating interpretations of what it means to be Hmong for individuals, families, clans, and an enduring culture. As a teacher, I have come to see *paj ntaub* as a form of narrative art, a living art that tells students in the twenty-first century the story of how memory is made in Hmong culture. While it may be true that "in the designs and patterns of the Hmong dress and costume are hidden important clues to their identity as a people," I am even more interested in *paj ntaub* as an art of memory-in-the-making. What, how, and why to sew are inseparable from who is sewing together: mother and daughter on quiet evenings after fieldwork is done for the day; young women in a village happily preparing for a New Year celebration; a college student in Milwaukee getting ready for her class presentation. Always open to interpretation, memory helps us to answer Lue Vang's question, "What is it to be Hmong?" with a new appreciation of how the past resides in the present.[14]

Origin of Story Cloth

Women in refugee camps first began to make story cloths in the 1970s because they wanted to remember and pass down what they had learned growing up in Laos and what they had witnessed during the war. To support their families, they also sent cloths to relatives for sale overseas. The market expanded with the help of missionaries and refugee aid workers, who collaborated with the women in blending traditional designs with modern colors and materials. Most commonly depicting the Vietnam War, story cloths after resettlement outside Laos also show Hmong New Year, daily rural life, village festivities, and folktales. Usually words are not sewn into the designs, but sometimes English captions are included for an intended international audience.[15]

Through ethnic festivals, school presentations, and public exhibitions, many Westerners have become familiar with story cloth as emblematic of Hmong culture. The first glimpse that non-Hmong have of Hmong culture could be through children's books featuring photos or illustrations of story cloths. Indeed, early exhibitions of and related commentaries on story cloths emphasized their value in opening up a new culture for viewing by an American public just beginning to realize that Hmong refugees were here to stay. However, as my students and I found in our class research, story cloths need to be read with an appreciation of the deliberate experimentation and gradual refinement in design that have led to contemporary patterns. That is, from the very beginning, Hmong women have creatively imagined and reimagined the potential forms that story cloths could take.[16]

For example, examining story cloth production from 1976 to 1996, June Anderson discovered Hmong women tried out at least four approaches,

Story cloth depicting peace time for Hmong people in Laos (15.5 inches wide and 16.5 inches long, circa 2000). From author's personal collection. Photo courtesy of Daniel Meissner.

which became progressively more challenging for the needleworkers in terms of the skills required and the effects achieved. First, from 1976 to the early 1980s, women sewed simple human and animal shapes on small cloth panels, chain-stitching these figures on plain backgrounds; Anderson described the design as "more like disconnected words rather than whole sentences" in overall composition. Second, from the mid- to late 1980s, they transitioned to more lifelike figures with more detailed backgrounds in horizontal rows; to my eyes, as if sentences were being formed in fabric. Third, in the early 1990s, Anderson noticed "more dynamic freeform composition, often with a diagonal or winding path leading the viewer from one episode to the other" in the creation of full stories, even stories of "epic proportions." Finally, from the mid-1990s on, women developed "the intricate stitching, the skill at texturing, the complexity and sophistication of the designs, and the general high quality of workmanship" that we associate with story cloth today.[17]

Now story cloths are collected by university and public museums that realize their inestimable value as art and history (e.g., the John Michael Kohler Arts Center, Sheboygan, Wisconsin; Michigan State University Museum, Lansing; and the Minneapolis Institute of Art, Minnesota). However, we should not forget that story cloths originate with Hmong women creative and courageous enough to put their highly developed traditional sewing skills to a bold new use. As Nora Murphy acknowledges, "Inside a stitch . . . lies the paradox of the ordinary, everyday textile hero. Her simple stitch helps keep the story of humanity alive." Learning to read story cloth with an eye for the interweaving of personal choices with group needs is an important lesson relevant across cultures, where indeed "every stitch matters" in women's life-bearing, life-saving creative work for their families and communities.[18]

Story Cloth: Memory and Survival

In this section I will focus on what we have observed in our class study of story cloths depicting Hmong experience of the Vietnam War, particularly how that experience has shaped important aspects of Hmong identity up to the present day. As Dwight Conquergood emphasizes, story cloths function to rewrite history—more specifically, to expose history "not as organically unified and continuous, but as a series of upheavals, disruptions, repeated displacements, negotiated struggles, border crossings, adjustments and inventions." Ban Vinai, a refugee camp built in 1975 to house twelve thousand Hmong soldiers and their families, by 1985 sheltered fifty thousand people whose future had been deracinated by political directives serving no one but the leaders who had left the land to burn. Then and there, "a distinct refugee culture [was] shaped in the crucible of . . . radical disruption, displacement, exile and domination." According to Lynellyn Long, women in Ban Vinai made *paj ntaub Hmoob* (traditional articles of clothing) for their families and *paj ntaub Amerika* (story cloth) for missionaries and international relief agency workers to take out of the camp. Other researchers believe that story cloth originally was called *paj ntaub dab neej* (flower cloth of life, including the customs and traditions of a people). In any case, from Ban Vinai, story cloth went all over the world— to other countries in Asia, to the United States and Europe, to Australia, and wherever else Hmong kinship connections could be found.[19]

Most striking, story cloth exposed the devastating reality of the Secret War waged by the United States in Laos for more than ten years. From 1960 to 1975, the war claimed the lives of thousands of Hmong, including ten-year-old boys conscripted and handed guns taller than they were; brothers forced to fight brothers; fathers never returning from the Plain of Jars; mothers trying to save babies and grandparents from starvation, Vietnamese soldiers, and U.S. bombardment. Who would know this if Hmong people did not tell their own story?

In an essay entitled "Toward a Theory of Cultural Trauma," Jeffrey Alexander presents insights that I find directly relevant to story cloth production. He explains, "Cultural trauma occurs when members of a collectivity feel they have been subjected to a horrendous event that leaves indelible marks upon their group consciousness, marking their memories forever and changing their future identity in fundamental and irrevocable ways." To make meaning out of trauma—for themselves no less than for others—group members must engage in retelling what they have experienced by "constructing a compelling framework of cultural classification" to make sense out of senseless tragedy. In my reading of story cloth, it does indeed function in this way, meeting the four requirements that Alexander sets for "bridging the gap between event and representation": showing "the nature of the pain" (what happened in Laos); leaving no doubt as to "the nature of the victim" (who was hurt); making the "relation of the trauma victim to the wider audience" a serious consideration for people who might otherwise turn away from what happened; and turning "attribution of responsibility" (who caused the suffering) into a subject of public as well as personal inquiry.[20]

Equally important, in my view, is the function of story cloth in transforming voiceless victims to outspoken advocates of justice not only for Hmong people but also for other indigenous people whose history and heritage have been trampled in the dust of war. Conquergood points out that Hmong language refers to refugees as *neeg tawg rog* (the war-broken people). In the twenty-first century, the number of refugees worldwide is climbing into the millions. Confronting that reality, student Ger Xiong told our class, "The more I learn about Hmong history, the more I see how it is connected to world politics and world history. Native people are the first silenced and the last heard." Yet, when they make themselves heard, their voices can subvert dominant narratives of history and reveal its missing chapters.[21]

Story Cloth: Stylistic Qualities

Most story cloths have noteworthy stylistic qualities in common, suggesting the contribution of each woman to a larger community project of remembrance. As Sally Petersen observed in Ban Vinai and other refugee camps of Thailand, Hmong women assessed the quality of each other's story cloth production in terms of "style, technique, and level of detail" but most of all for its representation of shared truth. According to her research, story cloth artists were placed by the very nature of their work in "the reflexive position of looking at us looking at them; they must decide what is appropriate for us to see, and in what form we should see it." By "we," Petersen meant non-Hmong (as did many, if not most, scholars of Hmong textiles in the 1980s and 1990s); certainly story cloths were first made with an acute awareness of their potential appeal to an international market.[22]

Equally important, as my students and I have come to appreciate, story cloths also originate in and continue to express women's consciousness of how their needlework is likely to be viewed by other Hmong. Moreover, in the twenty-first century, that imagined relationship extends to Hmong they will never meet but who recognize their shared membership in a global Hmong community. Here I see a crucial turn in the development of women's cultural creativity, motivated for generations primarily by needs and desires within families and clans. Whether expressed in *paj ntaub* or story cloth, "What is it to be Hmong?" has new meanings from 1975 to the present that it could not have held when the "Hmongness" of daily life was created mostly out of face-to-face relationships.[23]

With few exceptions, artists do not sign names to story cloths. Characters in a story cloth likewise have no names; instead, figures are representative or archetypal. Rarely are faces seen from the front; instead, profiles are shown. Women follow men, and children follow adults. No one walks alone; no one makes his own path. People zigzag down the page with each turn marking a change in time or place. Narratively and spatially, the deliberate compression of time and space indicates the urgency of telling a story whose full meaning far exceeds the available means of expression. As Conquergood observes, the "seams are exposed" with graphic depiction of "devastation and dignity, horror and humanity, suffering and survivor strength." Commenting on story cloths that students had brought to our class from their homes, student Jasmine Kalani reflected, "Somehow each story cloth is beautiful, although hard to look at up close. Women didn't give up on being Hmong. They did something to show that being Hmong was worth fighting for."[24]

As Alexander points out, "The cultural construction of trauma begins with . . . an exclamation of the terrifying profanation of some sacred value, a narrative about a horribly destructive social process, and a demand for emotional, institutional and symbolic reparation and reconstitution." For Hmong people, one "sacred value" is their rightful place in world history, including ancestral origins in China. Thus, story cloth narratives often wind down the fabric from China (represented by the Great Wall) to Southeast Asia (suggested by rural rooftops) and the Laos highlands (indicated by verdant farmland). Then, as if the fabric of the story is being torn apart, the Mekong River comes to fearsome life. People run from the war to the riverbank, desperate to cross over to Thailand; they plunge into the river, clinging to rafts, inner tubes, hollow bamboo sticks, and each other. Finally, if they are not swept away or shot, they climb exhausted from the dark water, emerging as people who belong nowhere in the world. While artists commonly deemphasize background scenes such as mountains, fields, or battlegrounds, the detailing of human experience is unflinching and graphically revealing. Faces are contorted, clothing is ragged, feet are bleeding. From the Mekong to the barbed-wire refugee camps to the stark reprocessing stations to the eerily deserted airfields, Hmong people walk on. Like other survivors of international wars, they walk on to new homes on far horizons, making the future itself possible for generations to come.[25]

Overall, the only way to understand any part of this story is to learn the whole story—yet the whole story is always in the process of being composed. Those who lived through it debate to this day what the Vietnam War meant and means; across generations, its impact is painfully inscribed in heart and mind. Although story cloths on the same subject may at first appear identical, no two cloths are ever exactly the same; not only do artists vary thread and fabric colors, they also change details as subtle markers of their individual perspective. For example, an attentive reader of a story cloth may notice a woman giving birth during wartime or a child taking shelter behind his father as a soldier aims a gun at their family. The story is every Hmong survivor's story, and yet it is uniquely different for each person.

In the story cloth shown opposite, two words are stitched for Hmong and non-Hmong to read and remember: "Phoubia" (at the top) and "Banhinher" (at the bottom). The first refers to the mountain base of the Chao Fa resistance movement, which continued fighting the communists in Laos after U.S. forces withdrew. Men and women who joined the resistance sought shelter with their families in this rugged territory for many years; some say even up until the present. If few Westerners know of Phoubia, still fewer know of Banhinher. In this town, not far from the capital city of Vientiane, Pathet Lao soldiers massacred Hmong refugees who were making their way to Thailand after Hmong military officers had been airlifted by the United States out of Laos in 1975. Surely the woman who dared to sew this story was grief stricken; she made the vortex of violence so graphic that any possibility of hope for Hmong people seems to be torn apart before our eyes. Yet her creative purpose goes far beyond evoking pity for the massacre victims or survivors. In this story cloth, as men, women, and even a child look directly at us, they seem to ask, "What will you do with what you now know?" For me, this is a profoundly compelling narrative of the aftermath of war brought forward in the anonymous artist's insistence that viewers not look away.[26]

Story Cloth: Individual Creativity and Collective Identity

What an individual artist chooses to highlight (usually with a purposefully subtle touch) depends on her perspective regarding what is true to the history of Hmong people. As student Nou Vang told us about her mother, a well-respected local story cloth artist, "She can't speak much English, but she knows the names of every kind of airplane that flew over Laos during the war and every type of bomb that was dropped on her village." These planes are stitched into her mother's fabric with glossy gray thread, which makes them stand out against the dark blue cotton background; additionally, behind the windows of some of the planes, blank white faces

Story cloth depicting Phoubia and Banhinher (32.5 inches wide and 30.5 inches long, circa 2005). From author's personal collection. Photo courtesy of Daniel Meissner.

are visible—a sharp contrast to the more common depiction of planes without pilots.

Another student, Pa Houa, told us that when she looks at her mother's story cloth, she realizes that the United States is "the latest stop on a long, long journey. Hmong people know that they could be forced to move and fight again for a place to stay." In her mother's view, every generation must take responsibility for "telling what you know to be true" in whatever form holds the most expressive potential at that time. In my view, this is a commitment to art shared by Hmong women who find authenticity in forms that are emotionally driven, collectively meaningful, and historically irreplaceable as representations of a reality that otherwise could be repressed or relegated to a footnote. Furthermore, story cloth as social, historical, and cultural revelation links Hmong women to indigenous women in other places and other times of critical truth telling. Salvadoran women threading their needles to depict the despair in Honduran refugee camps; Mexican women embroidering pilgrimages from war to peace; Inuit women sewing counter-stories to their complete assimilation by modern society—these and many more women around the world are combining vision, skill, and personal bravery to speak truths otherwise silenced.[27]

In my reading of their work, Hmong story cloth artists create histories, narratives, protests, arguments, and laments. Indeed, they create memories: sewing a landscape and touching again the land they once called home, weaving their own blood, tears, and hopes into a fabric strong enough to withstand whatever changes the future may bring.

No story cloth has a definite beginning or ending. Instead, as my students have observed, Hmong people "come from someplace else" at the top edge, and they "go someplace else" at the bottom edge of the fabric. From the river basins and mountain valleys of China to the highlands and villages of Southeast Asia, they have migrated around the world. The United States is now home to more Hmong people than anywhere else outside Asia. While they have lived on the edge of the landscape in many places, over two hundred fifty thousand Hmong people now are Americans, settled in this country for three or more generations, whose lives are closely stitched into the richly woven fabric of multicultural American life.

Hmong Identity: Cultural Continuity and Change

As Conquergood underscores, "The process of *pa ndau*-making—including the circumstances of production—is itself an open-ended text that draws together a complex weave of historical, economic, artistic, social, and political forces." Similarly, understanding how story cloth is made involves careful contextualization of what we see in each instance of it and in its collective impact. In my view, both *paj ntaub* and story cloth are not only to be admired as textile art but also to be more fully appreciated as forms of narrative art. Equally important, what they both communicate to students today is a powerful story of how Hmong women in their cultural creativity are stitching the fabric of Hmong lives together across generations.[28]

Their achievement reflects not only skill and resourcefulness but also refinement of their abilities over time and a commitment to turning their talents toward serving community needs. Women in older generations certainly honor traditional values of family and clan, yet they also are individuals with their own identities, no less so than women today. Those who have become *paj ntaub* and story cloth artists have done so not in choosing between individual and collective identity but in finding ways to blend innovation and tradition, the possible and the proven ways of being Hmong. In *The Woman Warrior,* Maxine Hong Kingston describes a Chinese mother who fears that her American-born children have "no memory and no feelings." This also worries many Hmong mothers today. How can children know the true feelings of being Hmong if they do not hold in their hearts the memory of what it has meant to be Hmong for generations before them?[29]

When they come back to the question "What is it to be Hmong?" after our work with *paj ntaub* and story cloth, students are much more attuned to history and heritage in their responses:

History is in people. I'm proud to be Hmong and American. I don't have to choose between them. I *am* both. (Tou Lee)

I see my mother and grandmothers in a whole new light. They show me how to be Hmong. They're strong, smart like women before them. (May Thao)

I will learn to sew, no matter how long it takes! That's being Hmong for me now. Just a part, but an important part. (Cindy Donaldson)

I can't sew, but I am learning how to sing from my mother. She cried when I told her that I wanted to learn. She has a beautiful voice, which I never listened to before. (Christine Moua)

In my other classes (art and English), I am going to bring *paj ntaub* and story cloth. I'm proud to show other students what I know. (Evangeline Her)

Lee and Tapp observe, "it is people who make their culture, not their culture that makes them." However, in teaching Hmong American Life Stories for fifteen years, I have found that students are very encouraged to realize through our work together that people and culture make each other. Like the ordinary Hmong women who have created extraordinary art, students can out of their daily choices and commitments create deeply meaningful lives for themselves, discovering (more often than not) their true individuality through their bonds with others. In fact, with every group of students, I see new possibilities emerging for what it means to be Hmong and American in modern society. Some will be artists, singers, or dancers. Some have their sights set on becoming doctors, lawyers, accountants, or entrepreneurs. I am happy to hear students talk about how much they would like to have families of their own someday. Most of all, I am heartened to see them walk with their heads held high and their eyes bright as they move into their own futures. As Blia Xiong, one of my most outspoken students, insists, "A Hmong is in every one of us." How fortunate we are in multicultural America to have Hmong people here to remind us of the best that we all can be.[30]

NOTES

1. Vincent Her, e-mail message to author, Jan. 28, 2011, regarding the significance of *qeej*. For an extensive discussion of Hmong "missing book" folktales and their significance, see John Duffy, *Writing from These Roots: Literacy in a Hmong-American Community* (Honolulu: University of Hawai'i Press, 2008).

2. For histories of Hmong people in Laos before and during the Vietnam War, see W. E. Garrett, "The Hmong of Laos: No Place to Run," *National Geographic* 145 (Jan. 1974): 78–111; Jane Hamilton-Merritt, *Tragic Mountains: The Hmong, the Americans, and the Secret Wars for Laos, 1942–1992* (Bloomington: Indiana University Press, 1993); Paul Hillmer, *A People's History of the Hmong* (St. Paul: Minnesota Historical Society Press, 2010); Gayle Morrison, *Sky Is Falling: An Oral History of the CIA's Evacuation of the Hmong from Laos* (Jefferson, NC: McFarland, 2007); Tim Pfaff, *Hmong in America: Journey from a Secret War* (Eau Claire, WI: Chippewa Valley Museum, 1995); Keith Quincy, *Hmong: History of a People* (Cheney: Eastern Washington University Press, 1988); Keith Quincy, *Harvesting Pa Chay's Wheat: The Hmong and America's Secret War in Laos* (Spokane: Eastern Washington University Press, 2000); and Nicholas Tapp, Jean Michaud, Christian Culas, and Gary Yia Lee, eds., *Hmong/Miao in Asia* (Chiang Mai, Thailand: Silkworm Books, 2004).

3. For course details, see Mary Louise Buley-Meissner, "The Spirit of a People: Hmong American Life Stories," *Language Arts* 79.4 (Mar. 2002): 323–31. Reprinted in *Hmong American Journal* (Apr. 2002): 22–29. All student names are pseudonyms; all student quotations are used with permission.

4. Lue Vang and Judy Lewis, *Grandmother's Path, Grandfather's Way: Oral Lore,*

Generation to Generation, 2nd ed. (Rancho Cordova, CA: Vang and Lewis, 1990), 8, emphasis added.

5. Detailed descriptions of *paj ntaub* techniques are included in Geraldine Craig, "Patterns of Change: Transitions in Hmong Textile Language," *Hmong Studies Journal* 11 (2010): 5–6; Joanne Cubbs, "Hmong Art: Tradition and Change" in *Hmong Art: Tradition and Change* (Sheboygan, WI: John Michael Kohler Arts Center, 1986), 21–29; Annette Hafner-Hoppenworth, *Hmong Paj Ntaub: A Comparison of Design Motifs, Color, Size, and Ornamental Construction Techniques Between 1977–1979 and 1981–1983* (master's thesis, Michigan State University, 1989); Gary Yia Lee and Nicholas Tapp, *Culture and Customs of the Hmong* (Santa Barbara, CA: Greenwood Press, 2010), 101–5; Norma J. Livo and Dia Cha, *Folk Stories of the Hmong: Peoples of Laos, Thailand, and Vietnam* (Westport, CT: Libraries Unlimited, 1991), 11–12; Jane Mallinson, Nancy Donnelly, and Ly Hang, *Hmong Batik: A Textile Technique from Laos* (Seattle, WA: Mallison/Information Services, 1988), 29–39; Ava L. McCall, "More Than a Pretty Cloth: Teaching Hmong History and Culture through Textile Art," *Theory and Research in Social Education* 25.2 (Spring 1997): 146–50; Marsha McDowell, *Stories in Thread: Hmong Pictorial Embroidery* (Lansing: University Publications, Michigan State University, 1989), 1–3; and Patricia V. Symonds, *Calling in the Soul: Gender and the Cycle of Life in a Hmong Village* (Seattle: University of Washington Press, 2004), 48–50.

6. The creative variety of *paj ntaub* designs can be seen in an excellent collection of drawings provided by Anthony Chan, *Hmong Textile Designs* (Owings Mills, MD: Stemmer House, 1990), and in numerous exhibition catalogues of Hmong textiles, such as C. Kurt Dewhurst and Marsha MacDowell, eds., *Michigan Hmong Arts: Textiles in Transition* (Lansing: The Museum, Michigan State University, 1984); *Hmong Art: Tradition and Change; Textiles as Text: Arts of Hmong Women from Laos* (Los Angeles, CA: The Woman's Building, 1987); and Joan Randall, ed., *Textiles, Silver, Wood of the Hmong-Americans: Art of the Highland Lao* (Davis: University of California, 1985).

7. Gina Corrigan, *Miao Textiles from China* (London: British Museum Press, 2001). Tomoko Torimaru, *One Needle, One Thread: Miao (Hmong) Embroidery and Fabric Piecework from Guizhou, China* (Honolulu: University of Hawai'i Art Gallery, 2008). Georgia Pabst, "MIAD Students Use Art to Transmit Old Hmong Tales," *Milwaukee Journal Sentinel,* Apr. 20, 2009, www.jsonline.com/news/milwaukee/43321707.html (accessed Jan. 23, 2011). Lee and Tapp, *Culture and Customs,* 99–100. Abby Remer, *Enduring Visions: Women's Artistic Heritage around the World* (Worcester, MA: Davis, 2001), vii.

8. Robert Cooper, ed., *The Hmong: A Guide to Traditional Lifestyles* (Singapore: Time Editions, 1998), 98. Nancy D. Donnelly, *Changing Lives of Hmong Refugee Women* (Seattle: University of Washington Press, 1994), 197. Mallinson, Donnelly, and Hang, *Hmong Batik,* 68. Symonds, *Calling in the Soul,* 49.

9. Cubbs, "Hmong Art," 21. "Hmong Traditional Artists" in *Hmong Art: Tradition and Change*, 135–44. Ten additional biographies are presented by Amy Catlin, "Textiles as Texts: Arts of Hmong Women from Laos," in *Textiles as Text: Arts of Hmong Women from Laos*, n.p.

10. Cubbs, "Hmong Art," 21. *Paj ntaub* symbolism is discussed at length in Cubbs, 21–22; Anthony Chan, "Introduction," *Hmong Textile Designs*, n.p.; Dewhurst and MacDowell, *Michigan Hmong Arts*, 70–71; Michele Gazzalo, "Spirit Paths and Roads of Sickness: A Symbolic Analysis of Hmong Textile Design" (master's thesis, Northwestern University, 1986); and Hafner-Hoppenworth, *Hmong Paj Ntaub*.

11. Anthony Doerr, *Memory Wall: Stories* (New York: Scribner, 2010), 151. Vincent Her, e-mail message to author, Jan. 28, 2011, regarding Third International Conference on Hmong Studies, "Hmong Global Identities in the 21st Century," Concordia University, St. Paul, MN, 2010.

12. Lee and Tapp, *Culture and Customs of the Hmong*, 105.

13. Meredith B. McGuire, "Why Bodies Matter: A Sociological Reflection on Spirituality and Materiality," *Spiritus* 3 (2003): 3. This understanding of *paj ntaub* is supported by the research of Dia Cha, "The Sacred and the Secular: An Examination of the Relationship between Hmong Traditional Art and Religion," *Paj Ntaub Voice* 8.2 (2003) and 9.1 (2003): 4–10; Eric Crystal, "Buffalo Heads and Sacred Threads: Hmong Culture of the Southeast Asian Highlands," in *Textiles as Text*, n.p.; Gazzalo, *Spirit Paths and Roads of Sickness*; and Remer, *Enduring Visions*.

14. Lee and Tapp, *Culture and Customs of the Hmong*, 144.

15. According to Marsha McDowell, *Stories in Thread*, men sometimes assisted their wives by drawing outlines of story cloth designs directly on the fabric with chalk, pencils, or pens available in the camps; women then embroidered over the outlines. McDowell notes, however, that women "exercise[d] control of the story depicted, color of background fabric, color of thread or threads used, and the degree to which they [chose] to follow the premarked drawings" (5). Story cloths made in the camps ranged in size from three-inch squares to wall hangings nearly eight feet by nine feet. Conditions of story cloth production in refugee camps are discussed in June Anderson, *Mayko's Story: A Hmong Textile Artist in California* (San Francisco: California Academy of Sciences, 1996), 28–37; Craig, "Patterns of Change," 8–9; C. Kurt Dewhurst, Yvonne Lockwood, and Marsha McDowell, "Michigan Hmong Textiles," in Dewhurst and McDowell, *Michigan Hmong Arts*, 18–20; Donnelly, *Changing Lives of Hmong Refugee Women*, 88–91; Lee and Tapp, *Culture and Customs of the Hmong*, 115–20; Lynellyn D. Long, *Ban Vinai: The Refugee Camp* (New York: Columbia University Press, 1993), 85–86; McCall, "More Than a Pretty Cloth," 150–56; and McDowell, *Stories in Thread*, 3–7.

16. See, for example, Dia Cha, *Dia's Story Cloth: The Hmong People's Journey of Freedom* (New York: Lee & Low Books, 1996); Jewell Reinhart Coburn with Tzexa

Cherta Lee, *Jouanah: A Hmong Cinderella* (Fremont, CA: Shen's Books, 1996); Rosalie Giacchino-Baker, *The Story of Mah: A Hmong "Romeo and Juliet" Folktale* (El Monte, CA: Pacific Asia Press, 1995); Ava L. McAll, "Hmong *Paj Ntaub*: Using Textile Arts to Teach Young Children about Cultures," *Social Education* 62.5 (Sept. 1998): 294–96; Peggy Deitz Shea, *The Whispering Cloth: A Refugee's Story* (Honesdale, PA: Boyds Mills Press, 1995); Randy Snook, *Many Ideas Open the Way: A Collection of Hmong Proverbs* (Fremont, CA: Shen's Books, 2003); and Blia Xiong with Cathy Spagnoli, *Nine in One Grr! Grr!: A Folktale from the Hmong People of Laos* (San Francisco, CA: Children's Book Press, 1989). Also, Anderson, *Mayko's Story;* MacDowell, *Stories in Thread; Textiles as Text;* and Randall, *Textiles, Silver, Wood of the Hmong-Americans.*

17. Anderson, *Mayko's Story.*

18. Nora Murphy, *Knitting the Threads of Time* (Novato, CA: New World Library, 2009), 4, 179.

19. Dwight Conquergood, "Fabricating Culture," in eds. Elizabeth C. Fine and Jean Haskell Speer, *Performance, Culture and Identity* (Westport, CT: Praeger, 1992), 208, 235. Long, *Ban Vinai,* 85–86. See, for example, McCall, "More Than a Pretty Cloth," who translates the Hmong phrase as "flower cloths of people, customs, and traditions," 152; and McDowell, *Stories in Thread,* who translates it as "flower cloth of people and customs," 3. The translation I use here is by Vincent Her via e-mail correspondence on Sept. 29, 2011.

20. Jeffrey C. Alexander, "Toward a Theory of Cultural Trauma," in eds. Jeffrey C. Alexander, Ron Eyerman, Bernhard Giesen, Neil J. Smelser, and Piotr Sztompka, *Cultural Trauma and Collective Identity* (Berkeley: University of California Press, 2004), 1, 12–15, includes a detailed explanation of his four requirements across groups and events in world history.

21. Conquergood, "Fabricating Culture," 234.

22. Sally Petersen, "Translating Experience and the Reading of Story Cloth," in ed. Franklin Ng, *Asian Women and Gender* (New York: Garland Publishing, 1998), 183, 184. Originally published in *Journal of American Folklore* 101.99 (1988): 6–22.

23. For a detailed discussion of Hmong global identity, see Gary Yia Lee, ed., *The Impact of Globalization and Trans-nationalism on the Hmong* (St. Paul, MN: Center for Hmong Studies, Concordia University, 2009).

24. Conquergood, "Fabricating Culture," 234.

25. Alexander, "Toward a Theory of Cultural Trauma," 11.

26. My appreciation of this story cloth has been enhanced by discussion with Vincent Her and Hmong elders (particularly veterans at Lao Family, Inc., in Milwaukee, Wisconsin) about the history of Hmong people in Laos after the official end of the Vietnam War. The Chao Fa resistance movement remains controversial among Vietnam War historians.

27. For a discussion of the artwork of indigenous women in a global political context, see Abby Remer, "Introduction," in *Enduring Visions,* vi-ix. Remer's bibliography provides many useful references on this subject.

28. Conquergood, "Fabricating Culture," 210.

29. Maxine Hong Kingston, *The Woman Warrior: Memoirs of a Girlhood among Ghosts* (New York: Knopf, 1976), 115.

30. Lee and Tapp, *Culture and Customs of the Hmong,* 118.

Contributors

Mary Louise Buley-Meissner, associate professor of English at the University of Wisconsin–Milwaukee, has been involved in cross-cultural education and teacher education for many years. Since 1996, she has taught courses in Hmong American and Southeast Asian American life stories as part of the wide range of Asian American literature courses that she has developed at UWM. She also has taught in China as a Fulbright professor and will be returning there for a life stories research project. With Vincent Her, she coauthored "Hmong Voices and Memories" (*Journal of Asian American Studies* 13.1 [2010]: 35–58) and "'Why Would We Want Those Students Here?'" (*Hmong Studies Journal* 7 [2006]: 1–43).

Amy DeBroux, a graduate student at the University of Wisconsin–Oshkosh, is pursuing her certification as an English Language Learner (ELL) teacher. A member of the Unpolished Gems writers' group, she has enjoyed performing readers' theater with the group at local venues. Her poetry has been published in *Free Verse* and *The Wisconsin Poet's Calendar.*

Jeremy Hein, a professor of sociology at the University of Wisconsin–Eau Claire, has studied the experiences of Southeast Asian refugees since 1983. His publications include *States and International Migrants: The Incorporation of Indochinese Refugees in the United States and France* (Westview Press, 1993); *From Vietnam, Laos, and Cambodia: A Refugee Experience in the United States* (Twayne Publishers, 1995); and *Ethnic Origins: The Adaptation of Cambodian and Hmong Refugees in Four American Cities* (Russell Sage Foundation, 2006).

Vincent K. Her is an assistant professor in the Department of Sociology and Archaeology at the University of Wisconsin–La Crosse. His teaching includes courses on Hmong American history and culture; ethnic and racial minorities; visual culture; and peoples and cultures of Southeast

< 261 >

Asia. Over the past decade, he has done extensive research on Hmong culture and has come to recognize how Hmong ideas, values, and traditions continue to be relevant to the lives of Hmong Americans. That work has resulted in a book entitled *In Search of Hmong Roots: Social Meanings in Hmong American Funerals* (forthcoming from Edwin Mellen Press).

Don Hones is a professor in the College of Education and Human Services at the University of Wisconsin–Oshkosh. Together with Txawjthoj Vang, he teaches Hmong Language, Culture, and Learning, a course designed for teachers that attracts increasing numbers of Hmong American students from all fields. With Shou Cha, he is the author of *Educating New Americans: Immigrant Lives and Learning* (LEA, 1999).

Gary Yia Lee, who was born in Laos, pursued university studies in Australia, earning a PhD in cultural anthropology from the University of Sydney. He taught at Macquarie University and the University of New South Wales; was a visiting fellow in anthropology to the Australian National University in 2001–2; and became the first scholar-in-residence at the Center for Hmong Studies, Concordia University, St. Paul, Minnesota, in 2006–7. For his lifetime record of extensive publication on the Hmong, he received the Eagle Award from Concordia University in 2006 and an honorary Doctor of Letters degree in 2008. He has lived in Australia with his wife and four children since 1975.

Song Lee is an assistant professor at California State University, Fresno, in the Department of Counseling, Special Education, and Rehabilitation. She earned her PhD in counselor education from North Carolina State University. Lee has been involved with the community by serving as an advisor for student organizations, providing pro bono counseling services to non–English speaking Hmong clients, cohosting a radio show for the Hmong elderly population, and conducting research on the needs and concerns of the Hmong elderly. Recent research includes a coauthored book chapter (in press) on counseling diverse clients.

Pao Lor is an assistant professor in the Professional Program in Education at the University of Wisconsin–Green Bay. His main professional focus is advancing Hmong education through involvement in school administration, international education, and other educational activities. His research has been published in journals such as *Multicultural Education* and *The American School Board Journal*. He works with the Office of the Basic Education Commission, Ministry of Education of Thailand, to create and establish international projects and collaborations. With his wife and four children, he lives in Kimberly, Wisconsin.

Bic Ngo is an assistant professor of culture and teaching in the Department of Curriculum and Instruction at the University of Minnesota. Her research examines culture and difference in the education of immigrant students and their implications for theorizing immigrant identity, culturally relevant pedagogy, and anti-oppressive education. Her work includes exploration of the experiences of Hmong American high school students, college students, parents, and community leaders.

Keith Quincy is the former chair of the government program at Eastern Washington University. He is trained in philosophy, political science, and economics; his books span many disciplines. His most recent works are *Der* (GPJ Books, 2007, his third work on the Hmong) and *Plato Unmasked* (GPJ Books, 2011, a new translation of Plato's dialogues). Another forthcoming book is an exposé of Washington's manipulation of the nation's economic data.

Chan Vang earned a BA in art from the University of Wisconsin–Oshkosh. In the near future he hopes to visit his birthplace in Thailand, continue painting, and attend graduate school.

Hue Vang earned a BS in biology from the University of Wisconsin–Oshkosh. He plans to pursue a career in medicine and to continue producing animation about the Hmong culture.

Ka Vang was born in Long Cheng, Laos. A playwright, fiction writer, and poet, she is a recipient of the Archibald Bush Artist Fellowship and several other fellowships. She performs frequently across the country and is actively involved in Asian American community issues, particularly those affecting Asian American women. She is currently a columnist for the *Minnesota Women's Press*. Her writing has been included in several anthologies, including *Riding Shotgun* (ed. Kathryn Kysar, Borealis Books, 2008); *Haunted Hearths and Sapphic Shades* (ed. Catherine Lundoff, Lethe, 2008); *Bamboo Among the Oaks* (ed. Mai Neng Moua, Minnesota Historical Society Press, 2002); and *Charlie Chan Is Dead 2* (ed. Jessica Hagedorn, Penguin, 2004). Among her many plays, "DISCONNECT" is the most well known and has been performed across the country, including in New York.

Kou Vang is an artist, writer, activist, advocate, wife, and mother. Vang has an MA in visual studies from Cardinal Stritch University, where she is creative director. Her art has been exhibited in several groundbreaking shows in Minnesota and has been published in two issues of *Paj Ntaub Voice*, a Hmong literary arts journal. Ms. Vang is a board member of the Hmong Cultural Center of Wisconsin (HCCWI) and owner of Inspiring Elements Photo.

May Vang, a doctoral student in the Urban Education program at the University of Wisconsin–Milwaukee, is researching bilingual education with a special emphasis on curriculum and instruction. She earned her MA in reading/language arts at Cardinal Stritch University.

Ma Lee Xiong attends the University of Wisconsin–Oshkosh with a major in elementary education (grades 1–8) and a minor in ESL (bilingual and Japanese). She is a student assistant in Human Services and Educational Leadership.

Shervun Xiong earned a BS in education from the University of Wisconsin–Oshkosh. She plans to be an elementary bilingual teacher and write children's books about the Hmong culture.

Kao Kalia Yang is the author of *The Latehomecomer: A Hmong Family Memoir* (Coffee House Press, 2008). She earned an MFA in creative nonfiction writing at Columbia University in New York. As an adjunct faculty member, she has taught creative writing at Concordia University in St. Paul, Minnesota, and other schools. As writer-in-residence at the University of Wisconsin–Eau Claire, she teaches courses in poetry, fiction, and creative nonfiction. In addition, her current projects include a venture into children's literature through her own creative nonfiction.

Kou Yang is professor of Asian American studies in the Department of Ethic and Gender Studies, California State University, Stanislaus. He has published extensively on the Hmong, Hmong Americans, Hmong diaspora, and the Hmong/Miao in China. He has contributed to many books, including *Passages* (ed. Howard Katsuyo, California State University, Fresno, 1990); *The Hmong: An Introduction to Their History and Culture* (Center for Applied Linguistics, 2004); *Emerging Voices* (ed. Huping Ling, Rutgers University Press, 2008); and *Hmong/Miao Migration* (ed. Gu Wenfeng, published in China). Professor Yang holds an EdD in educational leadership from the Joint Doctoral Program of Educational Leadership at California State University, Fresno and University of California at Davis.

Index

< 267 >